The Kurdish Women's Freedom Movement

Amidst ongoing wars and insecurities, female fighters, politicians and activists of the Kurdish Freedom Movement are building a new political system that centres gender equality. Since the Rojava Revolution, the international focus has been especially on female fighters, a gaze that has often been essentialising and objectifying, brushing over a much more complex history of violence and resistance. Going beyond Orientalist tropes of the female freedom fighter, and the movement's own narrative of the 'free woman', Isabel Käser looks at personal trajectories and everyday processes of becoming a militant in this movement. Based on in-depth ethnographic research in Turkey and Iraqi Kurdistan, with women politicians, martyr mothers and female fighters, she looks at how norms around gender and sexuality have been rewritten and how new meanings and practices have been assigned to women in the quest for Kurdish self-determination. Her book complicates prevailing notions of gender and war and creates a more nuanced understanding of the everyday embodied epistemologies of violence, conflict and resistance.

Isabel Käser is a Visiting Fellow at the LSE Middle East Centre and Research Associate at the University of Bern. She gained her PhD at SOAS University of London and has previously worked in journalism and diplomacy, most recently leading the research project 'Art in Peace Mediation' for the Swiss Federal Department of Foreign Affairs. She has lectured at the University of Bern and the University of Kurdistan Hewlêr (UKH), and is currently the Principal Investigator of a collaborative project between the LSE and the UKH titled 'The Kurdistan Region of Iraq Post-ISIS: Youth, Art and Gender'.

The Kurdish Women's Freedom Movement

Gender, Body Politics and Militant Femininities

Isabel Käser

London School of Economics and Political Science

Shaftesbury Road, Cambridge CB2 8EA, United Kingdom

One Liberty Plaza, 20th Floor, New York, NY 10006, USA

477 Williamstown Road, Port Melbourne, VIC 3207, Australia

314–321, 3rd Floor, Plot 3, Splendor Forum, Jasola District Centre, New Delhi – 110025, India

103 Penang Road, #05–06/07, Visioncrest Commercial, Singapore 238467

Cambridge University Press is part of Cambridge University Press & Assessment, a department of the University of Cambridge.

We share the University's mission to contribute to society through the pursuit of education, learning and research at the highest international levels of excellence.

www.cambridge.org
Information on this title: www.cambridge.org/9781009011112

DOI: 10.1017/9781009022194

© Isabel Käser 2021

This publication is in copyright. Subject to statutory exception and to the provisions of relevant collective licensing agreements, no reproduction of any part may take place without the written permission of Cambridge University Press & Assessment.

First published 2021
First paperback edition 2023

A catalogue record for this publication is available from the British Library

Library of Congress Cataloging-in-Publication data
Names: Käser, Isabel, author.
Title: The Kurdish women's freedom movement : gender, body politics and militant feminities / Isabel Käser.
Description: Cambridge ; New York, NY: Cambridge University Press, 2021. | Includes bibliographical references and index.
Identifiers: LCCN 2021008901 (print) | LCCN 2021008902 (ebook) | ISBN 9781316519745 (hardback) | ISBN 9781009022194 (ebook)
Subjects: LCSH: Partiya Karkerên Kurdistanê. | Women, Kurdish – Political activity – Turkey. | Women, Kurdish – Turkey – Social conditions. | Women and war – Turkey. | Nationalism and feminism – Turkey. | Militia movements – Turkey. | Government, Resistance to – Turkey. | BISAC: POLITICAL SCIENCE / World / Middle Eastern | POLITICAL SCIENCE / World / Middle Eastern
Classification: LCC HQ1726.7 .K38 2021 (print) | LCC HQ1726.7 (ebook) | DDC 305.409561–dc23
LC record available at https://lccn.loc.gov/2021008901
LC ebook record available at https://lccn.loc.gov/2021008902

ISBN   978-1-316-51974-5   Hardback
ISBN   978-1-009-01111-2   Paperback

Cambridge University Press & Assessment has no responsibility for the persistence or accuracy of URLs for external or third-party internet websites referred to in this publication and does not guarantee that any content on such websites is, or will remain, accurate or appropriate.

To my father Peter Käser (1955–2019)

Contents

Figures

Map

Tables

Acknowledgements

I initially had the idea for this project in 2012, when the first images of the Rojava Revolution started circulating. At the forefront of the colourful protests were women: waving flags from the back of pickup trucks, marching in Qamişlo and standing guard to demarcate the boundaries of the new Kurdish cantons in Syria's northeast. Since then, some parts of Kurdistan have undergone profound transformations and at the heart of this process were and are women. Over the course of the past seven years, I have managed to witness and put into writing some of these dynamics, a process that would not have been possible without the help of many wonderful friends, colleagues and family members.

At the School of Oriental and African Studies (SOAS), my intellectual home during the project, I want to thank Nadje Al-Ali who was not only an indispensable mentor but also became a great friend along this tumultuous journey. Her unfaltering support played a huge part in the successful completion of this project. Charles Tripp, Gina Heathcote Cynthia Enloe and Hamit Bozarslan influenced this project with their critical questions and encouraging nudges. Doctoral fellowships granted by the Janggen-Pöhn Foundation and the Swiss National Science Foundation are also gratefully acknowledged.

A research project like this one depends on people making introductions and opening doors. I am indebted to Estella Schmid, Kerim Yildiz, Özlem Yasak, Murat Bayram, Nazmi Gür, Evin Kışanak and Meral Çiçek for their time and trust. I would also like to thank the many people who hosted me so generously during fieldwork – between Diyarbakir, Istanbul, Erbil, Maxmûr and Sulaymaniyah – particularly Melis and Magnus Bischofberger for providing a home in Istanbul (and then again in London), Siham Mamand for organising my stay in Erbil, Neslihan Yaklav and Choman Hardi for hosting me in Sulaymaniyah, and Şehrivan Durmaz who opened her home in Maxmûr Camp. Most of this book was written at 83 Bartholomew Road, the late Cynthia Cockburn's house in London, a place that was home to generations of feminist academics and activists.

I am grateful to my friends and colleagues, the brilliant Paniz Musawi Natanzi, Sabiha Allouche, Haje Keli, Serhat Keser and Arzu Yılmaz who have read earlier drafts of this manuscript and with their criticality have made this work better. I would also like to express my gratitude to my Kurmancî teachers – Maldin Heidar, Murat Bayram, Zozan Yaşar and Aladdin Sinayic – for teaching me the ways of their beautiful language. Lukman Ahmad generously agreed to let me use one of his paintings for the book cover, the *Face of Crystal*, to me, touchingly captures many of the dynamics that I describe in this book.

A lot of life happened alongside this project over the course of the past seven years and I owe much to my family in Switzerland for their support along the way: my late father Peter Käser, for believing in me and for always encouraging my curious mind, and to my mother Myrta Grob who taught me everything, but in particular her very own brand of feminism. My aunt Monika Grob provided a home full of warmth and compassion whenever I needed time to write or recuperate. Without her love, generosity and that fireplace, I would not be where I am today. I am thankful to my family and friends, Eva and David Käser, Anne Hasselmann, Micheline Maire, Christine Baumgartner, Teresa Mitchell, Daniel Marwecki, Ayşe Tekagac, Corinna Drossel, Myriam Gaitsch, Bejan Matur, Pınar Balıkcı, Houzan Mahmoud, Suna Parlak, Asmin Beri and Lilly Ladjevardi, who were there with me as I went from excited nerd, to restless militant, to traumatised researcher, before eventually finding a way to write this book. This work is dedicated to all the struggling women and men who shared their time and experiences with me. I am indebted to your generosity and hope this work does justice to your life stories. And lastly, this is to Ares and our journey together – and to a love that has persevered against all odds.

Note on the Text

Because of the sensitive nature of this topic and the ongoing repression of politicians and activists linked to the wider Kurdish Freedom Movement, I have used pseudonyms for some of my informants, and have anonymised them fully if requested. I have mentioned the names of certain key public figures if they have been quoted on similar issues elsewhere.

Abbreviations

AKP	*Adalet ve Kalkınma Partisi*, Justice and Development Party
DBP	*Demokratik Bölgeler Partisi*, Democratic Regions Party
DFLP	Democratic Front for the Liberation of Palestine
DÖKH	*Demokratik Özgür Kadın Hareketi*, Democratic Free Women's Movement
DTK	*Demokratik Toplum Kongresi*, Democratic Society's Congress
DTP	*Demokratik Toplum Partisi*, Democratic Society Party
DTSO	*Diyarbakır Ticaret ve Sanayi Odası*, Diyarbakir Chamber of Commerce and Industry
EPLF	Eritrean People's Liberation Front
HEP	*Halkın Emek Partisi*, People's Labour Party
HDK	*Halkların Demokratik Kongresi*, People's Democratic Congress
HDP	*Halkların Demokratik Partisi*, Peoples' Democratic Party
HPG	*Hêzên Parastina Gel*, People's Defence Forces
HPJ	*Hêzên Parastina Jin*, Women's Defence Forces
Hüda-Par	*Hür Dava Partisi*, Free Cause Party
KCK	*Koma Civakên Kurdistanê*, Kurdistan Communities Union
KDP	*Partiya Demokrat a Kurdistanê*, Kurdistan Democratic Party
KDPI	*Hizbî Dêmokratî Kurdistanî Êran*, Kurdish Democratic Party of Iran
KJA	*Kongreya Jinên Azad*, Congress of Free Women
KJK	*Koma Jinên Kurdistanê*, Kurdistan Women's Union
KNK	*Kongreya Neteweyî ya Kurdistanê*, Kurdistan National Congress
KJAR	*Komalgeya Jinên Azad ên Rojhilatê Kurdistanê*, Eastern Kurdistan Free Women's Society
KODAR	*Komalgeya Demokratîk û Azad a Rojhilatê Kurdistanê*, Eastern Kurdistan Free and Democratic Society

Komala	*Komalay Şoreşgerî Zahmetkêşanî Kurdistanî Îran,* the Society of Revolutionary Toilers of Iranian Kurdistan
LTTE	Liberation Tigers of Tamil Eelam
PAJK	*Partiya Azadiya Jin a Kurdistanê,* Free Women's Party of Kurdistan
PÇDK	*Partiya Çareseriya Demokratîk a Kurdistanê,* Kurdistan Democratic Solution Party
PFWAC	Palestinian Federation of Women's Action Committees
PJA	*Partiya Jina Azad,* Free Women's Party
PJAK	*Partiya Jiyana Azad a Kurdistanê,* Kurdistan Free Life Party
PJKK	*Partiya Jinên Karkerên Kurdistanê,* Kurdistan Women's Worker's Party
PKK	*Partiya Karkerên Kurdistanê,* Kurdistan Workers' Party
PUK/YNK	*Yekîtiya Nîştimaniya Kurdistan,* the Patriotic Union of Kurdistan
PYD	*Partiya Yekîtiya Demokrat,* Democratic Union Party
RJAK	*Rêxistina Jinên Azad ên Kurdistanê,* Kurdistan Free Women's Organisation
SDF	*Hêzên Sûriya Demokratîk,* Syrian Democratic Forces
THKO	*Türkiye Halk Kurtuluş Ordusu,* People's Liberation Army of Turkey
THKP-C	*Türkiye Halk Kurtuluş Partisi-Cephesi,* People's Liberation Party-Front of Turkey
TJA	*Tevgera Jinên Azad,* the Free Women's Movement
YAJK	*Yekîneyên Azadiya Jinên Kurdistanê,* Free Women's Union of Kurdistan
YDG-H	*Yurtsever Devrimci Gençlik Hareketi,* Patriotic Revolutionary Youth Movement
YJA-STAR	*Yekîneyên Jinên Azad-Star,* Free Women's Units STAR
YJWK	*Yekîneyên Jinên Welatparêz ên Kurdistanê,* Unit of Patriotic Women in Kurdistan
YPG	*Yekîneyên Parastina Gel,* People's Protection Units
YPJ	*Yekîneyên Parastina Jin,* Women's Protection Units
YPS	*Yekîneyên Parastina Sivîl,* Civil Protection Unit
YPS-Jin	*Yekîneyên Parastina Sivîl a Jin,* Women's Civil Protection Unit
YRK	*Yekîneyên Parastina Rojhilatê Kurdistanê,* Eastern Kurdistan Defence Units

Map

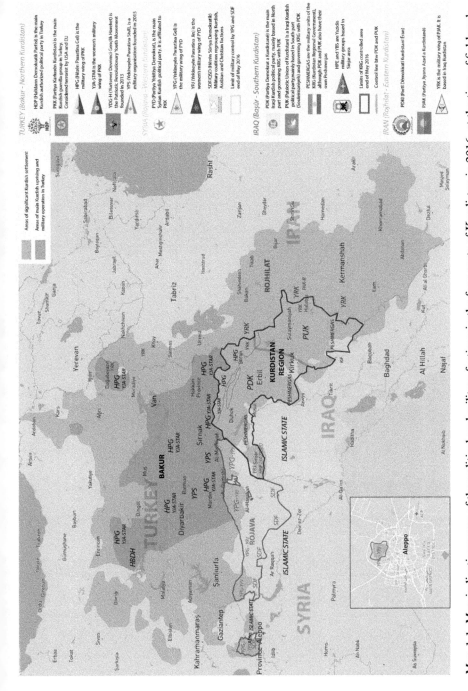

TURKEY (Bakur - Northern Kurdistan)

HDP (Halkların Demokratik Partisi) is the main Kurdish authorized political party in Turkey

PKK (Partiya Karkerên Kurdistan) is the main Kurdish guerrilla group in Turkey. Considered terrorist by USA and EU

HPG (Hêzên Parastina Gel) is the military wing of PKK

YJA-STAR is the women's military wing of PKK

YDG-H (Yurtsever Devrimci Gençlik Hareketi) is the Patriotic Revolutionary Youth Movement founded in 2013

YPS (Yekîneyên Parastina Sivîl), is a military organisation founded in 2015

SYRIA (Rojava - Western Kurdistan)

PYD (Partiya Yekîtiya Demokrat), is the main Syrian Kurdish political party. It is affiliated to PKK

YPG (Yekîneyên Parastina Gel) is the military wing of PYD

YPJ (Yekîneyên Parastina Jin) is the women's military wing of PYD

SDF/QSD (Hêzên Sûriya Demokratîk) Military coalition regrouping Kurdish, Arabian and Christian factions

Limit of military control by YPG and SDF as of May 2016

IRAQ (Başûr - Southern Kurdistan)

PDK (Partiya Demokrat a Kurdistanê) is the main Iraqi Kurdish political party, mainly based in North part and governing KRG with PUK

PUK (Patriotic Union of Kurdistan) is a Iraqi Kurdish political party mainly based in South part (Soulaimaniyeh) and governing KRG with PDK

PESHMERGAS are the military units of the KRG (Kurdistan Regional Government), although PDK and PUK also have their own Peshmergas

HPE and YBS are Yazidis military groups based in Sinjar area

Limits of KRG-controlled area end of May 2016

Control line btw PDK and PUK

IRAN (Rojhilat - Eastern Kurdistan)

PDKI (Partî Dêmokratî Kurdistanî Êran)

PJAK (Partiya Jiyana Azad a Kurdistanê)

YRK is the military wing of PJAK. It is based in Iran Kurdistan

Areas of significant Kurdish settlement

Areas of main Kurdish uprising and military operation in Turkey

Map 1.1 Map indicating some of the political and military factions in the four parts of Kurdistan in 2016, at the time of fieldwork.
Source: Emmanuel Pène in the Maghreb and Orient Courier

Introduction

'When I struggle for my freedom with women, I feel free and I feel equal. Maybe if we weren't organised, I wouldn't feel like that. But freedom is so far away, that I know, we need hundreds of years' (Ayşe Gökkan, 14 November 2015). We were sitting in the office of KJA, the Congress of Free Women (*Kongreya Jinên Azad*) in Diyarbakir, the largest Kurdish city in Turkey, when Ayşe Gökkan told me what equality and freedom meant to her. Our interview was often interrupted by the war planes roaring overhead and rattling the windows,[1] Ayşe's phone ringing and people walking into her office for a quick consultation. Ayşe seemed unfazed by all the commotion, the recent collapse of the peace process between the Turkish state and the Kurdistan Worker's Party (PKK, *Partiya Karkerên Kurdistanê*), and the ensuing outbreak of the urban wars in Turkey's southeast in the summer of 2015. She had been active in the Kurdish Women's Freedom Movement[2] for thirty years – as a journalist, politician and member of KJA – and had seen it all: the early years of the PKK, the prison resistance in the 1980s, the emergence of the Kurdish political parties in the 1990s, the establishment of women's structures and the implementation of the women's quota in the 2000s, and the hope that came with the Rojava Revolution in 2012. From 2009 to 2014 she served as the mayor of Nusaybin, a Kurdish city bordering Syria. When we met, she was responsible for the diplomacy of KJA, which meant building peace initiatives with Turkish feminists, creating international networks, welcoming foreign delegations, and speaking to researchers like me. KJA served as an umbrella structure to

---

[1] These planes took off in Diyarbakir to bomb positions in the Medya Defence Zone, the PKK-controlled area on the Iraqi/Turkish/Iranian border. According to my respondents, the planes deliberately flew low over the city in order to demonstrate Turkish state power and intimidate the population.

[2] Kurd. *Tevgera Azadiya Jinên Kurdistanê*, engl. Kurdistan Women's Freedom Movement. The name of the whole movement (Kurd. *Tevgera Azadiya Kurdistanê*) translates to Kurdistan Freedom Movement. I use shorter versions for the women (Kurdish Women's Freedom Movement or Kurdish women's movement) and the whole movement (Kurdish Freedom Movement or just Freedom Movement).

1

unify and streamline 'women's work' in Turkish Kurdistan/Bakur[3] and implement the ideas around women's liberation according to the writings of the Kurdish Freedom Movement's imprisoned de facto leader Abdullah Öcalan. During our interview Ayşe told me her personal story but also highlighted some of the cornerstones of the women's liberation ideology: the importance of devoting yourself to a unified struggle led by and for women, against a 'capitalist system' and a 'patriarchal society'.[4] She also explained the difference between 'being free' and a 'free life'; being free is achieved by participation in an everyday struggle, a process of liberation that is geared towards a vision of freedom situated in a future utopia. In order to achieve that 'free life' women have to liberate themselves from the shackles of a racist, misogynist and capitalist society, a process in which they will not only free themselves but the fragmented and oppressed Kurdish nation as whole.

This centrality of women in the struggle of the Kurdish Freedom Movement is represented by 'Women, Life, Freedom!' (*Jin, Jiyan, Azadî*), one of the main slogans[5] of the women's movement that was not only present on banners and posters in the KJA office but was chanted at demonstrations, after speeches and reiterated during my interviews across the fieldwork sites in different parts of Kurdistan.[6] This slogan is also

---

[3] I refer to the Kurdish geography as 'four parts of Kurdistan'; Turkish Kurdistan or Bakur, Iranian Kurdistan or Rojhelat, Iraqi Kurdistan or Başûr and Syrian Kurdistan or Rojava. In Kurdish language Bakur, Rojhelat, Başûr and Rojava refer to north, east, south and west, respectively, and are usually used as e.g. *Bakurê Kurdistanê* (North Kurdistan).

[4] 'Patriarchy' is a broad term that describes 'a political-social system that insists that males are inherently dominating, superior to everything and everyone deemed weak, especially females, and endowed with the right to dominate and rule over the weak and to maintain that dominance through various forms of psychological terrorism and violence [...]. Women can be as wedded to patriarchal thinking and action as men' (hooks n.d.). Cynthia Enloe further conceptualizes patriarchy as 'a system – a dynamic web – of particular ideas and relationships [...]. Patriarchy can be updated and modernized. It is stunningly adaptable' and might invite a few select women into the boardroom but only on the condition that they internalise masculinised ways of thinking and act in a way that does not threaten masculinised privilege (Enloe 2017, 16). The Kurdish women's movement uses the term 'patriarchy' (*baviksalarî*) or 'male mentality' (*zîhniyeta zilam*) to describe that adaptable web of power relations, linking the forms of everyday domination and violence it creates to capitalism and the nation state.

[5] I borrow 'slogans' from my interviewees, who would refer to reoccurring expressions that the PKK uses at public events, on banners and in party publications as 'slogans'. They also use the Kurdish word *şiyar* for slogan, which translates to 'warning' or 'promise'.

[6] Kurdistan is divided between four states – Turkey, Iraq, Syria and Iran – and is not exclusively Kurdish but is also home to Yezidis, Armenians, Arabs, Turkmen, Assyrians, Chaldeans, Chircassians, Laz, among others ethnic groups. No exact figures exist but estimates suggest that the number of Kurds in the Middle East and diaspora is close to 30 million; 12–15 million Kurds live in Turkey, more than 8 million in Iran, 5 million in Iraq, and approximately 1 million in Syria, and almost 2 million in other Middle Eastern countries, the former Soviet Union (Armenia, Azerbaijan, Russia) and Europe (Bozarslan 2008, 334).

a central aspect in Democratic Confederalism,[7] the political paradigm penned by Abdullah Öcalan, which links the liberation of women to national liberation and foresees a non-state nation based on gender equality, radical democracy, ecology and self-defence (Öcalan 2011). Running with this ideology, women in the political branch of the movement were able to push through a 40 per cent women's quota and the co-presidency system in the mid-2000s and have since been elected in great numbers into local and national political party structures in Turkey. Even more prominently, women who have been fighting in the armed branches of the movement have gained significant visibility since the PKK's sister party, the Democratic Union Party (PYD, *Partiya Yekîtiya Demokrat*) and its armed wings, the People's Protection Units (YPG, *Yekîneyên Parastina Gel*) and the Women's Protection Unit (YPJ, *Yekîneyên Parastina Jin*) took control of Rojava, the Kurdish northeast of Syria in 2012. The role armed women played in the defence of Kobanî (Rojava) and Şengal (Iraq) against the onslaught of the so-called Islamic State (colloquially known as *daesh*) in 2014 led to much media and scholarly attention on the female fighters. Often depicting smiling and attractive young women with Kalashnikovs, the female fighters of the YPJ became the antithesis to the barbaric other: *daesh*, the many jihadi groups fighting in Syria, the Syrian regime and the Turkish army. This representation of the female fighters has been criticised as essentialist and orientalist, as it objectifies and sexualises the women, brushing over what they stand and fight for (Dirik 2014; Shahvisi 2018). The party's own propaganda and the activist literature published in the wake of the 'Rojava Revolution', while providing important insights into the Rojava project, mostly idealise and glorify the struggle and its revolutionaries, without much space given to the critical voices or reflections on the true cost of war for those who fight it (Demir 2017; Flach et al. 2016; Lower Class Magazine and Unrast e. V 2017; Strangers in a Tangled Wilderness 2015; Tax 2016). Rather than assessing the representation of the female revolutionary, I want to introduce the female revolutionary through women's embodied experience of becoming and being a militant of the Kurdish Freedom

---

[7] Democratic Confederalism, Democratic Autonomy and Democratic Nation are three inter-related political concepts coined by Abdullah Öcalan. Democratic Confederalism is the council-political form, based on radical democracy, sustainable ecological, gender equality and self-defence. It foresees a collaboration between different regional assembly and self-governance structures, the smallest entity being the commune. Democratic Autonomy is the political principle of self-determination. It refers to the practices in which people produce the necessary conditions for collaboration with one another. Democratic Nation (instead of states) can accommodate ethnic, religious and linguistic differences. Ideally, Democratic Nations organised along the parameters of Democratic Autonomy would form Democratic Confederations, surpassing ethnic, religious, linguistic and state boundaries. In practice these concepts are still new and are often conflated or used interchangeably (Ayboğa 2018; Guneser 2018; Jongerden & Akayya 2013, 171; Öcalan 2016, 2017).

Movement, as politicians, activists and fighters. I discuss the specific ways in which this particular transnational women's movement has fought for, created and used emerging spaces since 1978, when the PKK was founded. In order to think beyond the sensationalist and sexualised representation of women at the political and military front lines, I examine how women filled the political, activist and militarised spaces with particular organisational practices and ideological claim making: how they operate on a continuum of violence and resistance in the everyday, and what kind of hegemonic femininity has been formed and is being practised in the different spaces between the mountains and the cities I had access to during my fieldwork: the legal Kurdish parties in the cities (Bakur), the women's guerrilla training camps (Başûr) and the martyr mothers in Maxmûr Camp (Başûr).

Ayşe and most of the other women I interviewed are part of the Kurdish Women's Freedom Movement, a transnational secular women's movement that is active in Turkey, Syria, Iraq, and Iran, as well as Europe and, to a lesser extent, Latin America and Russia. The women's movement is part of the larger Kurdish Freedom Movement and both are officially organised under the umbrella structure of the Kurdistan Communities Union (KCK, *Koma Civakên Kurdistanê*). Parallel to the KCK structure runs the female-only Kurdistan Women's Union (KJK, *Koma Jinên Kurdistanê*). Within the KCK/ KJK, there are three main spheres of work: the social and political sphere, the ideological sphere and the armed sphere. This complex and ever-changing party structure is visualised in the tables in the Appendix and will come into sharper relief in the following chapters; however, it is important to note that the Kurdish Freedom Movement is more commonly referred to as the PKK. The PKK, initially a Marxist-Leninist national liberation party, was founded in eastern Turkey in 1978 and has since 1984 been engaged in a guerrilla war against the Turkish state, fighting for an independent Kurdistan. In 1999, the party leader Abdullah Öcalan was arrested and, while in prison, has rewritten the liberation ideology from fighting for an independent Kurdistan, towards establishing Democratic Confederalism. He also demanded the party's organisational restructuring from PKK to KCK, so that today the PKK is only an ideological party within the greater KCK construct. Despite party restructuring from PKK to KCK, members of the movement themselves still refer to it as 'the party', 'the PKK' or 'the movement', and I use them interchangeably.

The historical transformations of the Kurdish Freedom Movement are intimately interwoven with the history of the Kurdish women's movement. The latter, however, has its very own historical and ideological references that need further attention, as I map out the trajectories of the women, as well as their complex challenges within the organisation. One of the movement's own ideological claims is that of sustainability and difference, emphasising that their movement is aware of the shortcomings of previous national liberation wars, in which women actively participated but were pushed back into the domestic sphere following the conflict, when peace- and policy-making were left up to men. When making this argument, my interviewees often referred to the Russian Revolution or the Algerian War of Independence to illustrate how women were unable to hold on to their wartime gains post-conflict because their institutions were not organised independently from men. This resonates with the ideological canon in which Öcalan points out that

the struggle for women's freedom must be waged through the establishment of their own political parties, attaining a popular women's movement, building their own non-governmental organisations and structures of democratic politics. All these must be handled together, simultaneously. The better women are able to escape the grip of male domination and society, the better they will be able to act and live according to their independence initiative. The more women empower themselves, the more they regain their free personality and identity. [...] I have full confidence in that women, irrespective of their different cultures and ethnicities, all those who have been excluded from the system, will succeed. The twenty first century shall be the century of women's liberation. (Öcalan 2013a, 60)

Members of the women's movement argue that because their struggle is deeply rooted in a forty-year history and ideology of resistance in the armed, political and personal spheres, and because women's liberation and the building of autonomous women-led structures are at the core of the movement's political identity and strategic efforts, their women's movement will endure. Moreover, the implementation of these new structures requires women's self-defence and will allow them to work and live as active members in their community and participate in political decision-making processes and conflict resolution during and after armed conflict, so the women of the movement argue. Öcalan links this claim of difference to the Neolithic matriarchal society (approx. 10,200–8,800 BC), a time when women of Upper Mesopotamia were strong and independent. He evokes the symbol of Îştar the goddess, an important Mesopotamian deity of female love, beauty, fertility, war and political power, saying that today's female freedom fighters all need to become like *Îştar* – fearless, dedicated and independent of men (Çağlayan 2012; Duzel 2018). The claim of sustainability and need for self-defence, as well as the relationship between official party discourse and practice raise further questions about how historical references are used, how the party's female identity of the 'free woman' is constructed, how that identity is translated into everyday practise, and how this challenges or reinforces existing hierarchies of power. This ideology and practice of women's liberation is two-sided as the journey towards liberation goes hand in hand with the renunciation of particular freedoms. For instance, women and men who join the armed branch of the party pledge to abstain from romantic or sexual relations. The trainee guerrillas learn to become desexualised freedom fighters, an endeavour that requires a strict ideological education but also much coercive power and discipline under the watchful eye of the party.

According to existing post-colonial and transnational feminist literature there is ample evidence that militarisation of societies not only leads to greater gender-based violence, but also shows how women's wartime gains are often marginalised and that women are pushed back into the private sphere in post-conflict settings and nation-building efforts. Subsequently, patriarchal structures that predated independence struggles are often further entrenched by militarism and war (Al-Ali 2007, 2009; Al-Ali & Pratt 2009, 2011; Bayard de Volo 2001; Bernal 2000; Cockburn 2004; Enloe 1988, 2014; Hale 2001; Kampwirth 2002; Mojab 2004; Viterna 2006; White 2007). This study, following the women's own claim of difference and sustainability, revisits the linkages between gender, war and militarism (Cohn 2013; Enloe 2000; Parashar 2009; Parashar & Shah 2016; Sylvester 2001, 2011; Sjoberg & Via 2010; Tickner 1992, 2011; Wibben 2010, 2016), asking in what ways the study of female revolutionaries who are fighting for gender-based liberation and justice through an armed and political struggle complicates existing Feminist International Relation (IR) literature on gender and war? Secondly, what does a critical analysis of this movement, which follows a male ideologue but has women at the forefront of all of its military and political struggles, contribute to transnational, post-colonial and geopolitical feminist literature on nationalism and feminism and militarism and body politics?

Aside from a case study on the Kurdish women's movement and gender and war, this research also contributes to broader debates about sexuality and war, speaking to an emerging boy of theory that attempts to decolonize the discourse of sexuality in the Middle East (Najmabadi

2005; Sehlikoglu 2016; Zengin & Sehlikoglu 2016; Sayyegh 2017). This means that I go beyond the usual tropes of militarized masculinities, armed women as agents in patriarchal structures, or women as victims of gender- and sex-based violence. Instead, I deconstruct and reassemble gender, sexuality and conflict and embed it within the meanings and signs that my interlocutors have shared with me, theorizing how the desexualized militant body becomes a vehicle to cultivate comradery, community, solidarity and resistance. This offers new insights into the myriad ways in which my interlocutors live and embody war, revolution and freedom.

In order to do that, the ethnographic insights trace women's armed and political presence in the Kurdish Freedom Movement, as well as the different trajectories to and within the movement. I map out not just women's place in the political and military structures and social and economic relations (Enloe 1990), but also the embodied dimensions of their journey, asking where and who the women are but also 'what keeps them here?'. How did women gain leading roles in the activist, political and armed spheres of the Kurdish Freedom Movement? What tools and mechanisms have the women developed to manoeuvre their movement on the continuum of violence and resistance and to make their hard-won gains last beyond the battlefield or the immediate political challenges? To what extent has this movement challenged prevailing gender norms and relations in the territories it controls, and which forms of (patriarchal) control remain uncontested?

Feminist analyses of IR aim to understand gender relations, meaning the configuration of masculinities and femininities within a certain context, and how they intersect with sovereignty, power, security and conflict (True 2010). What specific femininities and masculinities are needed to support the militarisation process of a society? What powers go into maintaining these structures? How do women navigate their way through conflict and war? (Enloe 1988, 1990). All the struggles that the Kurdish Freedom Movement is leading at the political and armed fronts in different parts of Kurdistan are to a large extent led by women. Spending a year with these women and asking questions about their trajectories, I was confronted with complex stories of how women got to play such central roles within the PKK, but also noticed a particular femininity that women obtained once they joined the party. Despite the fluid boundaries between armed and political, illegal and legal, the mountains and the cities, I started to see patterns: patterns of mobilisation, participation and, most importantly, subject formation. In order to put this particular kind of femininity into conversation with theories on gender and war and the everyday struggle of the women, I propose the concept of *militant femininities*. Militant femininities consist of the term 'militant', which has a specific meaning in the PKK: how one has to become and perform to be a successful militant (*militan*) is a prescribed process. And it consists of femininities, meaning that women operate within a set framework of liberation, living and implementing a neatly constructed idea and ideal of what it means to be a female revolutionary in the armed, political and activist branches of this movement. While acknowledging the boundaries of liberation as set out by the party, I will refrain from setting this study in a false juxtaposition of freedom and oppression, of agency versus coercion (Alison 2003; Parashar 2009; Schäfers 2020; Weiss 2010); clearly the socio-political reality is much more complex than that. Instead I discuss women's activism and their configuration of liberation in the movement's particular framework of reference. Also, I raise certain tensions along the way that result from the contradictions between theory and practice, which I can merely discuss but not resolve: the promise of freedom in exchange for the strict control over body and mind, the aspiration to a 'truth' held by the leadership, and the essentialised and binary gender norms and relations that are upheld by the movement.

Militant Femininities, Interrogating the Concept of the 'Free Woman'

Analysing the party ideology is key to understanding the subject formation or the process of 'becoming' a militant of people who join the PKK and fight at the armed or political fronts. In the PKK party program and charter, published in light of the fifth party congress in 1995, the party member was described as follows:

A party member accepts the party program and is responsible for implementing it, based on the will of the party and by gradually internalising this will, participating in party life and tactical practice all day in a party organ. A party member analyses himself/herself and changes himself/herself according to party style, party speed and party language for the main party purpose. A party member is a person who works with no self-interest and with deep enthusiasm and with endless sacrifice and who dedicates his/her life to the party struggle. (PKK 1995, *my translation*)[8]

A person who joins the party and lives based on these rules is considered a militant (*militan*). The gender-neutral concept of a militant is a signifier

---

[8] The charter has been adapted since then; after 1999, the struggle for the liberation of Öcalan, and after 2005, the struggle for gender equality and ecology were added.

for those who follow the party leader Abdullah Öcalan and his ideology and, through the internalising of his teachings, become 'PKK'cised' (*PKK'leşme*). In party literature militants are further described with adjectives such as honest, dedicated, steadfast, principled, abstinent, communal, sincere, self-critical, loyal, committed, and prepared to dedicate their lives and deaths to the struggle, freedom, humanity, people and the leadership. A successful militant is she or he who accepts this leadership; follows its path and obtains *îrade*, the will to resist; and sacrifices themselves for the cause. A bad, or 'fallen' (*düşkün*), militant is he or she who questions the leadership, doubts the liberation ideology and still shows traits of individualism. All meaning is given by the leadership and all struggles are carried out for the leadership (Öcalan) and thereafter for the freedom of people and all of humanity (Öcalan n.d., Serxwebûn 2015).

Upon joining the movement, women all become revolutionaries (as do the men), who are fighting for a specific vision of a free and gender-egalitarian society, no matter if they work in a political party or at the military front line. Everyone becomes a militant, but this means something very specific to different women, who bring their personal embodied experience and ideas of what it means to be 'a woman' to the party. The hegemonic femininity produced over the years by the militarised culture in the party does not exist in a vacuum but in relationship with a hegemonic masculinity (Connell 1987; Schippers 2007; Segal 2007, 2008) and is influenced and inspired by other revolutionary, leftist, national liberation movements that emerged in the second half of the twentieth century. Here, the universalised and genderless soldier body is tasked to dedicate his or her life to an all-embracing ideology and through repetitive performances sustain unity, loyalty, comradeship and sacrifice. The ideal (male) revolutionary, Lorraine Bayard de Volo found in her work on revolutionary war in Nicaragua and Cuba, expresses both deep love for the people and his comrades and fierce hatred for the enemy, and he is at the same time capable of immense tenderness, while committing fearless actions of revolutionary violence (Bayard de Volo 2012, 422). Each revolutionary movement rewrites gender norms and creates new femininities and masculinities, 'new men' and 'new women' that are reinforced by military hierarchies, revolutionary violence and a bespoke liberation ideology. In the case of the PKK, women have to unlearn false notions of femininity and become fearless goddesses of war and strength (*Îştar*), following in the footsteps of the many female revolutionaries who came before them and died a heroic death as martyrs, as I will discuss further in the next chapter. Subordinate masculinities (effeminate, weak) and femininities (vulnerable, seductive, dependent on men) are critiqued and marginalised in party education and practice. Crucially, different from other conceptualisations of masculinity and femininity (Connell 1987, Connell & Messerschmidt 2005), in the PKK, the relationship between men and women is not defined by desire for the 'other', but by the absence of desire; the new gender norms and relations are based on seeing the 'other' as a comrade on equal footing. While these desexualised revolutionary gender norms seek to shape masculinities and femininities to allow for comradely communal life, and subjects that can be mobilised for the purpose of war (Dietrich Ortega 2012), they are also in place so that hegemonic forms of masculinity can be challenged and thus make room for women's ascendance.

To grasp the performance of ideology through practice in the empirical context discussed here and do justice to the myriad of stories and experiences of women in the party, I introduce the concept of *militant femininities*. I conceptualise militant femininities as the dominant femininities desired by the party leadership and ideology, a set of norms and practices that allows women to challenge patriarchal, statist and capitalist norms in all its guises. Feminist scholars, particularly within IR, critical military studies and critical masculinities studies, have cautioned against simplified notions of hegemonic militarised masculinities (militarism, statecraft) or hegemonic femininities (victims of male violence, agents in patriarchal structures) (Connell 2005, Gentry & Sjoberg 2015, Parashar 2009), and have argued for the inclusion of disruptions, silences, the 'in-between' moments (Chisholm & Tidy 2017; Henry 2017). Similarly, I do not seek to simplify and create new labels of hegemony with my concept of militant femininities, but to create a framework that illustrates how gender, war, militarism and revolutions intersect (Enloe 1993, 2000) and create specific subjectivities between the political, activist and armed sphere of the Kurdish women's movement. In order to do that, I ask what are the characteristics and practices valued when educating new militants? What character traits and habits do they have to unlearn because they are considered disruptive or contaminating? What are the shared characteristics and practices that both men and women learn? How do women position themselves vis-à-vis men or other women's movements? How do conceptions of militant femininities shift between the armed and the political struggle? And to what extent can these norms be contested? Militant femininities according to my conceptualisation here consist of the process of joining the party and becoming a subject by means of education and discipline; the performativity and policing of militant femininities through ideology (knowledge production), direct military action (self-defence), and communal living (criticism and self-criticism); organisational separation in semi-autonomous women's structures; and a history and everydayness of violence and resistance. As such, the cornerstones of militant femininities and reoccurring themes in the following chapters are perseverance, dedication, self-control (*oto-kontrol*), the will to resist (*irade*), ownership over the body, self-sacrifice, desexualisation and communal love. My ethnographic analyses, which are the basis of the following chapters, allow for a grassroots perspective on how people learn, live, embody, implement and sometimes disregard these principles.

This concept of militant femininities is situated at the intersections of post-colonial, transnational and geopolitical feminist literature on gender and war, violence and resistance, feminism, nationalism, as well as militarism, body politics and sexuality. I put this research in a tradition of feminist ethnographers who try to move away from static tropes of 'what happens to women in war time' and thus challenge both the notions of women as 'victims' or 'pawns in male a male game', and the 'exceptionalism' of women as participants in armed resistance and perpetrators of violence (Al-Ali 2007; Al-Ali & Pratt 2009, 2011; Alison 2003, 2009; Bayard de Volo 2001, 2012, 2018; Cohn 2013; Enloe 1988, 2000, 2014, 2017; Giles & Hyndman 2004; Hale 2001; Jacobs, Jacobsen & Marchbank 2000; Kampwirth 2002; Lanzona 2009; Kaufmann & Williams 2010; Lorentzen & Turpin 1998; MacKenzie 2012; Moser & Clark 2001; Riley, Mohanty & Pratt 2008; Sjoberg & Via 2010; Sylvester 2011, 2013; Viterna 2013). This research also speaks to feminist IR literature that pays attention to how ordinary people are involved in wars and particularly women who engage in politically motivated violent acts (O'Keefe 2013; Parashar 2009, 2014; Gentry & Sjoberg 2015). This burgeoning literature, however, does not mean that the conundrum between militarism, masculinity and women's participation in liberation wars has been resolved. Swati Parashar argues that 'there is a tension that exists for feminists: to understand and engage with "militarised masculinity" while simultaneously accepting women's multiple roles and participation in militarised projects' (Parashar 2014, 8). Furthermore, women's participation in revolutionary liberation movements continues to puzzle feminist researchers who look at the inherent contradictions in 'revolutionary war': revolution promises to uproot the status quo, while war relies on militarised structures, loyalty, compliance and hierarchical commands, as opposed to democratic values such as free expression, consensus, and transparency in decision-making processes. Moreover, wars usually favour militarised masculinities, which enhance long-term gender inequality, instead of challenging gender norms and relations, as promised in many post-colonial national liberation movements (Bayard de Volo 2012, Enloe 1988, 2000, 2007; Kampwirth 2002; White 2007).

The Kurdish women's movement argues to be different from previous national liberation struggles that saw women pick up arms, not only because it claims sustainability but also because women do not fight in a men's war. Instead, they have created their own epistemology, and autonomous and semi-autonomous ranks in the armed and political spheres, while building a new gender-equal system in those societies it seeks to revolutionise. By focusing on particular empirical contexts, I reflect on the everydayness of these claims and their practices. Throughout, I examine to what extent the study of this women's movements ideology and practice allows us to rethink certain elements of 'gender and war' and where the movement operates along the same lines previously sketched out by post-colonial, transnational and geopolitical feminist research. In order to do that, I frequently zoom into the human body as an emotional and thinking entity that can touch and is touched by war and violence (Butler 2004; Sylvester 2011, 1).

In the following section I will provide a historical and transnational comparison of previous national liberation movements, in which women played key roles. Then, I sketch out the building blocks of militant femininities and situate this study methodologically and reflect on the challenges of doing a feminist ethnography in a war zone.

To Some Women Non-Violence Is Not an Option

> We argue that violent women are violent people, who, like all people, violent or not, live in a gendered world. *Women* have always been, and continue to be, among the people engaged in violence in the global political arena. Whether they are organizing attacks, leading insurgent groups, perpetrating martyrdom, engaging in sexual violence, committing war crimes, hijacking airplanes, or abusing prisoners, women can be found among the ranks of insurgent, rebel, terrorist and illicit economic groups across the world.
>
> (Gentry & Sjoberg 2015, 2)

Women are at the heart of conflicts and millions of women are partaking in wars across the globe. Due to their specific positioning within a region shaped by post-colonial border-drawing, ongoing wars, occupations, sanctions and embargos, non-violence was and is not an option for many of my interviewees. Taking this quote mentioned earlier as a departure point, I contend that women have always been warring, and armed women are nothing out of the ordinary. Yet the particular case of the Kurdish women's movement and its unique liberation ideology with its distinct focus on gender equality does call for a transnational and historical comparison. This is important, among other things, because the movement sets itself apart from previous national liberation wars, saying it has learned from the women who have struggled before them, for instance in Algeria, El-Salvador and Palestine, but that they are going further than anyone before them in their quest for liberation, by organising autonomously and establishing mechanisms of self-defence in the political, activist and armed spheres.

The Kurdish Women's Freedom Movement is not the first revolutionary movement in the Middle East to have women in its ranks. There is a rich tradition of women's involvement in political and armed struggles in different parts of Kurdistan; both Kurdish parties in Iraqi Kurdistan, the Kurdistan Democratic Party (KDP, *Partiya Demokrat a Kurdistanê*) and the Patriotic Union of Kurdistan (PUK, *Yekîtiya Nîştimaniya Kurdistan*) have had women in their military forces (*peşmerga*) since the 1970s. Komala in Western Iran or Rojhelat has had women fighting in its ranks since the late 1960s. However, in both cases women were mostly kept in supportive roles such as underground activities, nursing and logistics, rather than active combat or decision-making positions (Begikhani et al. 2018, 11; Fischer-Tahir 2012). Furthermore, these wars of national liberation were set in a strictly patriarchal system; that is they were driven by male-led political, economic and social relations, and especially since the 1980s, set in a region very much tied to the local history of consecutive wars, genocides, sanctions, and since 2003 an invasion and occupation (Al-Ali 2009, 53; Al-Ali & Pratt 2011; Mojab 2000, 2004). As seen in so many other post-liberation settings, 'patriarchy' endured, and women's equality was postponed in favour of the greater goal of national unity and the liberation of Iraqi Kurdistan (Al-Ali 2009, 45; Fischer-Tahir 2009).

The emergence of the Palestinian women's movement before the first *Intifada* in 1987 offers a valuable comparative perspective into women's mobilisation, as women played an active role in the political and armed resistance (Hasso 1998, 2005). An analysis of the ideologies and mobilisation strategies of the leftist-national Democratic Front of the Liberation of Palestine (DFLP) and the Palestinian Federation of Women's Action Committees (PFWAC) in the ten years predating the first *Intifada* shows that these organisations were successful because they opened new spaces for women to participate politically on a grassroots level. Women's presence was encouraged by the (male) leaders' assumption that the international community would perceive an active women's participation as proof of 'modernity' and would support Palestinian self-determination (Abu-Lughod 1998). Frances Hasso lists women's roles as 'actors, symbols, and authors – using, being used by, and constructing nationalism on their own terms' (Hasso 1998, 454). Similar to my study, this quote shows that women not only used emerging spaces for their own ends but were also markers of 'the other', in this case a modern Palestine (Hasso 1998, 2005, 92–97; Sharoni 2001). The Syrian-backed DFLP, among others, trained the first fighters of the PKK from 1980 in different DFLP camps in Lebanon, including in the Syrian-controlled Beqaa Valley.[9] Here the PKK learned from the Palestinians about the need of having the backing of organised civilians, such as 'civil militias', committees for youth and women, and martyr ceremonies, in order to expand (logistical) support and control among the population the PKK depends on (Marcus 2007, 58).

Other Marxist-Leninist movements such as the Communist Party of India (Maoist) have a long history of women's participation. Particularly during the Naxalbari Uprising, a peasant revolt (1967–1972), women were active as recruiters, supporters, activists and fighters. This still holds true for the contemporary Maoist insurgency (Naxalites), which has an increasing number of women combatants in its ranks (Shah 2018). The growing popularity and legitimacy of the movement, but also a genuine hope for a better life, paired with the economic marginalisation of the Indian countryside, which results in an exodus of men in search for labour elsewhere, provide strong motivations for women to join the insurgency. Moreover, the movement's ideological focus on women's emancipation and the active participation of women in combat provides coping mechanisms and alternatives for predominantly marginalized rural women (Parashar & Shah 2016, 449). Similar to the Kurdish Women's Freedom Movement, the Maoist movement uses occasions such as the International Women's Day to commemorate its martyrs, using slogans such as 'no revolution without women', in order to recruit more women for the cause and publicise the Maoist agenda of gender equality. Yet Parashar and Shah found that despite women's inclusion in the CPI (Maoist) as women combatants and a progressive approach towards 'the women's question', the movement operates along the norms of militarised masculinities; women remain absent in the upper echelons of power and are subject to gender-based violence within the movement's ranks (Parashar & Shah 2016, 452).

The Liberation Tigers of Tamil Eelam (LTTE), a militant movement that fought for a separate Tamil homeland in Sri Lanka (1976–2009), encouraged women to take up arms against their oppressors, namely the Sri Lankan state and the Sinhalese people. The LTTE has actively recruited women since the mid-1980s, also through its ideological canon, which included women's liberation as a necessary parallel struggle

---

[9] The DFLP was one of the largest Palestinian groups within the umbrella of the PLO. This collaboration was nothing out of the ordinary; the DFLP had at other times trained Greek communists, Iranian leftists and Nicaraguan Sandinistas (Marcus 2007, 54–56).

towards political and economic freedom. Before its defeat in 2009, 25 per cent of LTTE's force consisted of women, some of which engaged in deadly suicide bombings and armed attacks. Similarly, to the Maoist struggle in India, women were indispensable to the struggle; however, their inclusion into the military ranks did not necessarily result in 'empowerment'; forced conscription was widespread, patriarchal structures prevailed, and women remained absent from decision-making positions within the LTTE (Parashar 2009, 240–41). However, feminist scholarship has shown that the binary of victimhood and agency is not analytically fruitful when trying to understand women's motivations to join or to assess their roles within an armed struggle. Instead, they describe an 'ambivalent empowerment' an 'in-between' (Rajasingham-Senanayake 2001, quoted in Alison 2003, 52). Similarly, Parashar found that '[t]he same woman who was forced to join, and had no choice when she left, was often able to realise her potential during training, gain a sense of identity and feel empowered due to her association with the LTTE' (Parashar 2009, 244). This 'ambivalent empowerment' influenced my own analytical framework put forward in the following chapters, which shows how a unified struggle also opens spaces for women to organise, politicise, theorise and fight.

Liberation struggles in Central America in the second half of the twentieth century provide further insights into female mobilisation and participation in armed conflicts. Karen Kampwirth (2002), Jocely Viterna (2006, 2013) and Margret Gonzales-Peres (2006) have asked 'how did women get here?', unpacking the interplay between structural, ideological, political and personal factors that lead women into guerrilla movements in Nicaragua, El Salvador or Mexico. Viterna identifies three different mobilisation paths – the politicised, reluctant and recruited guerrillas – and argues that these arose from the patterned intersections of individual biographies, networks such as families, and situational contexts like living under heavy state repression (Viterna 2006, 2013, 38). Margaret Gonzales-Perez argues that the traction of guerrilla movements depends mostly on its ideology: if an ideology is based on domestic grievances and promises to challenge power structures, women are more likely to take up arms and will achieve higher leadership roles (Gonzales-Perez 2006).

While some of these studies suggest that women's motivations to join an armed movement are specific to their gender, others have argued that women participate in armed groups for similar reasons as men: nationalist desires, economic and political suffering and injustice, and a wish for revenge (Flach 2007; Mazurana 2013, 148). Dara Kay Cohen shows that women not only join armed groups for similar reasons as men, but also have similar experiences during the conflict and commit the same violent acts as men. She refutes the notion of the peace-loving woman and the fighting man, showing that women are just as capable of committing spectacular acts of violence during times of conflict as her case study of rape during the civil war in Sierra or during the Rwanda genocide illustrates. She highlights the tensions this causes, as female perpetrators are often pushed back into the private sphere post-conflict and are not held accountable for their wartime crimes (Cohen 2013, 388; Steflja & Darden 2020).

I have observed that women join the PKK or its sister parties across the region for a multitude of reasons, some similar to men and some for reasons unique to women. Similar reasons include nationalist fervour, an adherence to Öcalan's liberation ideology, the need to defend and protect their land and family, and wanting to avenge (state) violence inflicted on their community. Women-specific reasons are fear and anger about sexual or state violence and repression against women, the struggle for the emancipation of women via equal opportunities and rights, access to education, or escaping the sphere of paternal or male control over their life choices (Alison 2003, 2009; Enloe 1988; Flach 2007; Mazurana 2013). Pinar Tank argues that women's reasons to join the PKK or its regional branches can be divided into roughly five categories: social (urban migration, poverty), personal (forced marriage), idealistic (national liberation, women's emancipation), key event (experience of state violence, racism) and revenge (Tank 2017, 418). Clearly, the reality of Kurdish women and their reasons to join an armed struggle are more complex than these five categories indicate. My findings, as discussed in the following chapters, suggest that it is rarely just one of these factors that push a woman to join the party, but rather a culmination thereof. I argue that while an intersectional analysis of mobilisation patterns is important, it is more analytically fruitful to pay attention to what happens to women once they join; what they do in the party structures in the everyday; and what keeps them engaged in the many armed, socio-political and intellectual struggles the party is fighting.

'Militant' has also been the marker of many feminist movements, in the European context most notably so the Militant Suffragettes (Collette 2013; Pankhurst 2015). However, the women of the Kurdish Freedom Movement set themselves apart from European and US traditions of feminism. Most of my interlocutors would acknowledge the important work their feminist foresisters in the United States, Europe and the Middle East did, before explaining why their approach is different from previous feminist struggles for women's liberation. During my interview with Commander Leyla Agirî, at that time the head of the Eastern

Kurdistan Free Women's Society (KJAR, *Komalgeya Jinên Azad ên Rojhilatê Kurdistanê*), she told me: 'We have had many discussions with feminists who have visited us in the mountains. We are probably closest to Ecofeminism', referring to the struggle of Ecofeminists to simultaneously end the exploitation of women and the domination of nature (Daly 1978; Tong 1998). What makes this women's liberation ideology more radical than most feminisms is that they are en route to challenging the whole system of Capitalist Modernity, by dedicating their lives to the struggle for Democratic Modernity, a system of bottom-up self-government built on gender equality and ecology. Contrary to other utopic feminist theories (Bahng 2018; Hester 2018), this utopic society demands of its militants complete dedication and total self-sacrifice, as activists, politicians and fighters, in order to dismantle the patriarchal and oppressive division of labour and build an egalitarian political system in unison with the environment.

Gender, Violence and Militarism

> But Black women and our children know the fabric of our lives is stitched with violence and with hatred, that there is no rest. We do not deal with it only on the picket lines, or in dark midnight alleys, or in the places where we dare to verbalize our resistance. For us, increasingly, violence weaves through the daily tissues of our living – in the supermarket, in the classroom, in the elevator, in the clinic and the schoolyard, from the plumber, the baker, the saleswoman, the bus driver, the bank teller, the waitress who does not serve us.
>
> (Lorde 2007, 119)

What Audre Lorde describes so poignantly here is the interconnectedness of race with other power structures such as gender and class, showing that, due to her being seen as black, violence is not contained in certain spaces or limited to times when she foregrounds her gender in her struggle for emancipation. Black feminist thought has shown that violence takes structural, political, symbolic and everyday forms (Collins 1996, 2000; hooks 1984), which for Kurdish women means everything from economic marginalisation, and institutional racism, to domestic violence and the urban wars that broke out between PKK-affiliated youth and the Turkish army in mid-2015 in cities across the Kurdish southeast of Turkey.[10] In

---

[10] I am aware of the problems and limitations that arise from comparing two very different political geographies, not least because it distracts from the consistent violence black women still live with and die of in the political, legal and economics system in the United States (Nash 2014, 2019). However, the challenges Kurdish women face are partly a result of the same transnational capitalist patriarchal system and the conceptualisation thereof is analytically useful in other contexts as well.

a context of war and conflict, infrastructures of power and violence on the micro and macro levels become most visible when analysed through a gendered lens: both the journey to and the performance of power or violence are intimately shaped by the body politics in which subjects find themselves. In the context under investigation, the encounter of subjects with power and violence informs their subsequent systematic transformation into militants, as violence in the context here shapes militants who leave their civilian life, or 'system life'[11] as many of my interviewees called it, behind and in turn perpetuate violence on their own quest to liberation. The late Cynthia Cockburn conceptualised this omnipresence of violence with the 'continuum of violence' (2004), demonstrating that the continuum spans from economic distress, to militarisation and arming, ideological shifts, to mobilisation, and 'post-conflict' processes of peace and trauma, always paying attention to the gendered dimensions of body politics on everyday lives. She argues:

First, gender links violence at different points on a scale reaching from the personal to the international, from the home and the back street to the maneuvers of the tank column and the sortie of the stealth bomber: battering and marital rape, confinement, 'dowry' burning, honour killings, and genital mutilation in peacetime; military rape, sequestration, prostitution, and sexualised torture in war. (Cockburn 2004, 43)

Thus, according to Cockburn, it is the omnipresent continuum that connects different locations and forms of violence, and it makes little sense to make distinctions between pre- and post-war, or war and peace. Furthermore, this continuum runs through the political, personal, economic and social relations, aggravated by global processes of economic marginalisation, political disempowerment and social inequality (ibid.). This concept helps to think of violence as entrenching every aspect of the social, economic and political life of individuals as the driving force leading marginalised and oppressed women and men to the PKK. Cockburn's work allows to consider the domestic and intimate relations as we try to understand the workings of violence as opposed to power. The Kurdish Freedom Movement is not governing over territory recognised as a state; however, violence, or 'self-defence' as the movement calls it, is one of its major tools in the pursuit for governmental power. It informs the party ideology, its organisational structures, and the everyday practices of politicising and organising. As such, self-defence is used as a 'strategic' tool to reach the 'future utopia', free of violence.

---

[11] System life (Kurd. *jiyana pergalê*) refers to the capitalist life guerrillas have left behind, the civilian life they wish to revolutionise.

Broader than violence and war, militarism is being made up of a system of cultures, practices, institutions and values that extends into social and political life. War, conflict and consequent militarisation become part of the normal (Sjoberg & Via 2010, 7), and people live their life in anticipation of violence (Bayat 2013; Hermez 2017). Importantly, the rhetoric of national security, often accompanied by censorship laws, and limitations of freedom of expression go hand in hand with the privileging of a certain kind of militarised masculinities (Al-Ali & Taş 2017, 357; Enloe 1988, 2014). Militarism is reflected in the identity of people and their everyday interactions such as loyalties, jargon, cultural production and mourning practices. Women and gender relations are at the heart of militarisation processes, not only to demarcate boundaries of 'us' versus 'them', but also because women are needed to maintain any militarised system. Women's bodies also become battlefields for nationalist policies and are directly affected by changing educational policies, marital law or reproductive rights (Al-Ali 2007, 168). As such, Kurdish women's bodies constitute a site of struggle for competing discourses of belonging and ideas around womanhood, freedom and agency.

In the case discussed here, militarisation does not only affect civilians or create militarised masculinities but also creates a specific kind of militarised femininity. Both men and women, mothers and students are expected to struggle against the enemy and repeatedly enact their militancy and loyalty, more so in times of heightened conflict. In the Kurdish Freedom Movement, women are equal in fighting and dying for the cause, in inflicting violence and being violated, as long as they do not deviate from the guiding revolutionary principle.

Cockburn clearly posits herself against female empowerment in militarized male structures. She argues that women do not achieve equality through participation in war and that neither the hierarchies of armed forces nor the culture of militaries becomes more feminine because of women's presence, concluding that '[i]f they did, they would no longer fulfil their current functions' (Cockburn 2004, 34–35). Women have both accommodated national movements and have been used by militarised states or national liberation movements; however, many feminist scholars have demonstrated that militarised societies are necessarily undemocratic (ibid., 31) and sketched out the ways in which wars reinforce gender inequality (Bayard de Volo 2012, 414; White 2007). Yet the context in which this study is situated is one shaped by decades of war and displacement, where the armed movement is perceived as the 'liberator' and the only force that stands between the communities and barbarism (e.g. in the form of *daesh*). This allows me to rethink the binary between the civil and the military, as the boundaries between the two spheres are fluid at best, as the examples of the women's personal trajectories, life in Maxmûr, the martyr funerals and the norms around the militant femininities demonstrate (Pugliese 2016). To do so, I pay attention to the 'becoming' of the women and their ideology: how they used the liberation ideology to change the party from within and how they deal with the militarisation of their everyday lives? This includes the rituals of mourning the dead, as a location where a sense of belonging, sacrifice but also a vision and hope for a future nation to be liberated are negotiated (Khalili 2007).

Caron E. Gentry and Laura Sjoberg acknowledge that feminist IR has asked where the women are, but that women are still largely absent in theories of people's violence or included with reference to masculine standards of people's conduct. The authors advocate for a 'relational autonomy' framework, instead of a separation of men's and women's violence – the recognition that freedom of action is defined and limited by social relationships such as gender, race and class, as well as religious and political contexts. In relational autonomy, identities of the self and other are mutually dependent, and choices are often gendered and never entirely free or constrained. 'Gendered lenses' recognition of human interdependence and relational autonomy shows that all decisions are contextual and contingent, not only women's and all decisions are made, not only men's' (Gentry & Sjoberg 2015, 46). Warring women are still seen as exceptional because they threaten a system that is based on stable masculinities and femininities, where men go to war and women mourn at home and make peace. I argue that paying attention to context and relationality, but most importantly women's own narratives, allows for a more nuanced feminist IR theory on women and war, that does not ask why women commit political violence, but how on a daily basis they operate within spaces of violence and resistance, paying attention to how revolution and freedom are embodied, lived and fought for.

Space, Body Politics and Sexuality

The body and the experiences of embodiment in war have been put forward by feminists across disciplines. Judith Butler argues that the 'body implies mortality, vulnerability and agency: the skin and the flesh expose us to the gaze of others, but also to touch and to violence, and bodies put us at risk of becoming the agency and instrument of all these as well' (Butler 2004, 26). Due to the centrality of the body as a subject of wars, conflicts and militarisation, the body becomes a carrier of what Jennifer Hyndman has described as 'embodied epistemologies' of violence and invites us to 'undo' through ethnography 'embedded identities and strategic ways of seeing conflict and its consequences' (Hyndman 2004, 314). A 'strategic' reading is a reading aware of essentialist notions but refers to them in order to take apart the authoritative voice from within, as the extensive work of post-colonial feminist scholar Gayatri C. Spivak shows (1988, 1990, 2009). As I approach the body and its environments through ethnographic research, I dissect the scale of violence and agency that builds and sustains militant femininities among generations of female revolutionaries.

My work also draws on a growing body of literature on body, space and politics, which since the so-called Arab Uprisings and the coup attempt in Turkey in summer 2016 has examined the important links between protest, public space and gendered politics (Gökarıksel 2017, Hasso & Salime 2016, El Said, Maeri & Pratt 2015). This body of literature acknowledges the fact that '[p]olitical power is never gender-neutral but works through gendered and sexual production of bodies that belong and that do not, that need protection and that are threats, and through the gendered and sexual construction of borders and territory' (Gökarıksel 2017). Banu Gökarıksel emphasises that a feminist critique can provide new insights 'into the production of an environment of increasing consolidation of masculinist power, rhetoric of national unity, violence, and militarism' (ibid.). To this I must add that the women's movement under analysis here has been engaging in a critique of the masculine and militarised nation state since the early 1990s and in that process has developed its own form of organising and knowledge production, such as Jineolojî[12], the movement's 'women's science', which I will return to in the next chapter. This process was invisible or inaudible to many (not just Turkish feminists), due to state repression, racism and the fraught relations between the Turkish and Kurdish feminist movements (Çaha 2011; Gökalp 2010; Ömer 2011; Sahin-Mencutek 2016; Yüksel 2006). However, this way of linking body, politics and space helps me to connect questions of power, gender and sexuality, because revolutions or uprisings are deeply bodily and affective affairs. They are moments of rupture; gender and sexual orders are publicly disputed, while a range of forces actively work on reasserting orderly gender norms and relations (Hasso & Salime 2016; El Said et al. 2015). The body becomes a political medium: especially, but not only, women's bodies in the 'Arab Uprisings' have been 'sites of dissent and revolution', even as they 'are disciplined and regulated through discourses of patriarchy, Islamism and secular modern masculinity' (Hasso & Salime 2016, 12).

---

[12] The term *Jineolojî* has its roots in the Kurdish word *jin* (woman), which is connected to *jin* (life) and *logos*, Greek for 'reason' or 'word' (Jineolojî Committee Europe 2018).

An important part of militant femininities and the liberation ideology as a whole is the aspect of desexualisation and abstinence. Upon entering the party, each member learns to refrain from sexual or romantic relations, based on the argument that all energy and focus must be directed towards the struggle. Before unpacking this seeming conundrum between the fight for freedom and this 'abstinence contract', it is important to stress that most members join this party voluntarily[13] and that there is a difference between the rules for cadres – those trained in the mountains and then sent to fight or organise in all four parts of Kurdistan or the European diaspora – and the politicians in the pro-Kurdish parties. Many politicians and activists in both Bakur and Rojava have husbands, wives and children. However, paying attention to the 'abstinence contract' raises crucial questions about the ways bodies are controlled and disciplined in the party and how this control is justified towards the party subjects. In party ideology, sexuality is not for militants, because it would keep women in a 'slave position', when instead they need to be fighting for a new society that brings freedom, equality and a communal life. Furthermore, being driven by sexual desires would hinder the focus of revolutionary duties (Öcalan 2010, 478–80). Critically analysing the notions of sexuality (or its absence) engenders questions about what forms of control remain or are reinvented when people join the party. Foucault argues that '[sexuality] appears rather as an especially dense transfer point for relations of power [...]. Sexuality is not the most intractable element in power relations, but rather one of those endowed with the greatest instrumentality: useful for the greatest number of manoeuvres and capable of serving as a point in support, as a linchpin, for the most varied strategies' (Foucault 1990, 103). By controlling sexuality, the party holds tremendous power over its members, as it controls the 'means', here the human body as the source of reproduction (Butler 1999; Connell 1987; Foucault 1990; Snitow et al. 1983), which is especially important in times of revolutionary change or political upheaval (Hasso et al. 2016; El Said et al. 2015).

Sex-positive feminists, since the 1960s and 1970s (de Beauvoir 1997; Friedan 1965; Irigaray 2011), have tried to reclaim women's sexuality by situating the body as a crucial site of political struggle, centring sexuality as a source of power, freedom and pleasure (Fahs 2010, 446). I argue here that sexuality is such a dense transfer point not merely because of

---

[13] 'Voluntarily' here needs to be problematized, as many women join because they do not see any alternative due to poverty, confinement to the domestic sphere (Darici 2011, 468), experiences of gender-based violence, existential threats, such as the onslaught of *daesh* or the continuous repression of the Turkish/Iranian/Iraqi/Syrian state. Hence, in some cases the party becomes the only viable alternative that promises a life free from sexism, racism and capitalist exploitation.

reproduction or because of the body as a site of competing political narratives, but also because of the subversive power and knowledge of sexuality. According to Audre Lorde, sexuality and the erotic bear the capacity for joy and potential for self-connection; it is a provocative force which enables the most intimate form of communication (Lorde 1993). Controlling or banning sexuality can then perhaps also be read as an ideological and tactical tool to withhold from people that intimate space. I am conscious of the fact that this argument does not consider all the socio-political and economic conditions that hinder people from experiencing romantic or sexual relations as equals, not just in the Middle East but across political geographies, yet the core of this argument remains relevant for my analysis: sexuality can be an anarchic place of subversion and freedom, and people who experience it are maybe less suitable for political functionalisation. Nevertheless, I will be asking how controlling one's sexual desire, according to PKK ideology, not only gives the party power over its members, but to what extent this process of desexualisation also gives power to women over their own bodies and their relations to men? One crucial aspect is that many of the recruits are from rural and conservative Muslim areas in the (Kurdish) Middle East, where ideas around shame and honour, albeit challenged by Öcalan and the PKK, prevail. Within the movement, the navigation of conservative gender and sex norms for the sake of equality and freedom is not an easy feat, and one that demands complete dedication from its militants.

To come to terms with this unique configuration of powers that play out on the body of both male and female revolutionaries, I propose that it helps to consider the processes that unfold within the party, such as refraining from sexual relations, as 'party bargains'. A party bargain describes the ongoing negotiation between the superstructure that is the KCK/KJK and its individual members, who join and learn to adhere to its rules. These rules set out a clear framework of dos and don'ts, and here I argue that sexuality is a key location of renegotiation. This concept of party bargain is inspired by Deniz Kandiyoti's patriarchal bargain (Kandiyoti 1988). An important aspect of Kandiyoti's concept is that women play an active role in manoeuvring their specific roles, within and beyond the household, and are not merely victims in a patriarchal system but are actively involved in perpetuating it. When Kandiyoti rethought 'bargaining with patriarchy' ten years later, she critiqued that her earlier institutional analysis was based on simplified assumptions of how certain rules define how gendered subjectivities are formed and develop strategies of collusion and resistance (Kandiyoti 1998). When it comes to the party bargain that I propose here, it is essentially an 'abstinence contract' that allows women to participate in a much bigger struggle for a future vision of society. The terms of negation or the framework of this bargain has distinct parameters. In that sense, Kandiyoti's earlier framework resonates with the context analysed here. Women henceforward do not bargain within the networks of patriarchal connectivity (Joseph 1993) but with a military patriarchy which has gender equality at its core. And by entering this bargain, the negotiation is not over; obtaining and maintaining militant femininities require constant vigilance on the path of women not only liberating themselves but the whole non-state nation as foreseen by Democratic Confederalism.

Democratic Confederalism: Beyond Nationalism and Feminism?

Much has been written about the multitudinous relations between feminism and nationalism and how the two 'isms' enable or hinder each other. Nira Yuval-Davis was one of the first feminist scholars to draw attention to the fact that nations are always gendered, in their repertoire, in their performativity and in the assigned gender norms. Men are typically depicted as the builders of the nation, while women represent the soil, the earth and home of the nation. Because women bear the new members of the nation, women's bodies serve as markers of national boundaries (Yuval-Davis & Anthias 1989; Yuval-Davis 1997). For Enloe, 'nationalism typically has sprung from masculinized memory, masculinized humiliation and masculinized hope' (Enloe 2014, 93). Studies that analyse ethnic/national identities with a gender perspective call attention to the fact that men speak and act on behalf of the community and that women have symbolic roles, their voices often remaining silent in the nation-building project. The discussion initiated by Yuval-Davis engaged many scholars who asked if nationalism categorically stands in the way of feminism (Abu-Lughod 1993; Cockburn 1998, 2007; Dirik 2018; Kandiyoti 1991; Jayawardena 1986; McClintock 1991 inter alia). Nadje Al-Ali and Nicola Pratt made an important contribution to this debate by showing that nationalism and feminism are not mutually exclusive per se, but that nationalist movements have often opened spaces for women (Al-Ali & Pratt 2011). To understand the make-up and potential of these spaces, it is crucial to ask what kind of feminism and what kind of nationalism are being practised and analysed and to examine the temporality of them: at what point does a nationalist struggle open spaces for women? What kind of spaces open for women? For which women? How do they use these spaces? At what point do these spaces become narrower again?

In her work on women's involvement in the Northern Ireland conflict (1968–1998), Theresa O'Keefe further challenges the notion that nationalist movements are, in themselves, unconstructive for women. Instead, she argues that feminist identities developed within nationalist movements have the capacity to transform those movements and affect change during and post-conflict: 'Nationalist movements are strong catalysts for feminist engagement and feminist activism. Politicised women struggling against interlocking, structural oppression are well-positioned to engage in feminist resistance that is directed both within the movement and external to it' (O'Keefe 2013, 14). This is not to say that women are not discriminated against or oppressed in national liberation movements and used as markers of 'us versus them' or their reproductive capacities. However, it would be wrong to suggest that women participate in these movements on male terms only. 'To construct women primarily as victims or men's pawns not only denies their agency but also masks the ways in which women are oppressed through their ethno-national identity. This is one of the crucial factors why women chose to engage in armed combat: ethnicity and oppression' (ibid., 7–8). O'Keefe notes that treating women as pawns in male games is unconducive because it glosses over specific motivations, roles and experiences of female combatants (ibid., 4–5). My findings of the women's struggle within the PKK resonate with that of O'Keefe's, who argues that feminist nationalism in Northern Ireland developed precisely because of the attempts to marginalise and silence women. It partly gained strength because of nationalism's patriarchal tendencies, and the attempts to suppress women encouraged them further (ibid., 186). My work is situated in this contradictory and complex field of women being active in a liberation movement, that was not initially based on gender-based equality and justice but became a powerful vehicle for women's emancipation as a result of the everyday struggle of women themselves, who changed the movement from within (Al-Ali & Taş 2018c, 20).

Different from previous national liberation struggles, the specific nationalism analysed here is a nationalism that is tied to statelessness and occupation, among dominant Arab, Turkish and Persian nationalisms. Kurds are nationalists without a state and Democratic Confederalism is a non-state liberation project, centring around women's liberation, self-defence, ecology and communal economy in order to realise the liberation of the nation. This is a discursive tool used over and over again by the movement itself but proven true, insofar as it is the women who are at the front and who do the political, social and military work and as such rearrange the division of labour. Different from previous nationalisms in the region, women no longer represent the home, or the honour that needs protection from man, and neither are they expected to stay at home to reproduce the nation (Yuval-Davis & Anthias 1989). Women are expected to get out of the house and actively participate in defending the honour of the home-land, either through a political or armed struggle. Their love is directed towards the struggle and the land; other physical or personal desires are curbed. Furthermore, women's voices are heard; they are not merely spoken about in the nationalist discourse (Chatterjee & Jeganathan 2000). Moreover, women are not only using spaces provided by a patriarchal order, but they are to a certain extent further rewriting and reorganising that order into separate women's structures. Jineolojî, for example, is an important location where this dialectic relationship between Öcalan, women and an evolving body of knowledge production can be observed, as I will discuss further subsequently.

As always, the messiness of social reality exceeds the explanatory power of our conceptual frameworks (Kandiyoti 1998, 150). Knowing these limitations, I argue that militant femininities, as introduced here, can serve as a conceptual lens to discuss the complexity that emerges from simultaneous processes of subjectivation, performance, docility and agency in war and armed conflict. It can be used to critically analyse the PKK's party ideology, women's roles in the different spheres of activism, as well as the creation of a distinct body politics. The following section will highlight how I situate this study methodologically and how I dealt with the messiness of social realities during fieldwork.

Methodology: Mapping Out Different Matrixes of Domination

There is a consistent duality reinforcing the persistence of contradictions when making sense of 'who the women are'. In the Kurdish Freedom Movement, women are not just bodies to be formed and deployed, but the formation of the militant is meant to give rise to a woman comrade who will serve the greater good of the Kurdish nation and give women a social place and labour in the struggle. This duality allows to conceptu-ally discuss the potentiality of obedience and agency intrinsic to militant femininities. The disciplining and formation of obedient bodies have been extensively read through Michel Foucault's chapter on 'Docile Bodies' in his study of Prussian soldiers in the late seventeenth century (Foucault 1991). In the late 1980s and increasingly in the 1990s, post-modern and post-structuralist feminists have criticised Foucault's under-standing of the formation of universalized male soldier bodies by locating bodies across political geographies. Spivak in her criticism of Foucault and other post-structuralist and post-modern thinkers emphasizes that 'these philosophers' fail due to their positionality to see the implications of body politics, difference and place on one's access to fair labour in the international division of labour (Spivak 1988, 274). To consider, methodologically, the power of bodies and the power of governance through the use of violence, this ethnography is situated within transnational feminism, which recognises that intersecting power structures operate at different levels and impact the relationships between genders, ethnicities and classes (Al-Ali & Pratt 2009; Alexander & Mohanty 2010; Collins 2000; Grewal and Kaplan 1994; Mohanty 1988, 2013; Mohanty et al. 1991). These power structures not only define the essentialised discourse about the Kurdish women's movement, which often leaves out the economic, cultural, social and political complexity of this particular context, but also shapes the women's own everyday realities (Al-Ali & Pratt 2016, 90). Transnational feminists, rather than limiting the analytical field to the boundaries of the nation state, trace the circulation of gendered power across different scales, thereby going beyond binary analytics such as war/peace, power/resistance, victim/perpetrator, national/international and male/female. Bringing together questions of representation and political economy, a transnational feminist lens pays attention to the intersectionality and transnational circulation of power relations against the backdrop of imperial geopolitics (Grewal & Kaplan 1994). Transnational feminism is rooted in the intellectual and political legacies of Black feminisms, in particular in regard to the 'intersectionality' of power relations (Crenshaw 1991) or the 'matrix of domination' (Collins 2000). Since the 1960s, black feminist thought has articulated and reconceptualised the relationship between domination and activism, or violence and resistance, using a critical intersectional framework. Intersectionality as an analytic tool is neither a new phenomenon, nor is it confined to struggles of North America and Europe. Globally, movements have used intersectionality analyses, some before 1991 when Kimberlé Crenshaw coined the term for the academy. Without naming it as intersectionality, the women of the Kurdish Freedom Movement know that axis of social division such as gender, class and ethnicity operate not as exclusive entities but work together (Collins & Bilge 2016, 3–4; Alinia 2015). The Kurdish women's movement calls it the 'triple oppression' of patriarchy, capitalism and nation states. Taking the movement's own intersectional framing as a departure point and linking it to existing transnational feminist literature and black feminist thought, I build on what Patricia Hill Collins calls the 'matrix of domination', which she defines as the overall organization of hierarchical power relations for any society. Any specific matrix of domination has (1) a particular arrangement of intersecting systems of oppression, for example, race, social class, gender, sexuality, citizenship status, ethnicity and age; and (2) a particular organization of its domains of power, for example, structural, disciplinary, hegemonic and interpersonal (Collins 2000, 299). Only by analysing how different matrices of domination overlap, mutually constitute each other and intersect with imperialism, authoritarianism and neoliberalism, and how all of them intersect with gender, can one start to make sense of the messy and contested grounds the women of the movement operate in, both on the local and national levels (Al-Ali & Pratt 2016, 92).

Intersectionality as an analytical lens has been criticised for treating black women's bodies as anachronisms (Nash 2014, 61) and for either having become too preoccupied with particularity, or being hinged on fictive fixity, treating gender, class and race as separable rather than intimately linked (Puar 2007). This allegedly fosters identity politics, which is seen as detrimental to struggles. However, and here I concur with Collins and Bilge, for marginalised groups, or movements operating in a context of ongoing war and conflict, a collective identity is not only a necessity but also an important part of their emancipatory power. For example, a collective identity shaped by shared social locations that is formulated as a project of political empowerment and achieved through consciousness-raising is key in the fight against the manifold oppressions faced by Kurdish women (Collins & Bilge 2016, 129). When analysing strategically essentialised identities (ibid.), intersectionality also helps to show that identities are always constructed, never static, and that despite a clearly fleshed-out framework, such as militant femininities that I propose here, the social location and the temporality of inquiry decide which aspect of the powers that shape an identity are being foregrounded. Sometimes that might be gender, sometimes ethnicity, depending on the political situation or the networks of solidarity needing to be forged. Having said this, the ideas around womanhood and manhood fostered by the party do have essentialist elements that go beyond movements organising around social justice projects in other parts of the world (Spivak 1996). There is a clear idea of who the 'free' women and men are, what a good revolutionary is, and the rules of what the individual has to contribute to the collective struggle are fixed. This creates tensions between the promise of liberation and its strict and policed processes, a complexity that I try to capture through militant femininities.

A critical analysis of overlapping matrices of domination and their intersecting power relations also means paying attention to the knowledge that is being produced by the Kurdish women's movement. For example, what is the epistemological significance of Jineolojî, the women's science? Proposed by Öcalan in 2008, and since developed in women's centres across different parts of Kurdistan and Europe, Jineolojî and its advocates have put into writing their collective experiences and knowledge, which emerged out of four decades of political and armed struggle, finding a new vocabulary for understanding the intersecting oppressions they are fighting, while also connecting their knowledges to other feminist movements across the globe (Al-Ali & Käser 2020; Herausgeberinnenkollektiv 2012, 103–108).

Methods and Fieldwork in a Divided Kurdistan

Initially, in 2014, when I started this project, I had planned to undertake fieldwork primarily in Rojava, at that stage made up of three Kurdish cantons (Qamişlo, Kobanî, Afrîn) under the control of the PKK/PYD and its armed wings the YPG and YPJ. Due to the attacks of *daesh* on Kobanî, Şengal, and the wider region in 2014, and the intensification of the Syrian civil war as a whole, I decided to shift my focus to other geographies where the Kurdish women's movement has been active for many decades, namely Bakur (mainly Diyarbakir), Maxmûr Camp[14] in Iraqi Kurdistan and the guerrilla camps in the mountains on the Iraqi/ Iranian border. What linked these different fieldwork sites was not only the challenges of doing fieldwork in a divided Kurdistan and my own intellectual journey, but more importantly the ways in which the move- ment operates transnationally across borders, how knowledge travels, and how the liberation ideology is performed and lived in each of these places.

Due to four decades of war between the PKK and the Turkish state, Eastern Turkey, and Diyarbakir, where I spent the first five months of my fieldwork, is highly politicised and polarised. I arrived at the tail end of the peace process between the Turkish state and the PKK (2013–2015), or what activists in Diyarbakir referred to as the 'golden years'. During that short time of relative peace, the pro-Kurdish political movement, which was in charge of most of the municipalities in Turkey's southeast, managed to get off the ground many political, culture and language initiatives, according to the structures set out by Democratic Confederalism. However, not everyone was organised behind 'party lines'. In Bakur many political parties were fighting for power: from the pro-Kurdish parties, such as the Democratic Regions Party (DBP, *Demokratik Bölgeler Partisi*), or the Peoples' Democratic Party (HDP, *Halkların Demokratik Partisi*), to Tayyib Erdoğan's Justice and Development Party (AKP), *Adalet ve Kalkınma Partisi*), the Gülen Movement (pre-2016)[15], to different

---

[14] The Kurmancî Kurdish letter X is pronounced at the back of the throat like the Scottish CH (as in loch).

[15] Turkey's government accuses the Gülen Movement of being the mastermind behind the attempted coup on 15 July 2016. As a result, the whole movement has been wiped out; its members have either been arrested or had to flee abroad; its institutions, such as schools,

Islamist parties, such as the Free Cause Party (Hüda-Par, *Hür Dava Partisi*), and the Kurdish Hizbullah (Kurt 2017). These political splits manifested themselves in every city, neighbourhood and sometimes families. Throughout my time in Diyarbakir, I built a broad network of contacts, not with the AKP or the Islamists but with academics, journalists, students and lawyers, from across the political spectrum. Within this fractured and contested urban space, my mobility became increasingly constrained by the deteriorating security situation. This meant that I could only very occasionally visit KJA or do interviews with its members from mid-December onwards, when the siege of Diyarbakir's old city (Sur) started. The women were either too busy managing their operations during the conflict and making sure their members were still out and protesting, or it was simply no longer safe to meet. Instead, I did interviews with members of civil society organisations, went to press conferences, taught English at a Kurdish Kindergarten, and generally stayed close to my experienced journalist friends, who knew how to navigate the territory subjected to numerous security threats (Pottier et al. 2011).

In October 2015, I went to Rojava for a week-long trip with an international delegation to participate in the 'New World Summit Rojava'.[16] Together with activists, academics, artists and journalists, I visited the new women's academies, cultural and media centres, women's cooperatives and historical sites. I am not using any of the data from this trip for this book as we were mainly shuttled around from one party institution to the other, and the trip was not long enough to conduct ethnographic research. I could have stayed longer but was so overwhelmed with revolutionary dogma and exhausted by the intensity of it all that I decided to leave with the group and return later in the year. In retrospect that was perhaps a miscalculation, given that the border between Iraqi Kurdistan and Rojava later became increasingly difficult to cross. Furthermore, towards the end of my fieldwork I no longer had the energy to build yet another research network that could transcend what I call 'party slogans', the official party ideology that was so often narrated to me during interviews, a narrative that took time, effort and trust to break through. I have, however, been following the developments in Rojava closely for the past ten years and have interviewed many party members who had previously

---

have been closed down and its assets have been taken over or frozen (Angey 2018; Jongerden 2018).

[16] The New World Summit is an artistic and political organization led by artist Jonas Staal that develops parliaments with and for stateless states, autonomist groups and blacklisted political organizations. In 2015, he and his team, together with the new autonomous administration in Rojava, built the 'People's Parliament of Rojava', the inauguration of which our delegation attended (In der Maur, Staal & Dirik 2015).

worked there. Rojava will thus feature as a comparative perspective in this transnational analysis.

Due to the urban wars, I had to leave Diyarbakir in February 2016 and spent two months in Istanbul, where I continued my interviews with both male and female activists and politicians of the legal parties, the People's Democratic Congress (HDK, *Halkların Demokratik Kongresi*), the DBP and HDP. From a research perspective this was not a productive time, as I found it challenging to continue my work with the same passion in a city that felt indifferent to the war in the east of the country. Thereafter, I relocated to Erbil in Iraqi Kurdistan, where I was hoping to rekindle my enthusiasm. The most challenging aspect of doing a multi-sited ethnography is the building of numerous and new networks (Coleman & von Hellermann 2013). I found it needs great perseverance and a daily motivational kick to continually make those phone calls and visits, not least because due to ongoing wars and conflicts, I often felt like an imposition to the women and their more pressing tasks. Friends and interlocutors from the movement in Diyarbakir facilitated this process by handing me over to their comrades south of the border. After I contacted the two main party cadres in Erbil and Sulaymaniyah, they arranged my first trip to the Maxmûr Camp. There I improved my language skills and learned how the political ideology of Democratic Confederalism is being put into practice. Maxmûr is a refugee camp for displaced Kurds from Bakur, who had to flee the war between the PKK and the Turkish state in the early 1990s (Yılmaz 2016). In total I stayed in Maxmûr for over a month, conducting semi-structured interviews and participant observation with fighters and party cadres who were in Maxmûr to organise the socio-political life or to defend the camp. As a woman I had access to women's domestic spheres where I did most of my ethnographic research by simply living, working, cleaning, cooking, eating and relaxing with them (Abu-Lughod 1993). In Maxmûr, the boundaries between military and civil life are non-existent, something I only got used to during my second visit: the simultaneity of mundane housework and revolutionary organising, the ideological speech of women's liberation coexisting alongside conservative gender norms, the high PKK commanders spontaneously walking into the living room to join us for tea. In Maxmûr, the party ideology is lived in the everyday, the project of changing people and society as a whole by unlearning 'patriarchy', while organising and farming independently from the constrains of Capitalist Modernity. This is not an easy feat, given Iraqi Kurdistan's rampant capitalist development, its financial crisis due to the ongoing budget dispute with Baghdad, and continuous wars at its borders. Daily life at the camp was structured around party work and remembering the martyrs, and it was here that I understood how the party ideology gives people hope in the everyday, in this seemingly never-ending costly fight for Kurdish self-determination.

For the last four months of my fieldwork I lived in Sulaymaniyah. From there, I went on shorter research trips to Erbil, Maxmûr and the guerrilla training camps on the Iraqi-Iranian border. In Sulaymaniyah I spent my days at the meetings, conferences and protests of the local Kurdistan Free Women's Organisation (RJAK, *Rêxistina Jinên Azad ên Kurdistanê*), interviewed their female members or those cadres passing through from Qandil to Şengal or Rojava, and worked in a local NGO to secure my visa. Sulaymaniyah is ruled by the PUK, and the Talabani family, challenged by the PUK splinter party, the Gorran Movement. Contrary to the KDP, which is run by the Barzani family, both the PUK and Gorran have a more amicable relationship with the PKK and its regional sub-groups; they give them the right of passage, grant them their mountainous terrain and issue IDs for those who need to go from the mountains to the cities. However, in the city itself the Kurdish women's movement was able to do little apart from providing education courses and building political alliances. Many civilians I spoke to had a lot of respect for the PKK and were tied to the party emotionally, especially if members of their family have joined, but they did not see them as capable of becoming a governing power. Instead they perceive them as admirable fighters and successful warriors on the battlefield. Some teenagers go for 'education' to the mountains and will march on the relevant days with Öcalan flags, and a small number of people joins the military ranks from Iraqi Kurdistan. Overall, Sulaymaniyah, from the perspective of the movement, seemed more like a hub city on the way from Qandil to Maxmûr, Kirkuk, Şengal or Rojava than a real focus for political change. This party's paradigm has historically placed most of its ideological and tactical focus on Turkish Kurdistan/Bakur, and more recently Syrian Kurdistan/Rojava, but only in the last few years has it started to tailor its knowledge production (linguistically, organisationally, or reading material) to the specific context of Iraqi Kurdistan/Başûr and Iranian Kurdistan/Rojhelat. Its revolutionary language and claims, as well as its attempts to recruit the youth from Başûr, sit uncomfortably with many. I was told repeatedly: 'Our revolution days are over, people here don't want war or instability again.' Some also clearly see the PKK as a foreign power with no business in Başûr, an external meddler standing in the way of Kurdish independence. Yet I believe the power of new imaginaries that the movement creates, especially when it comes to giving young women different role models – such as after the defence of Kobanî and Şengal in 2014 – should not be underestimated.

At the end of my fieldwork I spent two weeks in 'the mountains', one week in a military training camp and one week in an ideological education course. The mountains are where the revolutionary ideology is taught, lived and discussed. It was here that I fully understood what the saying 'mountain life is difficult but beautiful' that I had heard so often really means, why joining the armed struggle is a viable and sometimes the only alternative for so many young women from across the region, how experiences of individual violence and collective trauma are turned into active resistance, and how liberation is learned and performed through communal living, the memorising of Öcalan's books, the practice of criticism and self-criticism, and how one gains the seemingly unfaltering will to resist until death (*îrade*). I observed how bodies and minds become disciplined to march to the beat of the PKK drum of freedom, and how their liberation ideology and visions of communal living make sense so far away from the realities of civilian life.

Overall, I paid careful attention to build networks that cut across class, gender, sexuality and political affiliations. But most importantly I tried to foster relationships built on mutual respect, interest and sometimes friendship. These connections, especially with female members of the party, then helped me when I was moving from Diyarbakir to Istanbul, Erbil, Maxmûr and Sulaymaniyah and endured long beyond fieldwork. In total, I conducted eighty-four semi-structured interviews with activists, politicians, mothers, fighters, sympathisers and critics in Diyarbakir, Istanbul, Maxmûr, Erbil, Sulaymaniyah and the mountain camps. Seventy-five per cent of my interlocutors were women. Most of my interviews in the first six months were either conducted in English or in Turkish with a translator, as my Kurmancî was only good enough for in-depth conversations in the second half of the fieldwork. I also did five interviews with former commanders, ex-cadres who left the party between 2005 and 2019 and have sought asylum in Switzerland.[17] These last interviews provided the opportunity to ask certain sensitive questions around femininity and masculinity, body politics and sexuality that most active members, who are bound to the official party script, would not have answered in the same way. I recorded all of my interviews

---

[17] These informants (four women, one man) will be referred to as 'former commander' or 'former cadre' 1–5 in this following chapters, as all of them requested to remain anonymous – some out of fear of legal and political repercussion, others because they did not want to be seen to publicly criticise the party, at a time when it is under attack from all sides.

but found that I got the richest data when I turned off the recorder and just participated in the everydayness of my interlocutor's routines.

Reflections on Doing a Feminist Ethnography in a War Zone

'Why are you studying this?' 'Why are you interested in us?' 'Switzerland is so nice, what are you doing in this place?', I was often asked by my interlocutors. Some asked this question simply because they were intrigued by my presence; others were wary of the 'Westerner', and the influx of journalistic and scholarly attention on the Kurdish women's movement, particularly after Kobanî and Şengal. Either way, these are legitimate questions, particularly in a highly politicised geography such as Kurdistan, which has historically been affected by a 'state of statelessness'. This has shaped, among other things, how knowledge is produced by and about the Kurds, and asks of me, the ethnographer, to reflect critically about the power and privilege that shape my positionality and journey through a research and writing process (Baser et al. 2019, xiii–xxx). As a feminist I wanted to understand what makes these women stand and fight at the forefront of the ongoing battles in the region and how they persevere amidst tremendous hardship. As an academic I was interested in debates around gender and war, and the particular femininities and masculinities that are the backbone of this liberation movement. When asked these questions, I sometimes gave a lengthy answer about having grown up in a refugee village in Switzerland where I learned early on that there is a world that is plagued by war and conflict outside my native and seemingly perfect Alpenland, or how I studied Arabic in Damascus in 2008 and 2009, when the trials were held for the Kurdish activists who had asked for minority rights during the 'Damascus Spring' in 2000 and 2001.[18] This drew my attention to the Kurdish question in Syria, as a result of which I ended up working on the Syrian Kurds during my previous studies. My motivations behind this project were certainly also driven by the desire to make sense of a part of this world that I feel a deep connection to, and the wish to listen to and record some of the voices of, the women who are pushing this emancipatory project forward. Many of my interlocutors will probably never read what I have written and those who do might not agree with some of my

---

[18] The 'Damascus Spring' refers to a brief political opening prompted by the death of Hafiz al-Assad and the appointment of his son, Bashar al-Assad in 2000. For one year, Kurdish and Arab human rights and civil society organisations engaged in a public debate, bringing the opposition into the open, raising hopes for democratic reforms. The 'Damascus Spring' came to an abrupt end in August 2001, when the leaders of the movement were arrested (Allsopp 2015, 108–10).

observations and analyses. Because over the course of the past seven years, my thinking about this women's movement and the matrices of domination it operates in has shifted considerably. From the onset, I was sceptical of the unified and often repeated slogans but was drawn into their urgency of the struggle as I arrived in 'the field', where the human side of this incredibly imbalanced conflict (between the Turkish state and the Kurdish Freedom Movement) became painfully obvious. However, throughout my research I also became very aware of the 'greyness of violence' (Bourgois 2004), observing and witnessing the many ways in which the movement is dogmatic, authoritarian and strictly hierarchical, and I began to ask more critical questions about the process of 'becoming' the desired militant. Now, at the end of it all, I hope to have found a middle ground where it is apparent that I am in solidarity with the movement and the people fighting for it, but also acutely aware of the violence that goes hand in hand with the liberation project. Until today I oscillate between attachment, solidarity, discomfort and scepticism, as is reflected in the way I analyse my data, the stories I share, and the conclusions I draw.

Conducting ethically sound research in a conflict zone meant above all not harming anyone with my presence or through my work. This included ensuring the anonymity of my interlocutors if requested, keeping safe the information they provided, sticking to spoken agreements of confidentiality, and most importantly relying on local knowledge about safety (Pottier et al. 2011), such as people providing safe passage to and from Maxmûr or the mountain camps.

The main ethical challenges I faced first had to do with navigating the wish to stay and conduct research, while knowing that the situation was either becoming uninhabitable (Diyarbakir) or the respective activists had more pressing things to do (everywhere). I struggled with my own role as 'only' a researcher in the face of visible human suffering. Given the highly charged and volatile political and security situation, I usually felt more or less inadequate given my seemingly much less effective position, compared to the activists, politicians and fighters struggling at the front lines. This gap between the women who are giving their life for a struggle and me merely writing about them never became easy to bridge, the feeling of inadequacy being my constant fieldwork companion. After all, '[n]othing is stranger than this business of humans observing other humans in order to write about them' (Behar 1996, 5) and particularly in a conflict zone these dynamics becomes painfully obvious.[19] During my fieldwork,

[19] Not only is the notion of observation strange, but it can smack uncomfortably of colonialism and imperialism and contribute to a discourse of the 'Other' (Said 1987). Decolonising methodologies, curricula and universities is an ongoing process that I tried to contribute to by adhering to my feminist principles of being ethical, respectful,

I often remembered the work of Elisabeth Wood, who conducted her research in El Salvador during the civil war. She wrote that she solved this dilemma between wanting to be there but not fully knowing how and for how long, by accepting the endorsement of her respondents: as long as they were willing to take the time to share their stories, experiences and political goals, she felt that her presence was validated (Wood 2006). This became my marker of when it was time to go or perhaps return at a later date.[20]

Gaining initial access to the women's centres such as KJA in Diyarbakir or RJAK in Sulaymaniyah was easy; however, going beyond those first conversations and forging closer relations was not. At the centres, I was always warmly welcomed but after a short while kindly tolerated and happily sent on my way. The women's offices and centres are places where, among other things, loyalty with the Freedom Movement is performed, which also includes certain interactions and comportment I was initially unfamiliar with. Particularly in the beginning, I often felt embarrassed when feeling like I had asked the wrong question (Schäfers 2019), said the wrong thing or sat the wrong way, crossing or extending my legs at an inadequate time. Numerous times during fieldwork I was scolded by both female and male militants between the cities and mountains, who drew a clear line between acceptable and inacceptable physical composure, which applied to me as well. This is not to say that I was not welcome as a frequent visitor at the women's centres, meetings and demonstrations; however, linguistic barriers (Turkish in Diyarbakir, mostly Sorani in Sulaymaniyah), as well as my position as a Western researcher who was perhaps not 'militant' enough, meant that I stayed at a certain distance.

Another challenge during fieldwork was to go beyond the official 'party slogans', as I came to call them, something I discuss throughout the following chapters. The long-standing struggle, the uniform women's

---

reflexive, critical and humble and not to silence or 'other' the voices of my interlocutors (Smith 1999).

[20] This feeling of inadequacy was difficult to shed but the urgency of the struggle also meant that I was fully involved. Only towards the very end of my fieldwork did I comprehend that this is my work and not my life and that I could and should separate the two. During my second trip to the mountains for example, I kept whispering to myself, 'You are an ethnographer, this is your work, you can leave again in a week, relax.' It was only during the process of writing this introduction that I learned that other people do that too. Behar writes: '[M]ost professional observers develop defences, namely "methods", that "reduce anxiety and enable us to function efficiently." Even saying, "I am an anthropologist, this is fieldwork," is a classic form of the use of a method to drain anxiety from situations in which we fell complicitous with structures of power, or helpless to release another from suffering, or at a loss as to whether to act or observe' (Behar 1996, 6).

structures and its unified ideology also meant that initially there were only a few layers of practices and everyday experiences (rather than the ideological narrative about them) that were visible and accessible to me, as a non-Kurdish researcher, who had only been active on the fringes of the Kurdish solidarity movement in London for a number of years.[21] Going beyond the slogans and being able to write an ethnography that transcends the official narrative of resistance – perpetuated by both the women's movement itself and the international media and the activist literature, particularly after Kobanî – required time, patience, and perseverance.

Before I started this research, I spent many years reading and researching different aspects of the Kurdish question, as part of my previous studies and as an activist in London. Pre-fieldwork I had done all the preparatory readings about how to conduct research in a conflict zone and how to navigate 'dangerous fields' (Mazurana et al. 2013; Naples 2003; Pottier 2011; Wood 2006; Viterna 2009). However, once I arrived in Diyarbakir and was thrown straight into a context of escalating conflict, I realised that as an outsider, as someone who was not 'born in the struggle', perhaps nothing prepares you for the intensity of feelings that comes with conflict and injustice. In their introduction to an issue of the Contemporary Levant titled *Ethnography as Knowledge in the Arab Region*, Samar Kanafani and Zina Sawaf poignantly introduce the term 'overbearing' in order to characterise the weight of forces and circumstances: 'which materialize on the level of spatial arrangements, violent conflict and dominant discourses, as well as hegemonic political and economic regimes. Their overpowering effect on the ethnographic experience is such that the ethnographer is compelled or constrained to devise unanticipated ways of grappling with research in that moment' (Kanafani & Sawaf 2017, 4). This overbearing feeling became my constant companion as I began to settle into my fieldwork reality. I learned to adapt to what Lamia Moghnieh in the same issue calls 'living-in-violence' (Moghnieh 2017), a form of everyday violence during the curfews in Diyarbakir, in which the local communities read and assess violence and threats in the everyday, learn how to negotiate it and continue their daily lives. 'Living-in-violence is a condition of continuous re-inhabitation and re-assessment of a social reality that oscillates between terror and normality, danger and safety' (ibid., 34). However, Moghnieh shows in her reflections on her ethnographic fieldwork in Lebanon that not all violence necessarily needs to be traumatic. According to her,

---

[21] I volunteered for Peace in Kurdistan (PIK), where I familiarised myself with many of the struggles both in the region and the diaspora. PIK is a London-based organisation dedicated to advancing the rights of the Kurdish people and achieving a political resolution of the Kurdish question.

violence is both destructive and transformative; it can be a life force as well (ibid., 26). This is something I observed closely everywhere I went; when communities were under attack it was not the time for despair; instead resistance snapped into action; ranks were closed, local and communal initiatives taken, and grounds stood firmly, quite literally so.

Four decades of war and protracted conflict across Kurdistan have led to highly militarised societies, particularly in places like Rojava and Maxmûr Camp, the latter a key research site for me. Aside from checkpoints, shifting front lines, and updates of the war constantly being televised into living rooms, it was the ritualisation of death, suffering and martyrdom that was initially most unfamiliar to me. For example, the fifteenth of August is an important day in the party calendar, marking the day when the PKK started its guerrilla war in 1984. Across the mountain camps this was celebrated with theatre, dance, music and speeches. In Maxmûr where I was, there were – apart from the music and dance – small children shouting from the stage 'martyrs don't die' and Murat Karayılan, one of the PKK's co-founders and top leaders, sent a video greeting, reiterating the importance of this day, and saluting the people of Maxmûr and their heroic resistance, after which the whole crowd stood to clap and cheer 'Bijî Serok Apo!' ('Long live the leader Apo!' [Öcalan]) and 'Bê Serok Jiyan Nabe!' ('No life without the leader!'). On the one hand I was often uncomfortable with the militarisation of every aspect of life; on the other hand I observed myself becoming more and more militarised, accepting and normalising killing and dying as a normal part of my informants' lives, while personally being prepared to support and defend the armed struggle as a sheer necessity in a region shaped by violence. This mindset accompanied me long after my fieldwork, also because I stayed closely connected to many of my informants, some of whom had become good friends.

I am sharing these fieldwork vignettes because I believe it is important to talk reflexively about the emotive registers of fieldwork, such as discomfort, doubt, and fear, just as importantly as deep affinities, friendship and solidarity, and ask: '[W]hat kind of critical knowledge can attention to these aspects of the ethnographic encounter (and the methodological adaptions that ensue) generate?' (Kanafani & Sawaf 2017, 4–5). Reflecting critically about the width of my emotions in the field helps to read these experiences in a way that scrutinize the emotional and intellectual connection between the observed and the observer (Behar 1996, 14), hopefully leading to more nuanced insights about the world in which they occurred and the ways knowledge is produced and later presented in its written form (Abu-Lughod 2017, 68).

Of course, emotive factors alone do not suffice to describe my fieldwork experience and how it influenced my methodology or data analysis. There were also material, spatial and political registers that facilitated or prevented access. Most importantly, I am a woman with the financial means, conviction and institutional backing to spend a year in different parts of Kurdistan. My gender mattered, particularly when gaining access to the women's party structures, being able to stay in women's houses or training camps. Our shared rapport on the fringes of interviews or participant observations about politics, freedom, love, men, sexuality or hopes for the future created the most surprising and rich insights into the lives of the people behind this liberation in the making. My Swiss passport mattered insofar as I could leave at any point when the crackdown on the Kurdish movement started in mid-2015 and intensified in late 2015. However, this did not mean that I and my work were not directly implicated by the widespread crackdown of the Kurdish Freedom Movement. When trying to return to Turkey from Iraqi Kurdistan in May 2016, I was stopped at Diyarbakir airport, informed that my visa had been cancelled and that I had been labelled a 'threat to national security'. I received a five-year ban and was locked into a deportation room for two days, before being put on the next flight back to Erbil.

To me, there was no clear transition between fieldwork and life in London. I continued to be engaged in what happens to my friends in the movement or on its fringes, many of whom have fled Turkey or Iraq, some of whom are imprisoned in Turkey, have been killed in battle or left the party since then. What kept me going throughout the challenging process of researching and writing this book, apart from my undying stubbornness, was meeting and working with the women and men of the movement, who for different reasons give their life to this political or armed struggle. Many of my explorations in the following chapters are shaped by an attempt to understand how exactly they continue to organise, resist and create hope in the face of seemingly insurmountable adversity.

Outline

The book is structured into five chapters: Chapter 1 historically contextualises the Kurdish women's movement and traces the trajectory of its organisational structures and knowledge production from 1978 to the present. It situates the Kurdish Freedom Movement and its local political and armed branches in the regional and international matrices of domination: Turkey, Syria, Iraq and Iran. It zooms in on the main internal rupture points where the women resisted and fought against their male comrades in order to build their autonomous ranks within the larger liberation movement.

Chapter 2 examines how the claim of difference and sustainability was organised and implemented by the Kurdish women's movement in the political sphere of Diyarbakir, where the movement has a long-standing history of organising women according to party ideology and structures. I analyse how this struggle for space unfolded once the urban wars started in mid-2015, mapping out the tools and mechanisms of resistance used by the movement as a whole and the women's structures in particular. This chapter also gives space to the critical voices, residents not organised in party structures, as they were caught in the front lines between the PKK and the Turkish army.

Chapter 3 is an account of how PKK revolutionaries are educated in the mountains, analysing how the liberation ideology is learned and lived in the everyday. Here, women find a language to talk about their oppression and learn about their responsibility: to liberate themselves, their minds, and through armed and political struggle, other women in the region. I demonstrate how this process of learning to become 'free' is both emancipatory and coercive, arguing that while the liberation movement opens spaces for women, women can only participate in those spaces if they learn to become soldiers for the cause. The ethnographic data of this chapter adds another layer to my concept of militant femininities and puts forward a more nuanced analysis of gender and agency in the context of an armed liberation movement.

Chapter 4 turns to martyr mothers in Maxmûr. This camp, with its violent history, is highly militarised and a place where the boundaries between the armed and civil spheres are non-existent. Almost every week someone from the camp falls at one of the many front lines in the region, while the families in the camps, and especially the mothers, continue to live life according to the party's liberation ideology. I show how the militant mothers of the camp play an integral part in continuing not only camp life but the struggle for freedom according to the PKK more broadly. I map out three key sites of daily life for mothers; first, the martyr house and death wakes; second, camp work; and third, the private house. Throughout I discuss how mothers organise and perform rituals of mourning, remembrance and resistance. Hereby, the martyr culture is a key location where a sense of belonging and sacrifice but also a vision and hope for a future nation are negotiated.

Chapter 5 takes an in-depth look at body politics and sexuality and aims to do two things: first, to unpack the often sidelined aspect of the fighters' desexualisation. How is this part of the subjectivity produced, believed, maintained and policed? What are the tensions that emerge from creating a desexualised guerrilla army that comes down from the mountains to liberate society? Second, this chapter discusses what I call 'party bargains'. I argue that women break out of their particular societal constellations by joining the party and enter a new bargain, this time with the party. It discusses three sites of party bargains: the fighter, the civil activist or politician, and the mother, whereas the three categories are overlapping. I demonstrate that in each case these party bargains hold great emancipatory power and that chosen abstinence (for the guerrillas) can be seen as one of the main tools of women's resistance that strengthens the women's ranks. However, this process goes hand in hand with a strict process of discipline and coercion, and I ask whether the sex ban is in fact at the heart of the new gender norms and relations in the making and key to the party's ability to control its revolutionaries.

I conclude by arguing the party system, and all its militarly and political projects, are propped up by a highly gendered ideology that is institutionalised, taught, learned, practised and policed and which gives women a powerful tool to enforce and defend their rights, if they do it within the framework of militant femininities. While this movement challenges certain knowledges that we have about gender, sexuality, nationalism and war, it reinforces others. The claim of sustainability, the institutionalisation of gender-based equality and justice beyond the revolutionary moment are difficult to measure or anticipate, since there have never been enough consecutive peaceful years, and the system in Rojava is yet to prove that it can be democratic in the sense of including consensus and dissensus. Instead, the claim of sustainability is an important discursive tool to create difference and continuity, as the fight for freedom goes on.

1   The PKK – A Woman's Party?
A History of the Kurdish Women's Freedom Movement 1978–2020

On 30 July 1996, Zîlan, a female PKK guerrilla, detonated a bomb in the middle of a military parade in Dersim. Beforehand she sent a letter to the exiled party leader Abdullah Öcalan in Damascus that stated:

> I want to be part of the total expression of the liberation struggle of our people. By exploding a bomb against my body I want to protest against the policies of imperialism which enslaves women and express my rage and become a symbol of resistance of Kurdish women. Under the leadership of Apo [Öcalan], the national liberation struggle and the Kurdish people, will at last take its richly deserved place in the family of humanity. My will to live is very strong. My desire is to have a fulfilled life through a strong action. The reason for my actions is my love for human beings and for life! (Letter excerpt, Zîlan 1996)[1]

This suicide attack was the first of its kind and had a huge impact on the women, the party and Öcalan himself. With her suicide attack, Zîlan became the new symbol of women's resistance and determination for generations of women who came after her. Shortly after the attack, Öcalan started calling the PKK a 'woman's party', in order to make official women's important contributions and central role in the movement as a whole (interview with former commander, 14 May 2018). This signified an important shift for women who had spent years fighting for recognition within the male-dominated party structures. 'We had to fight in order to be able to fight', a former commander told me about her experience of the power struggles with men in the party in the 1990s. Zîlan's act, however, made it impossible for any male member of the movement to question her and, by extension, women's dedication to the cause. Yet, in the day-to-day struggle, many of my respondents recounted how their male comrades actively sabotaged the women and their nascent party structures, especially after Öcalan's arrest in 1999. The women nevertheless managed to establish their own army (1995) and party (1999) within the PKK. Since then, their party structures have developed and diversified into all cultural, political and military realms in different

---

[1] For the whole letter, see Zeynep Kinaci (Zilan). 1996. *PKK Online.*

parts of Kurdistan and Europe as well, most visibly so in the form of the
female fighters in Rojava, the co-mayors in Bakur and the development of
Jineolojî. Today, one can imagine the Kurdish Freedom Movement and
its organisational structure like a tree that over the past decades has grown
more and increasingly versatile roots.[2] Depending on the political space
available, the party and the women's structures can branch out more or
less in the respective regions. Until 2015, this was the case in Bakur and
continues today in Rojava and Maxmûr refugee camp, where the organisational structures go down to the neighbourhood level with communes
and cooperatives organising daily life. How much the party and its women
can do in each region is constantly changing, and the boundaries between
armed and political activism are often fluid.

I have chronicled elsewhere how the women's movement developed
between the mountains and the cities and how the struggle for political
space played out in different parts of Kurdistan (Käser 2021). This
chapter will continue to investigate how women got to play such
a central role within the PKK, how the 'free woman' came into being
and how that resulted in semi-autonomous organisational structures
and the development of Jineolojî. Analysing the women's struggle alongside the development as a movement as a whole will allow me to discuss
the duality reinforcing the persistence of women's everyday resistance
and Öcalan's ideological production (Al-Ali & Tas 2018c). This chapter
is based on existing (academic) literature, as well as ethnographic
research (2015–2019), namely in-depth interviews with both current
and former female members of the Freedom Movement, in the armed
and political spheres. The chapter is by no means a complete history of
the Kurdish women's movement, but is intended to be read in tandem
with other accounts that analyse the rich and complex history of
the movement and its individual members struggling to realise their
particular version of liberated women and a liberated Kurdistan
(Çağlayan 2020; Dirik 2021).

The PKK, a Short History

The history of the PKK and how it found ways to adapt to the shifting
political and military dynamics in the region is well researched (Aras

---

[2] Vera Eccarius-Kelly described the PKK as working in an 'octopus-like manner, extending
its tentacles into the neighbouring countries and Europe'. She divides the tentacles into
guerrilla, criminal and political (Eccarius-Kelly 2012, 238–39); however, my work shows
that the issue is more complex and that different spheres of labour are in fact fluid and
overlapping. For a diagram of the party as a whole and the women's structures in particular
refer to the tables in the Appendix.

2013; Bozarslan 2000, 2004; Chaliand 1993; Gunes 2012; İmset 1992; Jongerden 2017; Jongerden & Akkaya 2011, 2012; Marcus 2007; McDowall 2001; Olson 1996; White 2000, 2015 inter alia).[3] The women's history on the other hand, aside from a few notable exceptions (Çağlayan 2008, 2012, 2020; Mojab 2001), is poorly documented in academic literature; the women's struggle within the movement sometimes merits a chapter or subchapter at best (Çelik 2002; Grojean 2017; Gunes & Zeydanlıoğlu 2014; White 2015). However, the women's movement has documented its own history in the many books published by the party in Turkish and Kurdish, which are mainly used for educational purposes in the mountains (Garzan 2015). Apart from a few exceptions (Flach 2003, 2007; Herausgeberinnenkollektiv 2012), the women of the movement were only propelled into the gaze of the Westerner's (scholarly) eye with the defence of Kobanî and Şengal against the attacks of *daesh* in 2014. This fascination is reflected in an upsurge of academic and journalistic publications foregrounding the role of women in the Rojava Revolution (Demir 2017; Flach et al. 2016; Lower Class Magazine 2017; Strangers in a Tangled Wilderness 2015; Tax 2016). These books by and large paint a rosy picture of the developments in Rojava, idealising the women as the fearless goddesses of war and defenders of an anti-capitalist, post-statist and post-patriarchal revolution, which they often are. But their struggle is much more complex, messy and perilous as I aim to demonstrate in the following chapters. Jordi Tejel (2009, 2017), Oliver Grojean (2017) and Thomas Schmidinger (2014, 2018) have published more nuanced accounts of the Rojava Revolution and the wider movement, which discuss the party landscape in Rojava historically and highlight the contradictions that emerge due to the PKK's authoritarian structure versus the intended grassroots democracy (Leezenberg 2016). Turkey is the best-researched country in terms of how the Kurdish Freedom Movement operates, especially in the political sphere (Clark 2015; Watts 2010), which is also shaped by the fraught relationship between Turkish and Kurdish feminists (Al-Ali & Tas 2018a, b; Çaha 2011; Gökalp 2010; Küçükkıca 2018; Sahin-Mencutek 2016; Yüksel 2006).

The PKK emerged against the background of the 1971 military coup in Turkey, which cracked down harshly on the revolutionary left and civil society more broadly. Revolutionary groups were forced into the private

---

[3] This research is based on literature in English, German, French and Kurmancî. Many Turkish sources exist on the topic of the PKK and some on the women within the PKK, which, apart from a few exceptions, including issues of *Jineolojî* (www.jineolojidergisi.com/); Bingöl 2016; Çağlayan 2007; Özgür Kadın Akademisi 2016; Newaya Jin 2016; Öcalan 2013b, 2015; Yılmaz 2016, have not been consulted.

spheres, such as university dormitories in Ankara, where they formed 'friends' groups', reading and discussing politics. As early as 1972–1973, one of these groups started to assemble around Abdullah Öcalan, then a student in Ankara. At the time they referred to themselves as the 'Kurdistan Revolutionaries'[4] and started to build a dedicated group of cadres (Jongerden 2017, 235–36). Over the next four years, the group further developed its Marxist–Leninist ideology and the idea of Kurdistan as a colony that needed to be liberated through a people's revolution.[5] They agreed on the need for an armed struggle and expanded recruitment to different provinces in the Kurdish southeast of the country, where female cadres such as Sakine Cansız were at the forefront of mobilising women for the cause (Cansız 2015). The group that formally became the PKK in 1978 grew out of a regional and international context shaped by the Cold War and the Turkish student and workers' movements of the 1960s, and was inspired by the successes of anti-colonial and national liberation movements such as in Algeria, China, Cuba, Nicaragua and Vietnam. The intelligentsia of the movement was made up of Kurdish and Turkish students around Abdullah Öcalan, Haki Karer and Kemal Pir, while their social base in the early stages was the disenfranchised Kurdish population in the country's southeast. It is beyond the scope of this chapter to sketch out the complex history of Kurdish nationalisms or the highly fractured party landscape of the late 1960s and early 1970s in Turkey.[6] However, it is important to note that this era produced charismatic and influential political thinkers and leaders such as Mahir Çayan, Deniz Gezmiş and Ibrahim Kaypakkaya.[7] Mahir Çayan was the first to formulate the discourse of the 'New Man' in the Turkish context. In reference to Franz Fanon, he put the responsibility of resistance into the hand of the oppressed, a resistance that goes beyond the military and political struggle, towards becoming a 'free man'. Hereby, revolutionary violence was seen as the main tool to reach liberation and considered a cleansing force, freeing the native from his inferior position and restoring his humanity and self-respect (Fanon 1968, 94). Ibrahim

---

[4] The group was also known as *Apocular*, 'followers of Apo', the nickname for Abdullah Öcalan (Jongerden 2017, 236).

[5] To frame Kurdistan as a colony was not Öcalan's idea but he was influenced by Mahir Çayan and Sait Kırmızıtoprak (Bozarslan 2012, 7).

[6] For a detailed discussion of the origins of Kurdish nationalism, see Vali (2003), and for Turkey's political landscape in the 1960s and 1970s, see Bozarslan (2012) and Jongerden & Akkaya (2011, 2012).

[7] Mahir Çayan was the leader of THKP-C (*Türkiye Halk Kurtuluş Partisi-Cephesi*, Turkish People Liberation's Party-Front) and Demiz Gezmiş the leader of THKO (*Türkiye Halk Kurtuluş Ordusu*, People's Liberation Army of Turkey). Both were executed by the Turkish state in 1972 (Jongerden & Akkaya 2011, 127).

Kaypakkaya, a Turkish Alevi, Maoist and founder of the Communist Party of Turkey–Marxist–Leninist in 1971, was the first revolutionary who criticised Kemalism as a fascist regime that needed to be overthrown by an armed struggle.[8] Most of these ideas were later picked up by Abdullah Öcalan, who had, like most of the founding members of the PKK, a background in the revolutionary left and was informed by its discourse (Jongerden 2017, 235). After the military coup in 1971, the Kurdish groups became more radicalised and as of 1974 increasingly autonomous from the Turkish left, drawing in not only university students but also a new generation of politicised youth who had previously migrated from rural Kurdistan (Bozarslan 2012, 2–6).

The official history of the PKK starts on 27 November 1978, with the founding congress in Fis, a small village near Lice in the Diyarbakir district. The founding members included twenty-two Kurdish and Turkish students such as Abdullah Öcalan, Sakine Cansız, Kesire Yıldırım, Cemîl Bayık, Mazlum Doğan and Duran Kalkan (Jongerden & Akkaya 2011, 138). Sakine and Kesire were the only two women present at the founding congress. Sakine Cansız, who became an important figure of the women's movement, writes in her memoirs that she only briefly spoke at the congress and not about the topic that was closest to her heart: the role of women in the war of national liberation. Women, since the adoption of the Turkish Civil Code in 1926, had been important markers of the modern and westernised Turkish nation state and constituted the 'civilised' subject (Kandioğlu 1996; Kanidyoti 1996): they had the right to vote; polygamy was outlawed; child custody and the right to divorce were granted to both parents. However, these new laws for a long time remained formal, focused on urban centres and higher-class Turkish women. 'The state assigned women's rights only to a particular circle of women within society that was regarded integral to the national project built on the paradigms of "one state, one nation, one language, one flag"' (Burç 2018, 6; Kandiyoti 1987). Kurdish women were thus left out, and their plight was largely ignored by the state feminist organisations that emerged over the following decades. It was not until the 1960s and 1970s that Kurdish women were politicised as part of the revolutionary left and later as members of the PKK (Al-Ali & Taş 2018b; Yüksel 2006). Cansız being hesitant to speak at length amidst the more experienced male members present, the congress did not address further the ideological and practical position of women in the party (Cansız 2015, 393–400). In

---

[8] These three leaders are greatly admired by the PKK, especially Ibrahim Kaypakkaya's legacy is celebrated, not least with music. The song *İsyan Ateşi* by Grup Munzur is played everywhere between the mountains and the cities. See bibliography (multimedia).

1979, prior to the military coup, Sakine Cansız and many of her comrades were arrested (Cansız 2018, 14). To avoid meeting the same fate, Öcalan and a few of his followers escaped to Damascus, where the party's headquarters would be based for the next twenty years (Herausgeberinnenkollektiv 2012, 17).

Throughout the 1980s and early 1990s, the PKK developed into the only significant Kurdish party, which started to pose a military and political challenge to Turkey's authority in the Kurdish regions (Gunes 2012, 101). At that time many women were active in the guerrilla, as student organisers in Istanbul or Ankara and as so-called city guerrillas. City guerrillas were party-affiliated cadres who organised the civilian populations in the villages and towns. Many of the grassroots activities were carried out by female cadres because women could go undetected for longer than men who were known to the security forces. These city guerrillas were particularly active in cities like Cizre, where Kurdish consciousness was strong and people were sympathetic towards the PKK. They used important dates such as Newroz (Kurdish New Year) or 15 August (date of the first PKK guerrilla attack) to stage their opposition (interview with Zelal, 1 June 2018). One of these city cadres was Bêrîvan, who had been successfully organising and educating women in Cizre, building women's committees and militias that were able to operate between the different districts. In January 1989, Turkish police forces caught up with her and surrounded her house. Legend has it that she answered calls to surrender with slogans of resistance and fought to the last bullet in order to free her trapped comrades before being murdered (Binevş Agal 2011; Herausgeberinnenkollektiv 2012, 533). Her heroic death in January 1989, its commemoration a year later and the brutal state response sparked the uprisings (*Serhildan*) that continued and spread across eastern Turkey until 1993, mobilising large numbers of women to join the guerrilla force (Herausgeberinnenkollektiv 2012, 19).

However, the Kurdish women's movement, from the onset, was not only focused on an armed struggle. During our interview, Gültan Kışanak, a key figure in the pro-Kurdish legal parties and the former co-mayor of Diyarbakir, explained the emergence of the women's movement as a result of the political, economic and military violence that women faced:

When the Turkish state was targeting people, village, homes, and gardens, women's response was related to the principle of self-defence, they were defending their livelihoods and were politicised that way. The resistance started in prison and merged with the women defending their livelihood. They got politicised by themselves, because of the state violence, they went to the street and became political actors.

She emphasised that, contrary to other women's movements, it was not a top down effort of a group of intellectual women who tried to mobilise the masses, but that in Bakur it had worked the other way – from a grassroots movement to a political movement. According to Gültan Kışanak women, joining the guerrilla ranks also had a huge impact on society: 'Like in many patriarchal societies there were specific roles for women in the eyes of men. [...] But after they saw that women were leaving the village and joining the guerrilla they couldn't behave in the same way [...] and the classical roles started to be questioned within the family' (interview with Gültan Kışanak, 5 January 2016). Gültan Kışanak described an important dynamic that has been a dominant factor shaping the women's movement: the simultaneous struggle in the activist, political and armed spheres, taking place in the prisons, villages, municipalities and the mountains. She also brings up the specific targeting of Kurdish women's lives and bodies, something that has a long history in Turkish politics and can be observed to this day. The movement itself contends that this phenomenon (*feminicide*) and gender- and sex-based violence (GSBV) have increased a staggering 1,400–1,500 per cent under the AKP government (Herausgeberinnenkollektiv 2012, 49). Deniz Kandiyoti terms this darker and more violent form of authoritarianism 'masculinist restoration': a 'profound crisis of masculinity leading to more violent and coercive assertions of male prerogatives where the abuse of women can become a blood sport [...]' (Kandiyoti 2013). The organised women of the Kurdish movement (but not exclusively) are a direct target of this masculinist restoration. Thousands of activists have been arrested, particularly so with the start of the 'KCK trials' in 2009, when around 9,000 politicians, human rights and peace activists, union members and activists of the women and youth movements were arrested. Zelal, a London-based activist of the Kurdish women's movement, contextualised the KCK arrests as follows:

Because of Kurdish women's roles in the party, the state directly attacks them. They were caught and put in prison. The Kurdish women's movement at that point [2010] was not just one organisation but between the guerrilla, the parliament, the many associations, and the media it was a diverse entity. [...] It was a powerful identity to be a Kurdish woman. But the state attacked all the different aspects of the Kurdish women. They knew that the Kurdish women are the blood and heart of the movement. (Interview with Zelal, 1 June 2018)

The criminalisation of the Kurdish Freedom Movement, particularly in Turkey but also in Iran and to a lesser extent in Syria and Iraq, illustrates that Kurds, inside and outside of the party, are excluded from biopolitical care and security provided by the state and become subjects of necropolitical disciplining, imprisonment and eradication (Khalili 2013; Khalili and Schwedler 2010; Mbembé 2003). The criminalisation of Kurdish activists by the Turkish state denies the liberatory dimension of their actions as it is framed as an attack against the modern Turkish nation. Gültan Kışanak was arrested in October 2016 under alleged terrorism charges and has since been imprisoned together with many other female politicians, such as Sebahat Tuncel, another important member of the women's movement.

Liberating Women, on Paper and in Practice

While women started to organise in the political sphere and join the armed movement, Öcalan was based in Damascus and the Beqaa Valley in Lebanon. In the first party programme of 1978, the women's question was not yet formally addressed. Like other national liberation movements, it was thought that women would gain their freedom in the course of the anti-colonial struggle. From the mid-1980s, however, Öcalan put a lot of intellectual labour into the ideological creation of women's identity and role within the movement. It was after 1983 that first texts tentatively linked the liberation of Kurdistan to that of women. In 1986, the women's ideology was further developed, a process that went hand in hand with the foundation of the *Mahsum Korkmaz Academy* in the Beqaa Valley. Here, Öcalan's relationship with his wife Fatma (Kesire Yıldırım) and his struggle against the demeanour of traditional Kurdish women seem to have played a key role. During the third party congress in 1986, Fatma was accused of working for the Turkish state and was sentenced to death. She later left Syria and has since lived under a different name in Europe. Oliver Grojean argues that the early discussions about the 'women's question' should be seen less as an attempt to create equality and rather as a wish to 'correct' the unwanted women's behaviour that Öcalan had to deal with during his marriage to Fatma (Grojean 2017, 154–55). Öcalan's private musings aside, during the 1980s and early 1990s, due to the uprising in Bakur and the ongoing state repression, more women were educated in the Academy. Here the triple oppression of women was first discussed: the intersecting dynamics emerging from patriarchy, capitalism and nation states. As a result of these discussions, the first women's union, the Kurdistan Union of Patriotic Women (YJWK, *Yêkitîya Jinên Welatparêzên Kurdistanê*), was established on 1 November 1987, not in Kurdistan but in Hannover, Germany. This organisation educated Kurdish women in the diaspora and mobilised women to join the armed resistance in Kurdistan (Herausgeberinnenkollektiv 2012, 20).

Handan Çağlayan, whose analysis traces the development of the 'free women's identity' from the 1980s to the late 1990s, shows that the biggest challenge in the effort to mobilise Kurdish women for the armed struggle was to overcome the honour (*namus*) barrier, which links men's honour to women's bodies and sexuality. In earlier writings, Öcalan had described women as being 'pulled down' – referring to being locked up in the house, dependent on men and always in danger of damaging their honour. This barrier needed to be removed so that women could leave the house and join the movement, thus freeing themselves from their state as 'slaves of slaves'. In the 1990s, Öcalan changed this discourse so that the liberation of men and all of society was hinged on women's liberation (Çağlayan 2012, 10–11). In this process he linked women's powers to a mystical past, the Neolithic era when women of Mesopotamia were active and free. In this paradigm shift women needed to free themselves from the shackles of slavery in order to rediscover their inner goddess, while the men were tasked with killing the 'dominant man': 'Indeed, to kill the dominant man is the fundamental principle of socialism. This is what killing power means: to kill the one-sided domination, the inequality, and intolerance. Moreover, it is to kill fascism, dictatorship, and despotism' (Öcalan 2013a, 51). These ideas of revolutionary femininities and masculinities were needed to create a new class of vanguards who could mobilise, theorise and push forward the idea of a revolutionary society. According to Öcalan's ideology, women can only become 'free' by struggling and by participating in the collective actions of the party as desexualised goddesses. Yet, my data demonstrate that while some women would only repeat these party slogans, most skilfully used the official identity bestowed upon them to keep organising on a large scale. Çağlayan's work further demonstrates that while the powerful 'Kurdish women's identity' drew clear boundaries and rules to be obeyed, it was this identity that opened new spaces for women, which further enabled their social, political and legal activism. As a result '[w]omen's active and massive participation not only has shifted the gender conception within the movement but also inserted women's demands into the political agenda of the movement' (Çağlayan 2020).

In the 1990s, the Kurdish political space changed profoundly. The PKK had turned into a permanent and legitimate actor, and the People's Labour Party (HEP, *Halkın Emek Partisi*), the first pro-Kurdish political party, started to organise around 'Kurdishness' in Turkey. HEP was not founded by the PKK but shared a social basis with PKK supporters and martyr families. By entering electoral politics, HEP and its successors gained access to state-allocated legal, political and material resources and helped to legitimise the Freedom Movement through votes. The pro-Kurdish political parties were and still are heavily restricted by the PKK and the Turkish establishment's intolerance, a tension that plays out in power struggles within the legal parties over how closely to work with the PKK (Gambetti 2009, 54; Watts 2010, 14). The legal party could not adopt the radical discourse of the PKK or its military hierarchy; instead, it developed both as a Kurdish and as a left-wing party, advocating human rights and the democratisation of Turkey (Bozarslan 2012, 12). Zelal, who was serving a seven-year prison sentence in the 1990s, remembers the importance of HEP:

The Kurdish political parties gave hope to people because for the people it was easier to see their children being involved in the legal party, it meant they might live. Otherwise their children would join the guerrilla and after a couple of months or years they would lose their life. This was a new area for Kurdish people. The Kurdish legal party also had a big effect on people because for the first time they openly talked about the Kurdish issues. (Interview with Zelal, 1 June 2018)

Despite pressure from the PKK and the Turkish establishment, it was the Kurdish movement's efforts to diversify through civic organisations, trade unions, media outlets, women's organisations and international alliances that have turned the PKK's militaristic strategy into a social movement (Gambetti 2009, 54). The women were integral to this process. Similar to their comrades in the mountains, in 1996, they created a separate women's congress within the Kurdish political movement, established associations and published journals such as *Roza* (politically independent) and *Yaşamda Özgür Kadın* (linked to the Freedom Movement). These journals developed into important sites where the women's movement could set itself apart from the male-dominated Freedom Movement and from the feminist movement in Turkey (Yüksel 2006, 780–81). As part of the political work they also started to organise around the women's quota. The People's Democracy Party (HADEP) was the first political party in Turkey to introduce a voluntary 25 per cent women's quota in 2000. Over the next few years, women worked tirelessly to increase this quota to 30 per cent, before it was eventually set at 40 per cent in 2005 (Alkan 2018; Çağlayan 2020, 104).[9]

Apart from the political struggle in the cities, the 1990s were also a period of intense wars between the PKK and the Turkish army, as well as between the PKK and the Iraqi Kurdish parties (KDP/PUK). In the early 1990s, the

---

[9] In the 1990s and 2000s, numerous pro-Kurdish parties were shut down: HEP in 1993, DEP in 1994 and the Democratic Society Party (DTP) in 2009. HDP, founded in October 2012, had come under immense pressure in 2015 when it managed to win 13 per cent of the popular vote and entered the parliament with eighty MPs (Gunes 2019, 222).

Turkish army destroyed up to 4,000 villages in Eastern Turkey in an attempt to break the support and supply networks of the PKK. Millions of Kurds migrated to urban centres such as Diyarbakir, or the Western cities of Istanbul, Ankara and Izmir. Around 20,000 people fled to Iraqi Kurdistan and eventually settled near the town of Maxmûr, establishing the Maxmûr refugee camp (Yılmaz 2016). While more women were fighting, more were also dying, some of them committing spectacular acts of resistance. Those who left a particularly significant mark were Bêrîvan, Bêrîtan and Zîlan, each of them initiating a new era of female mobilisation. Bêrîtan fought during the Southern War against an alliance between the Turkish army and the KDP/PUK *peşmerga* in 1992.[10] Legend has it that she fought until her last bullet in Xakûrkê, when she was cornered by approaching *peşmerga* forces, who allegedly said: 'Surrender, we will marry you off and you will live like a rose.' To escape her capture, Bêrîtan jumped off the cliff she was standing on. Her death became a symbol of the will to resist (*îrade*) of Kurdish women and the symbol of the women's army that was initiated in 1993 (Herausgeberinnenkollektiv 2012, 535). While the resistance of Bêrîvan sparked the uprisings in Cizre in 1989, Bêritan's death leap in 1992 pushed Öcalan to initiate a separate women's army in 1993. While this was only a promise in the beginning, autonomous structures started to take shape with the preparation for the first women's congress in 1995. During this process, women formulated forty-five questions, for example: how do you develop into a determined fighter? What is the influence of Islam? Why do women get distracted by men? What does honour mean in a liberated society? What is the meaning of marriage? What is the meaning of love? How should sexuality in relationships be understood and lived? (Solina 1997, 336). These questions were discussed during the congress in 1995, and a twenty-three-member executive council was elected. They formed the Free Women's Union of Kurdistan (YAJK, *Yekîneyên Azadiya Jinên Kurdistanê*), under which women started to build their independent units, aiming to live and fight without assistance from their male comrades (Herausgeberinnenkollektiv 2012, 22). 'That was a very difficult time', commander Zaxo, whom I interviewed in Iraqi Kurdistan, recounted, 'we were like children, trying to walk but we kept falling down. But what we lacked in physical strength, we made up with our will to resist' (*îrade*) (interview with Zaxo, 17 March 2017). By the end of the 1990s, around 30 per cent of the PKK's members were women. They were involved in a constant battle

---

[10] The PKK fought against the Iraqi Kurdish parties and their peşmerga forces on different occasions during the 1990s: first in 1992 (against an alliance between the Turkish army and PUK/KDP), then again in 1995 (against the KDP/Turkey), in 1997 (against the KDP/Turkey), and in 2000 (against the PUK).

against their male comrades and remained absent in the leadership ranks of the party. Yet their presence and acceptance among the rank and file members had an impact on slowly challenging ideas around gender norms in the wider Kurdish society and politics (McDonald 2001, 148). This process, however, was not without its contradictions and setbacks, as will be further discussed in the next section.

The Formation of the PJKK

All my interlocutors emphasised that the early years, especially the 1990s, were a particularly difficult period, not only militarily but also internally: the 'battle of the sexes' being a constant feature of daily life and struggle. 'Just because we joined a revolutionary movement did not mean that the men in the party had changed. In the early years we struggled against the same hierarchies in the party as in society,' I was repeatedly told. Abdullah Öcalan was in Damascus, training cadres, producing ideology and sending reports with commands to the mountains, while brutal wars were raging on in Bakur and Başûr, and where women and men were mainly concerned with their own survival:

At that time, we weren't so critical and this [the women's movement] was not our priority. Our priority was the revolution, because there was a big war with a clear enemy; the Turkish government and the Turkish army, and our goal was to fight against the Turkish government. When I was a guerrilla in Bakur I can tell you honestly, I didn't think so much about the women's movement. Because our priority was different: you are in war, you have to survive, and you have to fight. (Interview with former commander 1, 14 May 2018)

This quote illustrates that often women joined and trained as combatants out of necessity and not out of a pre-existing feminist consciousness (White 2007, 869). Most of my respondents, who joined the party in the 1990s, confirmed that they joined because they wanted to do something for Kurdistan and only later, in education, learned that they are also liberating Kurdish women. Today, with televised wars such as Kobanî or Şengal and social media, this has changed and many young recruits know about the parallel women's struggle.

Another former commander describes the struggle to be accepted as equals in the 1990s:

We are women, so of course we have physical limitations. Men are stronger than women, that's a fact. In the mountains it was like a competition. We had to do everything like the men, or we didn't stand a chance. For example, if he carried 50 kg of flour then I have to do that too. Normally my body cannot carry 50 kg but in order to get accepted by the men I had to do it. We had to fight in praxis with men. If he goes and attacks a *karakol* [Turkish army outpost] then I have to do that too and then we can talk about equality. In the mountains we experienced this the hard way and fought for this equality physically. (Interview with former commander 3, 11 May 2018)

In March 1998, two years after Zîlan's death, Öcalan finally published his official 'Ideology of Women's Liberation' (*Bîrdoziya Rizgariya Jinê*). Öcalan had been in a constant discussion with women, talking about what a women's army would look like, how a women's party would be organised and according to what kind of ideology. However, he was the one who formulated the questions, structured the discussions and lectures, and it was those lectures that were recorded, transcribed and sent to the different mountain camps as educational material. Nevertheless, women's everyday struggle in the mountains, their resistance in the prisons and their deaths in protest of Turkey's oppression influenced him greatly. 'He saw women as a power and wrote the liberation ideology accordingly' (interview with former commander 3, 11 May 2018).

As was the case in other national liberation movements, prevailing ideas around masculinity and femininity had to be adapted, so as to fit the revolutionary agenda and the communal living in the party ranks. In 1998, Öcalan put into writing five undesired 'types of women', who due to their faulty or weak characters were holding the party back. In the official history of the women's movement this occasion is described as follows: 'For the first time in history, the women found out about their types. With this a new period started for us' (Garzan 2015, 120). These five types of women were (1) the type who does not abide by the women's liberation ideology (stubbornly holding onto old patterns), (2) the type who is a stranger to her own gender (too masculine), (3) the type who is too fragile and sensitive (too feminine), (4) the type who focuses on her individual freedom (power hungry, liberal) and (5) the type who misunderstands freedom or wants to create her own version of it (petite bourgeoisie) (Garzan 2015, 119–22). With these five types Öcalan explained to the women the roots of their oppression and laid out what can be done to resist them as a unified force. According to Garzan, the author of the educational book quoted here, these five types enabled the women to strengthen their ranks, as well as the party as a whole by determining what kind of femininity was wanted and needed. Women needed to distance themselves from their upbringing (both feudal and petite bourgeoisie), relearn their perception of femininity and how to put that to use for the goal of the greater good. Contrary to other national liberation movements, for example in Latin America, in the PKK, the feminine was not devalued, rejected or muted per se to maintain the privileged position of men (Bayard de Volo 2012; Dietrich Ortega 2012). Instead, militant femininity was reimagined and rearranged by Öcalan in order to respond to the conditions of 'mountain life' (female-male bonding, cohabitation) and to include women on equal footing as men.

Öcalan not only told the women how they should not be, but also how they should become: like the famous martyr Zîlan who dedicated her life and death to the struggle, and who deeply loved her country and her people (Garzan 2015, 122). Zîlan is not only an example of female bravery and determination in the party, but also of the complexity that is reflected in the lives and deaths of the women. Multiple interviewees have told me that many people who can no longer bear living in the mountains and fighting for the party either commit suicide or choose a martyr's death. According to some of my informants Zîlan was one of them:

There are some people like Zîlan who staged a big suicide attack with a bomb in Dersim. After that she became a hero. But I know the background of Zîlan. She found it very difficult in the mountains and had big problems with the praxis [warfare]. Maybe she chose this attack to prove herself. [...] But we have to consider how brave this attack was, not everyone could do that. (Interview with former commander 3, 11 May 2018)

Despite her alleged human weaknesses, Zîlan became the modern-day *Îştar*, the goddess of freedom, a symbol for a new Kurdishness, and a key role model for generations of fighters who came after her (Çağlayan 2020, 72). Moreover, her death signified a crucial rupture point in how Öcalan viewed the women and their role in the struggle, which was reflected in the women's liberation ideology that was published shortly after.

The time between the publication of the women's liberation ideology in March 1998 and Öcalan's arrest a year later was crucial for the women's movement. 'Morale' was high, as more women were put into leadership positions and their organisational and military power grew. When Öcalan spoke to the commanders of a certain region, he always made sure to speak to the female leader as well:

Öcalan was a weapon for women, and women were a weapon for Öcalan. Öcalan was able to control the men through the women. Men are better at lying and could have told him something different [about the situation in an area]. But women had a good and special relationship with him. He was a weapon for us, we were a weapon for him. (Interview with former commander 1, 14 May 2018)

At the end of 1998, the sixth party congress was held in the mountains. In preparation for this congress, Öcalan sent his decrees in which he frequently discussed the formation of a new women's party. However, during the congress, on 15 February 1999, Öcalan was arrested, which sent shockwaves through all four parts of Kurdistan, as well as the

European diaspora. Despite the chaos, the proceedings in the mountains continued, and after the general congress ended, a woman's congress was held. Commander Zaxo remembered: 'Almost all women agreed that if we don't do it now [form their own party], we would never do it. Apo is in prison now, but we have his writings and his paradigm to support us' (interview with Zaxo, 17 March 2017). During that congress, the women decided to go ahead with the planned formation of a women's party and thus turned YAJK, a union, into the Kurdistan Women's Worker's Party (PJKK, *Partiya Jinên Karkerên Kurdistanê*). If PJKK was to be an independent party or a women's party within the PKK was not entirely clear at that point but remained a topic of discussion. The predominantly male leadership around Cemîl Bayık, Osman Öcalan and Duran Kalkan all tried to pressure the women not to go ahead with their women's party:

[They] said we are now going through difficult times, Öcalan was arrested and all the power needs to be united in the central committee. A separate party, an independent party can weaken us, and the enemy can use this situation. They argued like this and said we don't accept your [women's] congress. This resulted in a big fight between the women and the leadership. The 200 women who participated in the congress were kept in a valley and weren't allowed to do anything. It was like an open prison. (Interview with former commander 1, 14 May 2018)

Abandoned by the leadership, the women were kept hostage in a valley for a few months. Here, they tried to find a way out of their predicament. They did not want to speak against the party because their beloved leader had just been arrested, but at the same time, women's gains and strength could not be compromised. 'It was difficult to find a way. If you say we accept the general leadership it means you lost the women's struggle, and all the power will be in the men's hands. But if you resist, they respond with violence, psychological violence' (interview with former commander 1, 14 May 2018). After a few months of back and forth negotiations, joint meetings were held, during which the female leaders chosen by the women were punished and removed from their post. In their place they put women chosen by men. 'This was a big blow for women. This really broke the women's morale and was a turning point, like before and after Jesus. [...] We saw that men would leave nothing to us, and we saw them becoming more patriarchal again' (interview with former commander 1, 14 May 2018).

Why did Öcalan not support the women during this difficult time? After a few months in prison, he was able to send messages through his lawyers; however, those messages only greeted the women but said nothing to support their party. I posed the question to a former commander who assessed the situation as follows:

Many of us said, if Öcalan was still here, this wouldn't have happened. [...] After this he didn't say anything about women for a long time. I understand that well. On the one hand the women's movement was a tactical move for him but on the other hand he also knew the male leadership. If he would have said something in favour of the women, the men would not accept it, and this would weaken his authority. He considered that. This doesn't mean he was against women, but he was also not clearly for women. It was a balancing act, he had to do it that way. Politically, I understand it, as a woman I don't. (Interview with former commander 1, 14 May 2018)

Another former commander who attended the congress was more critical, recounting how they waited for four weeks, but all the notes that were sent back through the lawyer only concerned the war, politics or commands for the male leaders such as Duran Kalkan or Cemîl Bayık. 'I realised that we are not important for him. That the women's movement is not important for him. We are only a tool that you can use' (interview with former commander 2, 20 July 2018).

This power struggle between men and women, and women allied with men continued throughout the following year. During the seventh party congress in late 1999 and early 2000, women disagreed with the general direction Osman, Öcalan's brother was trying to take the party, as well as the names of potential leadership candidates that had been put forward. In protest they all cut their hair to shoulder length, a sign of 'having lost everything'. At that same congress, nineteen women refused to be part of the leadership and were put in detention in a valley yet again. The men accused them of working against the party and of collaborating with the enemy. They also put pressure on the women by withholding food and clothes (interview with Zaxo, 24 March 2017). Eventually, negotiations between the opposing factions resumed and women were told to hold their congress. During that congress PJKK became PJA (The Free Women's Party, *Partiya Jina Azad*). 'It became evident that slowly the women had lost their power, also because many of them changed their position and moved closer to the men, admitting that the decision to form PJKK as an independent party as wrong. [...] This was a great setback' (interview with former commander 1, 14 May 2018). Thereafter, the overt opposition to men stopped and it became clear that any women's party would exist within the framework of the PKK and not independently from men.[11] This is still the case today: the women are able to

[11] The women's movement underwent numerous name changes and processes of restructuring: 1987: YJWK, 1995: YAJK, 1999: PJKK, 2000: PJA, 2004: PAJK (Free Women's Party of Kurdistan, *Partiya Azadiya Jin a Kurdistanê*). Today PAJK functions as the ideological branch and is organised as a parallel structure alongside YJA-Star, the armed Free Women Units (*Yekîneyên Jinên Azad-Star*), YJA, the political front Union of Free Women (*Yekitiya Jinên Azad*), and the Women's Youth Organization (*Komalên Jinên*

operate within their autonomous ranks as long as they do not transgress the boundaries set by the umbrella of the KCK, as well as the parameters set by what I call militant femininities.

While the women's organisational structures in the mountains grew stronger throughout the 1990s, prior to Öcalan's arrest, so did the political parties in the cities. Most of the grassroots work was done by women, which strengthened their networks and expertise. Their everyday efforts were helped by the publication of the 'women's liberation ideology' in 1998, as Zelal recalled:

> That was very important. At that time, I was in prison and we celebrated this. Because before that whenever we talked about a special women's organisation, party or association, even in prison our male friends were telling us we are trying to separate the party, we are trying to spill the blood of the party. Or that we are taking the side of the Turkish government because we are attacking the party. But when this ideology was published, they couldn't say anything anymore. (Interview with Zelal, 1 June 2018)

Zelal speaks to the fact that the contention between the men and women of the movement over the place of women in the movement was not only carried out in 'the mountains' but extended into all spheres of activism, even into the prisons. After his arrest, Öcalan reformulated his vision for a democratic future of Kurdistan and Turkey. He abandoned the goal to establish an independent Kurdistan and introduced Democratic Confederalism. He presented this as part of his written defence, which was also sent to the European Court of Human Rights in 2002 and 2004. In it he advocated a democratic, ecological, gender-equal social system, a bottom-up system of self-government. Democratic Confederalism seeks to develop a mode of ordering beyond the nation-state and capitalism that goes hand in hand with a process of social reconstruction (Jongerden & Akayya 2013, 171–78). The guerrillas should hence forward no longer carry out a 'people's war' but only engage in 'legitimate self-defence' (Herausgeberinnenkollektiv 2012, 27). Naturally, many guerrillas and party cadres who had fought half their life for an independent Kurdistan and lost thousands of their friends in the struggle opposed this new ideology. At the same time, Osman Öcalan, who had previously tried to take on his brother's leadership role, proposed the 'reform of social relations', in an attempt to legalise romantic and sexual relationships within the party. All women I spoke to, current and former cadres, had vehemently opposed this reform, knowing it would only lead to the weakening of the women's structures, something Osman had intended all

---

Cîwan), all under the umbrella of the Kurdistan Women's Union (KJK, previously KJB, *Koma Jinên Bilind*); see Jongerden (2017) and the tables in the Appendix.

along. Due to ideological differences and the staunch opposition he faced, Osman left the party in 2004, together with thousands of others. One of the former commanders stated:

Maybe fifty people left with Osman, not more. Most people understood that he is a feudal man. Most people left because they didn't agree with the new politics of the party. I am one of them. I didn't lose all these friends for the democratisation of Turkey. Others had fallen in love and wanted to have a relationship. Others again had seen injustices and lost their trust in the party. (Interview with former commander 3, 11 May 2018)

In the years that followed his arrest, Öcalan might have not said anything specific about women, but that did not keep the women's movement in the cities from progressing. Having PJA, a (weakened) women's party in the mountains, supported their efforts in expanding their grassroots and cultural work. Women opened women's associations across the country, where they offered education courses to women in minority and linguistic rights, women's and children's health issues, Kurdish and Turkish language courses, and women's history.

During Newroz in March 2005, Democratic Confederalism was officially declared as the new party ideology. With this announcement, women's centrality in the struggle was finally official. Shortly after, Öcalan proposed the co-chair system, meaning that all political leadership positions should be occupied by a man and a woman. Zelal, who was working in media at that point, remembered:

And we took it [the co-chair system] from him. But the male members of the party told the PKK that this wasn't acceptable and unrealistic, and that it was against the rule of the Turkish party system. We women came together and thought why are they now thinking about whether the Turkish system accepts this or not? We never acted according to the Turkish system, we have always been defectors. Of course, they said this because they didn't want to share power with the women. Meanwhile we women had a big meeting and decided that we are going to choose ten candidates. We spoke with all of them and in the end, we chose Aysel Tuğluk. I was an editor and writer and I did a big interview with Aysel just one day before the Kurdish party's congress. We published it and said 'Kurdish women's candidate for co-chair is Aysel Tuğluk'. So, they [the men] couldn't say anything. Both the men in the legal party and the men in the illegal party didn't like the power we had at that time. So, they said the women's branch is old-fashioned, and they destroyed it. They changed the structure of the legal party [DTP][12] but they couldn't take back the co-chair system. (Interview with Zelal, 1 June 2018)

[12] The new party, which no longer had a women and youth branch was the Democratic Society Party (DTP, *Demokratik Toplum Partisi*), founded in 2005. The body that should govern these transitional processes was the Democratic Society's Congress (DTK, *Demokratik Toplum Kongresi*), another umbrella structure founded in October 2007, in order to unify all the political and activist organisations in Bakur. According to my

After this internal coup, which saw the youth and women's branches suddenly dismantled, women continued to organise and mobilise around the co-chair system and the 40 per cent women's quota. Women activists and politicians who were involved in this process stress that having Öcalan's support was important but did not shield them from the resistance they continued to face from their male comrades. Quite the opposite, due to internal resistance, it was only in 2007 that women were able to create their own election committee and select their own candidates. That same year, the women's movement managed to get eight female MPs elected, and the numbers have been rising steadily since then (Al-Ali & Taş 2018c, 15–16). Throughout the following decade women such as Gültan Kışanak, Leyla Zana,[13] Sebahat Tuncel and Aysel Tuğluk played key roles in keeping the pressure and the organisational structures alive. During our interview in Diyarbakir, Ayşe Gökkan recounted:

In 2010 we organised a big conference, where the men said we have solved the problem between men and women, you no longer need the separate women's organisation. And we said, really you solved it? How? At every conference we discuss this, still. At every conference we say, no we are not equal. The problem is not you, but the system, the state, the family. You and me don't have a problem, the system is the problem, so we have to continue our struggle. (Interview with Ayşe Gökkan, 14 November 2015)

This struggle reached another important milestone with the establishment of the Peoples' Democratic Party (HDP, *Halkların Demokratik Partisi*) in 2012, a broad coalition of Kurdish and Turkish leftist, anti-racist, anti-homophobic, anti-nationalist, anti-sexist and pro-peace organisations and parties. Within the HDP, women organise autonomously in the Women's Assembly, and the co-chair system is applied throughout (Burç 2018, 8). In the 2014 local elections, the HDP won 102 municipalities in the southeast of Turkey and in the 2015 general elections managed to pass the 10 per cent threshold to enter the Parliament of Turkey. The continuous pushback against patriarchal norms in society and the party was only possible due to the large-scale women's network and umbrella organisations that had been established over the previous decades and unified by umbrella organisations such as the Democratic Women's Movement

respondent, this restructuring under DTK was also aimed at curtailing women's power (interview with Zelal, 1 June 2018).
[13] Leyla Zana was an important political figure in Turkey, who came to her activism in the 1980s, when her husband was imprisoned in the notorious Diyarbakir prison. She joined HEP soon after it was established in 1990, and in 1991 she was the first Kurdish female politician to be elected as an MP. In 1994, when her party (DEP, Democratic Party, successor of HEP) was banned, she lost her parliamentary immunity, was arrested and was charged with treason and being a member of the PKK. She spent ten years in prison (Bruinessen 2001, 106f).

(DÖKH, *Demokratik Özgür Kadın Hareketi*, from 2003), later KJA (2015), and currently the Free Women's Movement (TJA, *Tevgera Jinên Azad*). The women's movement is active in all four parts of Kurdistan, both in its armed and political branches, working towards establishing a democratic, gender-equal and economic society. In an effort to put women's know-ledges into writing and build stronger transnational alliances, Öcalan, in 2008, suggested that women establish Jineolojî, a new 'women's science'. Jineolojî has since become central to the movement's organisational work well beyond the four parts of Kurdistan.

Jineolojî: Decolonising and Feminising the Sciences

The Kurdish women's movement does not frame its struggle as 'feminist' but instead as 'women's liberation' or 'struggle for gender equality'. Until the late 1990s, the movement rejected the label 'feminist', a movement and mode of organising that was perceived as elitist and petite bourgeoisie (Al-Ali & Käser 2020; Öcalan 2013a, 55). Since the 1990s, Kurdish women and Turkish feminists, as well as international feminist groups, have increasingly collaborated on issues related to peace, human rights abuses and anti-militarism, which has softened this stance somewhat (Çağlayan 2020, 130). Despite this shift, in party education 'feminism' is taught as a movement that has made important political and legal gains but failed to truly challenge the capitalist and patriarchal system. During my research with militants of the movement I was often asked, 'Are you a feminist?' in a slightly patronising tone, indicating that feminism did not achieve what it set out to do and has been corrupted by capitalism. Instead, the Kurdish women's movement has developed Jineolojî, which supposedly goes further than feminism, by building the scientific foundations of Democratic Confederalism, the new gender-equal society in the making. Instead of feminism, Öcalan suggested:

I believe that the key to the resolution of our social problems will be a movement for woman's freedom, equality and democracy; a movement based on the science of woman, called Jineolojî in Kurdish. The critique of recent woman's movements is not sufficient for analysing and evaluating the history of civilisation and mod-ernity that has made woman all but disappear. If, within the social sciences, there are almost no woman themes, questions and movements, then that is because of civilisation and modernity's hegemonic mentality and structures of material culture. (Öcalan 2013a, 56)

Proposed by Öcalan in 2008 and published as part of his book *Sociology of Freedom* (Öcalan 2009), the women's movement has since developed Jineolojî by publishing books (Özgür Kadın Akademisi 2016; Newaya

Jin 2016) and magazines (Jineolojî, since 2016)[14], holding conferences[15] and establishing Jineolojî committees across the four parts of Kurdistan, in Europe and more recently in Latin America, in order to spread the word among a wider feminist, anti-sexist, anti-racist audience (Exo 2020; Neven & Schäfers 2017; Sirman 2016). To outside observers the concept of Jineolojî often remains obscure and it is not altogether clear how exactly Jineolojî departs from post-colonial and transnational feminist knowledge production (Alexander & Mohanty 2010; Collins 2000; Harding 1986; Smith 1999; Wylie 2003). I put the question of what exactly Jineolojî does to Zozan Sinan, a PKK cadre who was building the Jineolojî Academy in Rojava when we met in Sulaymaniyah in 2016. She told me that because women face such big problems not only in the Middle East but globally, there is a need for a new perspective on women's liberation. 'The struggle the Kurdish women's movement has been engaged in for the last forty years, has a lot to offer other women's movements.' Their goal is to create radical solutions to the severe problems women face and to share that knowledge globally. She also emphasised the importance to include men in this process and that they aim to do more research into who the free men should be:

We want to strengthen and spread the women's revolutionary perspective because there is a great need for new ideas. Before it was socialism, then feminism, but they all failed the hopes of women. They are not radical. Now the capitalist system is not scared of feminism. Why? Because there is not a lot of dynamism and activism in it. But there is a big need for it. Look at *daesh*, their form of masculinity is a big problem for the whole world, not only the Middle East or Şengal. Every time fascism rises in the world, men also rise. And liberal movements cannot resist against this. As a women's movement we criticise that. For 300 years there have been women's movement, why didn't they achieve more? What guarantees do we have? Can we trust the state? Or the police? No. Our goal is that we can defend ourselves. Jineolojî creates the ideas for that. (Interview with Zozan Sinan, 21 July 2016)

According to Zozan Sinan, Jineolojî is a philosophical, intellectual and political endeavour to challenge male knowledge production and to rewrite history from a female perspective. In that process, women discover old histories and produce their own knowledge, using their voice to claim intellectual ground. By living a communal, anti-capitalist life focused on the struggle, a 'truth'[16] and women's power can be rediscovered (Jineolojî

---

[14] See https://jineoloji.org/en/2016/06/26/parameters-of-jineology-discussed-in-paris/
[15] See https://kjkonline.net/en/turkce-kadinlar-kolnde-jineolojiyi-tartisiyor/; http://revolutioninthemaking.blogsport.eu/
[16] 'Truth' in the movement's ideology refers to how things were in a pre-historical 'natural society', namely the Neolithic era, before men cemented their power over women, the

Committee Europe, 2018). In Jineolojî teachings, genders are essentialised and operate in a binary, women's bodies are seen to have become a commodity for capitalist consumptions, and sexuality (the identity and the practice) needs to be controlled so that women can focus on the struggle (Al-Ali & Käser 2020). Jineolojî resonates with certain elements of second wave feminist writings, such as the French 'woman's writing' (Irigaray 2011) or *écriture feminine* (Cixous 1976), which in the 1970s sought to rediscover the female voice in language, history and philosophy. Hélène Cixous writes: 'Woman must write her self: must write about women and bring women to writing, from which they have been driven away as violently as from their bodies [. . .]. Woman must put herself into the text – as into the world and into history – by her own movement' (Cixous 1976, 875). Moreover, Jineolojî's critique of capitalist commodification of sexuality reminds of feminist activism and literature that emerged in the United States in 1960–1970 and argued for asexuality in order to disrupt the intersections between sexuality and state politics. 'By removing themselves from sexuality, women assert an anarchic stance against the institutions that engender sex, thereby working toward more nihilistic, anti-reproduction, anti-family goals that severely disrupt commonly held cultural assumptions about sex, gender, and power' (Fahs 2010, 447). More research is needed to establish if Öcalan read this feminist literature in Turkey or Syria and later in prison, or whether 'becoming female' was influenced by his study of Derrida and Derrida's reading of Nietzsche (Derrida 1978), in which he discusses the convergence of the history of 'women' and the history of 'truth' (interview with former commander 4, 11 October 2017; Philips 2014), or whether his idea of women who seek a different 'truth' grew out of the local history and the everyday struggle of women. What is certain is that Jineolojî emerged as a result of an ongoing conversation between the women and Öcalan, who were corresponding regularly throughout the 1990s and 2000s, between the mountains, cities and prisons in Turkey, Syria and Iraq. I have further explored the meaning women attach to Jineolojî in an article with Nadje Al-Ali, where we found that 'there exists a complex dialectic between the women's reverence for the leadership, using Öcalan's writings for women's advancement, and trying to move beyond his dogma'. We argue that Jineolojî can be considered the epistemology of the Kurdish women's movement: an ongoing effort to put into writing and develop further the knowledge this movement has acquired through its everyday confrontation with different forms of patriarchy, state formations and capitalism. We remain sceptical of the 'new science' claim and instead consider Jineolojî to be

family, economy and politics (Jineolojî Committee Europe, 2018; Öcalan 2013a). In order to get to the bottom of this truth, women have to rediscover their lost histories.

a continuation of and contribution to transnational and post-colonial feminist knowledge production and key to the movement's local and transnational organising (Al-Ali & Käser 2020).

Conclusion

Women have played a key role in the establishment and development of the larger Kurdish Freedom Movement. Despite a strong pushback from the men in the PKK, women, with the backing of the leadership, managed to carve out important organisational spaces, such as PJKK and later KJK. Yet women were not a unified block in this process of emancipation. Both in the mountains and in the cities, they were and are divided into more or less militant factions, who were more or less close to or critical of the leadership or the way in which the PKK developed. However, in both spheres, so I was repeatedly told, it was the women's determination that drove the movement forward. Or as a former commander told me: 'If we didn't have this parallel struggle for the freedom of women and the freedom of our nation, women would become passive and the whole movement would lose its energy' (interview with former commander 2, 20 July 2018). One way the history of the Kurdish women's movement can be read is through its famous martyrs. Any women's centre or academy would have the pictures of the most famous ones on their wall: Bêrîtan, Bêrîvan and Zîlan are only a few martyrs heading a much longer list of women who had given everything to the struggle. As I traced the member's labour in the founding, manifestation and expansion of the PKK, this chapter discussed the gender politics that unfolded as women worked to create a space for themselves within the male-led movement, one example being Jineolojî, which lays out an idea of the right way to undo male-led knowledge production and relearn history and the politics of social and economic relations. The Kurdish women's movement has made tremendous gains in terms of gender-based equality and justice far beyond the guerrilla ranks, in Turkey's political sphere, and in Rojava as a whole. However, these gains usually remain in the framework of the KCK/KJK and the highest decision-making powers are still largely in the hands of men who are in the mountains (Duran Kalkan, Cemîl Bayık, Murat Karayılan). The KCK, aiming to implement Democratic Confederalism across the four parts of Kurdistan and perhaps beyond, is lacking democracy in its own ranks. One of the great paradoxes is that the PKK uses violence to implement a project of radical grassroots democracy (Jongerden & Akayya 2012, 5). All the women I spoke to are acutely aware of these contradictions and so their struggle continues in the armed and political spheres. One powerful way to do that is to employ the movement's liberation ideology, which has gender equality at its core. Living and organising according to militant femininities gave them a hard-earned field from which to navigate the perilous terrain that is Kurdish politics, as I will discuss further in Chapter 2.

2 Diyarbakir under Fire: Women at the Barricades

Introduction

> We are told to resist, keep resisting but I don't want to resist anymore, I could die. First, we had to resist every month, then every day, then every hour, now we have to find strength within ourselves to resist every second against these horrors, and I don't have that strength anymore. I don't know what to hope for anymore.

A friend and activist in Diyarbakir shared this bleak outlook with me in January 2016, exhausted and disillusioned by the political situation and the brutal state crackdown of the Kurdish Freedom Movement. The short-lived peace process had ended in mid-2015 and the ensuing urban wars had engulfed numerous cities in the Kurdish southeast, such as Diyarbakir, Cizre, Şirnak, Silopi and Nusaybin. Over the next months, this developed into a large-scale conflict between the Turkish state and the Freedom Movement, directed at the movement's political and armed branches, such as the HDP and DBP and the armed Patriotic Revolutionary Youth Movement (YDG-H, *Yurtsever Devrimci Gençlik Hareketi*)[1], the latter having built ditches and barricades in these Kurdish cities to prevent state forces from entering.

In September 2015, I had come to Diyarbakir to conduct research on how the Kurdish women's movement implements the liberation ideology of women's equality, ecology, and communal economy in the everyday, and simultaneously resists different forms of violence. The political situation, however, deteriorated so rapidly between the two general elections of 7 June and 1 November 2015, that the spaces, which had previously been claimed by the movement, shrank dramatically over the five months I spent in Diyarbakir. The week I arrived on fieldwork, the state had announced numerous curfews around the Kurdish southeast of the country. However,

---

[1] At the time of fieldwork, the legal Kurdish youth movement was called YDG-H. In late 2015, it was reorganised into the Civil Protection Units (YPS, *Yekîneyên Parastina Sivîl*) and the Civil Protection Women's Units (YPS-Jin, *Yekîneyên Parastina Sivîl a Jin*), a military organization, in order to repel Turkish attacks on Kurdish cities.

people I spoke to for the first few months were reluctant to acknowledge the failing of the peace process, not wanting to let go of the hope they had in those all-too-brief two years between 2013 and 2015. For a few months people tried to stick to business as usual, while a creeping sentiment of fear slowly descended on the city. Amidst this looming war, women continued to resist at a high cost, as the opening quote illustrates.

While militant femininities unfold in 'the mountains' were guerrillas are mobilised and trained according to the principles of the party ideology, this chapter highlights how militant femininities are lived and performed in the civilian sphere, in the predominantly Kurdish southeast of Turkey. In Diyarbakir, civilians and activists have political and legal rather than military leverage, albeit limited and fragile as the systematic persecution, imprisonment and targeted killings of Kurds in Turkey throughout the twentieth century to the contemporary era demonstrate (Aras 2013; Çiçek 2017; Gambetti & Jongerden 2015; Jongerden 2007). Acting in 'self-defence', civilians as well as activists in the political or legal branch of the party find themselves at the front lines of a transnational war against not just the Kurdish Freedom Movement, but any Kurd. In light of the difference among Kurdish women's roles in the movement, this chapter asks what tools and mechanisms the Kurdish women's movement had to keep the resistance alive in Diyarbakir, where the women's movement has a long history of activity and support, but also faced an even more violent state-backlash over the last five years. The data for this chapter were collected in Diyarbakir between September 2015 and February 2016. Diyarbakir is southeast Turkey's largest city and often referred to as the Kurdish capital. During the 1990s, when the Turkish army destroyed up to 4,000 Kurdish villages, approximately 500,000 displaced villagers moved to Diyarbakir. The city's population doubled in only a few years, with the urban migrants either populating the city's historical centre (Sur) or building new neighbourhoods on the outskirts of the city (Jongerden 2007). The city is geographically divided into more affluent suburban areas (such as Dicle Kent) where most of the new middle and upper classes reside and the central district where the urban poor live and most of the clashes during the urban wars took place (Sur, Bağlar). I conducted a broad first round of interviews with politicians, lawyers, journalists, academics, businesspeople and activists. From there I built my network focusing on the KJA women, but I also spoke to many people who were not linked to the larger structure of the Freedom Movement. I had not learned Turkish and my Kurdish was not yet good enough to conduct in-depth interviews. Hence, all the interviews were either conducted in English or with the help of translators. Furthermore, I collected data during participant observations at conferences and demonstrations, as well as my very personal observations of living and working in a city under such heavy attack. The spaces I had access to decreased continuously in those five months, due to the urban war and police repression of any larger gathering. Whereas in the beginning I was free to move around in every neighbourhood, I was steadily pushed into the domestic sphere. For my work this meant that I had to either meet my interlocutors at their houses or invite them to mine.

This chapter starts with a conceptual discussion that shows how the claiming and defending of urban space is an integral part of the continuum of violence and resistance in which the Kurdish women's movement operates and sustains militant femininities as a means of self-defence of Kurdish livelihoods. I then highlight the work of KJA, the women's umbrella structure at that time, before recounting how the urban war affected their work and everyone else in the city. I give space to the critical voices here, as a way to complicate the official 'resistance slogans' of women working in the legal spheres and argue that the 'performance of resistance' is an integral part of their everyday labour in the bigger structure of the KCK/KJK. This is by no means a full account of what the women's movement did in Diyarbakir as a response to the military violence, ensuing political crisis and economic hardship, but a snapshot of the spaces I had access to while 'encountering violence' as a researcher (Moghnieh 2017).

Resistance in Visibility and Audibility

'Where there is power there is resistance,' Michel Foucault famously said, continuing to argue that resistance is never external to relations of power; instead it operates within power and highlights the relational character of power relations (Foucault 1990, 95). Acknowledging the dynamic interactions and co-dependency between power and resistance is important in the context of Turkey, where, according to Hamit Bozarslan, Kurdish radicalism has been and still is largely a product of state coercion. He argues that violence is a consequence of power relations and authoritarian structures, the absence of integrative social contracts and the impossibility of challenging mechanisms of national and political domination by other means than violence (Bozarslan 2000, 9–11). The criminalisation of political, ethnic and sectarian identities and the resulting divisions have contributed to the formation of what he calls a 'tragic mind', that perceives violence as the surest provider of justice and hope (Bozarslan 2004, 15). Thus, the use of violence becomes a temporary necessity for those sympathetic to the PKK and an almost sacred deed for those in the armed struggle (Grojean 2014, 5). In a never-ending procession of violent incidents such as those that have occurred in Bakur since the 1980s, the past becomes an ensemble of traumatic events that follow one after the other and resist mental classification. The tragic past is never over and always remembered, while people struggle to grapple with more violence and death (Bozarslan 2004, 41–42). The future in turn becomes yet another period where atrocious things will happen, such as the urban wars that engulfed Bakur in 2015.

Studies on the militarisation of urban life and 'state of emergency' at the intersection of critical geopolitics, political geography and Feminist IR (Graham 2004; Gregory 2004; Mbembé 2003) and gender and body politics (Enloe 2014; Fluri 2009; Herold 2004; Katz 2007) emphasise how the city and the life and work routines of its subjects are shaped by war and the normalised use of violence. Domestic spaces, residential neighbourhoods, city centres and suburban areas are turned into front lines of 'insurgency' and 'counterinsurgency' in contemporary wars of states against other social formations (Khalili 2010; Shaw 2004; Sorkin 2004). Both the authoritarian state policies of Turkey and the PKK's war strategies cause the continuous cycle of violence in the city and the rural peripheries, in which the state, in its role as a recognised sovereign, intends to destruct the non-state actor (Foucault 1990, 1991). This confrontation, however, operates on different scales: the Turkish army can destroy whole towns, as seen in Cizre, Nusaybin and Şirnak, whereas the PKK and its affiliate youth in the cities can dig trenches and build barricades.[2] As mentioned in the introduction, the shortcomings of Foucault's understanding of bodies, insofar as he has an androcentric idea of difference, call for an interdisciplinary understanding of how bodies encounter violence as a continuum of reactions that intersectionally run through political, personal, economic and social relations and spaces (Cockburn 2004, 43; Crenshaw 1991; hooks 1989, 2001). Zeynep Gambetti and Joost Jongerden (2011, 2015) pay particular attention to the spatial production of the Kurdish issue and emphasise the importance to consider the actual production of space and 'the performativity of spatial practices, or how

---

[2] This is true for the city war as well as the guerrilla war in the mountains, where guerrilla tactics have more impact on the Turkish army, yet they are still faced with the superior power of one of the most advanced NATO armies. Especially (armed) drones have tipped the scale in favour of the Turkish army and have profoundly changed life in the mountains in the late 2000s, according to my respondents. Nevertheless, the PKK is able to commit spectacular actions: during my fieldwork a video showing how a guerrilla shot down a Turkish helicopter was particularly popular, and every time it showed on TV the party members would cheer and clap. See bibliography (multimedia) for a clip (Gençlerden Kobra Skeci 2016).

people experience and shape the places they live in, how social relations co-define and institutions occupy geographical location as territory' (Gambetti 2005; Gambetti & Jongerden 2011, 377; Massey 1994). It is within these spaces that war is experienced, state policies are felt, neoliberal economic pressures are negotiated, violence is embodied, resistance is performed, and symbols are appropriated (Wedeen 1999). The Kurdish struggle is, among many other things, also a struggle for territorial space and the possibility to make claims in these spaces. However, spaces do not have an authentic core; instead, we need to ask questions about their production, transformation and resilience by analysing the social processes that produce them (Gambetti & Jongerden 2011, 379–82). Furthermore, spaces are gendered insofar as they form and reproduce power structures and reflect social norms into the experience of the everyday (Nakhal 2015, 17).

The case of the Kurdish women's movement is a good example to highlight how we can understand that not only violence but also gendered resistance runs on a continuum, in terms of location (private houses, neighbourhood committees, party buildings, frontline) and scale (discourse, organisation, armed). The Kurdish women's movement is well aware of the continuum of violence, which they refer to as Capitalist Modernity, the interplay between the state, capitalist and patriarchal structures, and it has adapted its ideology and tools of resistance accordingly. First, the women fight against the state, capitalism and patriarchal mindsets simultaneously, and second, they do so in the armed, political and activist spheres. This happens in an audible, communal and highly organised way:

I cannot look at my own resistance, but my resistance is part of a bigger communal resistance. At the core of the success is our emancipation perspective, and that we want to create a different world. Our idea is not to establish a free Kurdistan first and then solve the women's issue, we want to make change now as these things happen. (Interview with Sebahat Tuncel, 28 March 2016)

Sebahat Tuncel, a long-term activist and politician, who in 2007 ran her MP election campaign from prison, emphasised that the only way women stand a chance in this often existential struggle for (political) survival is by standing shoulder to shoulder with each other. Their militancy and closed female ranks help them achieve this. I have defined militant femininities as the process of becoming a subject by joining the movement, going through education and being disciplined, a form of subjectivation necessary for the quest of 'freedom'. An integral part of this process is the performativity of the liberation ideology in the every-day and direct actions of self-defence (Butler 1988). In the political sphere, this does not mean armed struggle but building resilient women's structures. However, the political field is a contested one, where the PKK certainly holds a lot of power, but the movement does not operate as a fully unified block (Watts 2010). Marlene Schäfers further cautions against the presumption that just because actions and voices are visible and audible, they should be equated to women's agency. Instead she examines audibility as an 'ideological site that frames voices, produces subjects, and assigns meanings' (Schäfers 2018, 8). That is why it is important to ask which voices are being silenced and who are the women at the forefront in order to move beyond 'the dichotomy treating voice or silence as a sign for empowerment or suppression' (ibid., 20).

The militant femininities and masculinities are performed with varying visibility in specific spaces: between the mountains and cities, the front lines, villages, and the diaspora. Cynthia Enloe's work complicates the relation of bodies, space and labour, considering the increasingly complex international division of labour, using the example of a state-led military base, which is an intricate microworld dependent on a variety of women in various functions from being a soldier, an officer's wife, a sex worker or cleaner (Enloe 2014). Zooming into the different realms of labour in the Kurdish women's movement, the microworld of the party's urban women activists shows that their work and life routines, while based on the same ideological education that the armed militants absolve, are subjected to the laws of the city. The city, however, is itself subject to war, surveillance and military control over the Kurdish population. Meanwhile Kurdish lawyers, politicians, journalists and activists work with legal and political tools to mobilise and enforce civil rights against the criminalisation of Kurdish citizens of Turkey. Before and during the urban wars, this meant the continuous claiming and defending of spaces for women's centres, academies, cooperatives and municipalities. These spaces gained and defended were filled with particular practices, symbols, posters, slogans and speeches, creating a social imaginary of a group in a particular place. I treat this performativity and its power as a form of knowledge production that follows a pattern of being created (in the mountains and cities), distributed (cadres), performed (demonstrations, conferences, politics), defended (pickets, demonstrations, armed resistance), remembered (martyr cult) and further developed (daily practice, Jineolojî). Linking these spaces together via the proposed nexus of violence, militarisation and competing state and non-state ideologies are another way to acknowledge the relationship between the local and the global, and how they mutually constitute each other, 'for places are also the moments through which the global is constituted, invented, coordinated, produced' (Massey 2004, 11). In what follows I will focus on the specific forms of violence and resistance, and reciprocal violence that I witnessed in Diyarbakir, from KJA's ideological knowledge production, to women's embodied resistance at the barricades.

KJA: The Free Women's Congress

Apart from the municipalities, the most visible and audible driver of change in terms of gender-based equality and justice in Diyarbakir was KJA. Throughout my stay in Diyarbakir I spent time at their congress headquarters in Dicle Kent and went to as many of their events as possible. However, my access was hindered due to the fact that I had made the decision to learn Kurmancî, and all their events, discussions and training courses were held in Turkish. Furthermore, just as I arrived the political situation started to deteriorate rapidly, as the state started to put Sur, Diyarbakir's historical centre, under curfew. In the ensuing state crackdown women's structures were especially targeted, and the women I was supposed to work with were preoccupied most of the time. As of December 2015, it was too risky to attend their marches and rallies, not least due to my fear of being deported if I was too visible for the security forces. The following ethnographic data and analysis are based on semi-structured interviews with KJA activists, a number of days spent at their offices, participation at their events (women's conference, demonstrations) and their publications.

The movement's liberation ideology that I discussed in Chapter 1 is the cornerstone of women's activism in the cities. It is continuously discussed, taught, published and implemented in the women's centres and academies but also in the municipalities. Looking through their official documents, KJA, like any other KCK-/KJK-affiliated party or organisation, departs from a critique of Capitalist Modernity and the enslavement of women:

Nation-state in capitalist modernity developed all sorts of slaughtering policies for women with the purpose of undermining the essence of sociality [. . .]. Women as a gender have been undermined in society and have been prisoned in family, which is the smallest power unit of male-dominated system. Economic system based on profits and exploitation considered women's labour invisible, kept her as a non-waged worker, dispossessed her and even commodified her. Vulgarity of scientism contributes to the reproduction of male dominated world view. [. . .] It is no coincidence that violence against women, abuse, rape and slaughtering of women are more frequent under capitalist modernity. Rape has been systematized and politicized becoming part of a culture that has been legitimized in all spheres of social life including economical, social, political and ideological. Men have been identified as the supreme dominating power over nature and such understanding of power relations have been institutionalized paving way to a never-ending war waged against nature, society and women. (KJA n.d., 2, *language unchanged*)

In Öcalan's ideology, it is no longer the working class that needs to be liberated, but women who are the key to an all-encompassing liberation. In order to achieve this, society has to be organised around his proposed alternative system, Democratic Modernity, which will lead to the liberation of women, nature and humanity as a whole:

Democratic modernity is based on principles of radical democracy and consists of ecological and women's liberation values. [...] Democratic modernity is a democratic system of family and society in opposition to principally relations of domination between women and men and to all forms of relations based on sexism and domination. It is an ecological system that sees humans as part of nature unlike the system of industrialism based on destruction and consumption. With the goal of eradicating class differences, it is an egalitarian system based on communal economics to provide for social needs. It is a system of democratic autonomous self-governance of peoples and communities established by their own free-will to address social concerns and problems. Democratic modernity is a political and ethical society. Democratic modernity, as opposed to power relations of domination based on nation-state under capitalist modernity, upholds democratic nation based on principles of cultural diversity and egalitarianism in which diversity of communities live equally. (KJA n.d., 3, *language unchanged*)

These two dense concepts are the binary that was set out by Abdullah Öcalan in 2003 and formally adopted by the movement in 2005. Since then, the goal of the Kurdish Freedom Movement has been to strive towards Democratic Modernity, through activist, political and armed struggles. The implementation, however, is painstakingly difficult and depending on the context, the people on the ground face tremendous state-backlash or very limited political space. Rojava and Bakur are telling examples of what happens when these concepts are implemented, but also speak to the threat this political alternative, or alternative way of life (*jiyanek alternatif*), as members of the movement call it, poses. This alternative is under constant attack, mainly from regional powers that do not wish to see Kurdish self-determination become a reality.

In Diyarbakir, KJA was the main umbrella organisation that coordinated the efforts being taken by the Kurdish women's movement in the socio-political sphere: 'KJA addresses all societal problems within the framework of democratic, ecological and gender-egalitarian societal paradigm. [...]

It is a body of solidarity, self-determination and self-governing of women of all peoples from diversity of faiths, cultures and communities living in Mesopotamia' (KJA n.d., 11).

All actions are taken with the 'democratic-ecological women's freedom paradigm', meaning the centrality of women's liberation in all structures built, efforts taken and events planned. This involves women's self-organising, Jineolojî workshops, ecology projects, peace building, and the fight against gender-based violence, and oppressive, sexist social relations (KJA n.d., 12–14). What do women do in the everyday to implement these goals? How do they carve out spaces, fill and defend these spaces in southeast Turkey, and Diyarbakir in particular? These were questions I asked when I started working with KJA activists. During my first interviews with prominent representatives of KJA (Ayla Akat and Ayşe Gökkan), I was struggling to break through 'party slogans', such as the quotes mentioned earlier. I tried for a long time to disentangle speech and action and eventually realised that firstly, I would have to spend much longer with the women in order for them to tell me something beyond these official slogans, and secondly, that these slogans are part of their everyday labour, that speech is one of the most powerful tools they wield.

'For us it is our life to struggle. If we don't struggle, we are nothing.' With these words, Ayşe Gökkan, the former mayor of Nusaybin and in 2015 responsible for KJA's diplomacy, explained to me the urgency of their work. Again a party slogan (*Berxwedan Jiyan e!* (Resistance is Life!)), it also speaks to the everyday reality of KJA-affiliated women in Diyarbakir, who are involved in organising work 24/7. Their main objective is to build a unified block including all the women's organisations in order to have one voice and one objective in the greater political arena. All female activists or politicians linked to the larger Freedom Movement were automatically part of KJA. Each municipality worker had to pass a thirty-day KJA training course, essentially a crash course in Öcalan's liberation ideology. Municipality workers who were not sufficiently on party line were sent back to this training course. Each course finished with a criticism and self-criticism session, after which the instructors would decide whether the person had made enough progress to get a municipality position or get her old position back.[3] Second, KJA's purpose was to coordinate the implementation of

---

[3] Criticism and self-criticism are a common tool in Marxist-Leninist movements and were a central element of rule and control in the Soviet Union under Josef Stalin (Erren 2008). The Kurdish Freedom Movement uses it to review events such as training courses or conferences, both in the armed and political sphere. Each attendee has to stand in front of the group and criticise him- or herself for shortcomings and wrongdoings. Afterwards, the members of the group can criticise the person at the front. This exercise is used to create communal members who are capable of reviewing their progress of 'becoming' a militant. It is also a coercive tool to police the boundaries around militants.

grassroots activism and local political organisations, as foreseen by the com-munes-assembly-congress structure developed by Öcalan.[4] Third, KJA coordinated the committee work. Each area (e.g. neighbourhood) had up to twelve committees, which were the basic organising principles of Democratic Autonomy: politics, social affairs, ecology, economy, diplomacy, law and human rights, press and media, peoples and faith communities, language and education, culture, local governments, and self-defence (Ayboğa 2018). Furthermore, KJA was responsible for the implementation of the women's campaigns addressing issues of honour, rape, domestic violence and women's liberation (KJA n.d., 10).[5] These campaigns used to be one of the main tools of the struggle for gender-based justice and equality and over the course of a year included discussions, conferences, education courses and media campaigns, both in Kurdistan, but also in the European diaspora (interview with Zîn, 27 August 2016). These conferences, which were coordinated with the women cadres in the mountains, were an import-ant organisational tool to build community, stage visibility and claim urban space for a democratic confederation with gender equality at its core (Casier 2011; Gambetti 2005).[6]

The main goal of KJA's diplomacy committee was to forge regional and international bonds of solidarity. KJA was one of the first places visited by international delegations on their (solidarity) trips to Diyarbakir; apart from being the headquarters it also functioned as the foreign relations office. Ayla Akat, at that time one of the leading figures of KJA, told me about the movement's relationship with feminism:

When we started to struggle for women's rights we didn't know about feminism, we had never heard this word. But we struggled for our freedom and for women. In time, when we researched, read what is going on in the world, we saw that many women were struggling, feminism is a protest against men's authority. Now it is useful for us to know feminism and we take their experience and that is very

---

[4] The neighbourhood communes (ideally self-sufficient) send representatives to the district, city or regional assemblies. These assemblies elect members to represent them at the congress. The General Assembly of the Congress is made up of 501 delegates, who are elected for a two-year term. This assembly then elects 101 women for the Permanent Assembly, 45 for the Executive Coordination and 11 for Coordination. In Diyarbakir this structure was divided into the different districts such as Dicle Kent, Ofis, Bati Kent, Dikasum, Suriçi, Yenişehir and Bağlar, working in close collaboration with the munici-palities (interview with Ayşe Gökkan, 14 November 2018).

[5] The names of the four campaigns were as follows: We are women, not anyone's honour, our honour is our freedom; Let's overcome the culture of rape; Let's build a democratic free society; Massacre of women is the massacre of society; Say no to women's massacre; Towards a democratic nation with women's freedom (KJA n.d., 10).

[6] 2010: National Kurdish women's conference; 2012: The Socialist International Women's Regional Meeting; 2013: The first Middle East Women's Conference; 2014: The World Women's Conference Middle East Meeting; 2015: First Women's Congress & World March of Women IV (KJA n.d., 10).

important for our struggle. But we looked to find feminism, feminism never looked for us! (Interview Ayla Akat, 19 September 2015)

This quote reflects the reluctance of the Kurdish women's movement to adapt the 'F word' (Çağlayan 2020, 130), as well as the difficult relationship the Kurdish women's movement has had with other feminist movements, such as the Turkish one (Çaha 2011; Gökalp 2010; Yüksel 2006). Iclal Ayşe Küçükkırca divides the relationship between the two movements into four eras: the 1990s as the years of silence due to conflict; the 2000s as a start to renewed engagement; 2013–2015 as the resolution process as well as the resumption of armed clashes; and since 2015 as a time of despair (Küçükkırca 2018, 143–50). She argues that in times of relative peace the relationships between the two movements flourish, but as soon as war breaks out again, ruptures appear. This is due to the fact that the sociopolitical differences in the Kurdish region become more visible in times of war, as well as the fact that the Kurdish women's movement gets visibly closer to the larger Freedom Movement and Öcalan when the attacks on them intensify. Küçükkırca observes that Turkish feminists find it difficult to fully align themselves with the Kurdish women's movement and instead choose to work on issues more suited to western Turkey (Küçükkırca 2018, 151).

Ayla Akat continued:

> We didn't know feminism, but we knew the women's freedom ideology [. . .] All across the world many women's movement struggle, we tried to follow what they were doing. It is not enough to be a big umbrella of KJA, we need to struggle with the women across the globe, we are trying to touch all the women who are struggling, because it is not enough to be strong in Kurdistan. [. . .] We also got in touch with feminists in Turkey, as they are near to us. That time they had a class system; bourgeoisie and working class. Our category was different because the punishing of society is the same for all of us, we never think about who is rich and who is poor, we struggle together [. . .]. The state punishes us all the same. Our problems are the same, in the street every woman is the same.
>
> (Interview with Ayla Akat, 19 September 2015)

Here Akat hints at another tension between the two movements: Turkish feminists looking down on the Kurdish women's movement for its perceived backwardness and issues with honour killings. And in return the Kurdish women's movement considers some of the Turkish feminists as part of the Kemalist elite and therefore as part of the oppression. Turkish feminists often tried to persuade their Kurdish counterparts to distance themselves from the larger Kurdish Freedom

Movement in order to achieve a truly autonomous women's movement. A famous Turkish anthropologist who went to Kurdistan and met with the women there, trying to get her concern regarding this separation across, was brusquely rebuffed: 'I am sorry professor, but the PKK came here long before you did' (interview with Hişyar Özsoy, 20 February 2016).

It was not long into the interview that Ayla Akat articulated the movement's claim of sustainability, as well as the embodied knowledge that both violence and resistance operate on a continuum. She insisted that the state and men both try to oppress women and that only by struggling against both did they gain the experience of organising against 'men mentality' as Öcalan called it:

If they solve the Kurdish problem, it does not mean they will solve women's problems, so our struggle will continue. When we see the revolutions of this world, women go back home after. That's why we say, we will struggle, we will never go back home. And to counter this they have formed KJA as an umbrella organisation to coordinate women's work and to reach out to other struggling women across the world. (Interview with Ayla Akat, 19 September 2015)

As many of her comrades whom I was yet to meet, Ayla replied in the plural form 'we', signifying that this is a communal struggle and she is not giving me her personal opinion, but that of KJA, and by extension that of the women's movement and Öcalan. It was Öcalan, in discussion with the women, who found a really important shortcoming in previous women's struggles: that of organising separately. Realising how much of the struggle (visible to me) was repetition of discourse, I often wondered: can the women challenge the discourse? Can they come up with their own?

Women Vanguards and War in the Cities

In 2015, the Kurdish Movement started to declare Democratic Autonomy in different parts of Bakur, including Sur, Diyarbakir's old city. Democratic Autonomy is the political principle of self-determination and refers to the practices in which people produce the necessary conditions for collaboration with one another, rather than being dependent on state institutions and structures (Jongerden & Akayya 2013). In essence, this meant that certain parts of the city were declaring self-rule. This led to a violent backlash by the Turkish state that took it as an opportunity to crush the armed youth movement (YDG-H) that had barricaded itself in these areas and remove the elected mayors from their posts. This harsh state-backlash did not stop the movement from continuing to announce further areas of self-rule, always with the accompanying slogan: 'People will keep up their resistance in the neighbourhoods, and this resistance will spread everywhere.'

By September 2015, the attacks and counter-attacks between the YDG-H and the Turkish state were getting more frequent. Cities across the country's southeast were under siege, sometimes certain neighbourhoods, sometimes the whole town, as was the case in Silopi and Cizre. Large demonstrations were held regularly across the region to protest the war. Women were at the forefront of these demonstrations and were targeted specifically by the security forces. During a meeting at the KJA offices, the female MP Çağlar Demirel showed me her two big canister wounds on both her legs. She had been shot by the police, despite her parliamentary immunity. Çağlar emphasised that the isolation of Abdullah Öcalan, the non-intervention of Turkey during the attacks on Kobanî a year earlier, the curfews in Cizre and Sur, the attacks on Qandil, the forest fires around Lice, and the arrests of politicians, as well as the police's right to shoot live ammunition during demonstrations were all connected and part of Erdoğan's new military strategy, so that he can stay in his palace in Ankara (and become president). She assured me that this was all planned and worse than the 1990s, insofar as the war was now in the cities and fought with bigger weapons on both sides (fieldwork notes, 19 September 2015).

Police forces also verbally abused women, insulting them for being in the public sphere and not at home, married and taking care of the house, or for being ugly and that being the reason why they were not at home, married and taking care of the house. I asked Feleknas Uca, a Yezidi HDP MP who was very much at the forefront of the protests, how the state used women's bodies and how she as a female politician experienced violence:

Women experience so much violence because they stand at the frontline of our fight. Why do they stand there? Because they feel responsible for change in this country; for more rights, for equal rights. But also because the Kurdish freedom movement has changed the image and roles of women. Before women were mainly housewives, but with the Kurdish freedom movement, women became more confident and got more involved. The co-mayorship is only one of these examples. The quota is everywhere. We now have 104 municipalities and 104 women who are active. (Interview with Feleknas Uca, 29 February 2016)

At this stage in January, Feleknas experienced violence on her own body on an almost daily basis: 'At demonstrations the police walk towards me, hit themselves on the chest and shout "I am the state!"

So I say, You are the weapon of the state – but I am a representative of the state so show some more respect!' (Interview with Feleknas Uca, 29 February 2016). All these tactics she assured me are intended to make the women feel small and powerless, especially the MPs of the HDP: 'We are attacked; tear gassed, hit with water cannons and insulted by the police. Imagine the hate that they have for us! The state says, we will continue "cleansing the east until the last terrorist is dead". And we, we will continue to fight for a peaceful solution' (Interview with Feleknas Uca, 29 February 2016). Then she rushed off to attend yet another funeral of a person killed in the clashes during the urban wars. One year later Feleknas Uca demonstrated her defiance in the face of state violence again, when she protected a fellow demonstrator from a police officer (see Figure 2.1).

Women were standing their ground not only on the streets, but also in the municipalities. Februniye Akyol, the Syriac Christian co-mayor of Mardin explained to me how she used the women's liberation paradigm in the everyday: 'I have a baseball bat *[laughs]*, and when issues come up, I use that. In all seriousness, it needs a constant push back from the

Figure 2.1 Feleknas Uca during a demonstration in protest of Gültan Kışanak's arrest, Diyarbakir, October 2016. Photo: İlyas Akengin

women. But compared to previous generations it has improved; now men have a certain level of knowledge of gender issues. However, often their behaviour contradicts this knowledge because their way of thinking and working is so deeply engrained in them. Often, they belittle our efforts to be self-sufficient and autonomous.' When I asked her how she can win these arguments, she replied that certainly banging on the table [with her imaginary baseball bat] helps: 'We need to constantly remind them: if it is an issue that concerns women, you need to consult with the women.' She shared her co-presidency with Ahmet Türk, a senior member of the pro-Kurdish political movement:

He has been a politician for 40 years and he has been the party [DBP] leader for years. And he is a tribal leader! This has been educational for me as well. I had to struggle more with the people surrounding him, because they admire him, his background, what he stands for. The way I overcame this was with the women's movements paradigms [...]. The most effective method was to sit down with the co-mayor and talking to him about it. I would explain that we are in it together and have to solve it together [...]. Now he has changed the way he is. When something comes to him, he will always ask me to be present to solve the issues. He started to say 'we', not 'me'! (Interview with Februniye Akyol, 30 January 2016)

I also asked her about the potential and limitations of the women's quota, and she assured me that having a quota only does not mean that gender equality has been achieved (Al-Ali & Tas 2017). Instead, gender equality has slowly been introduced over the course of a forty-year struggle. 'But it still needs a great deal of education, especially for men,' she emphasised. Just like all other mayors, Februniye was removed from her post in November 2016, as part of the large-scale crack down on the Kurdish movement, which further inceased after the attempted coup in July 2016.

In late September 2015, when the first curfew in Sur was lifted, I visited the embattled streets with an international delegation. What caught my eye, apart from the destruction, were the various graffiti on the colourful walls that proclaimed allegiance with the PKK: stencilled heads of Öcalan, 'Join the resistance and the PKK' (see Figure 2.2), or 'Protect your language'. We met with the YDG-H in a tent in one of their central squares. The members of the group, clearly traumatised by the recent fight, reiterated their goal of self-rule, pledged allegiance to Öcalan and reassured us that they were organised and ready to fight the state.

Haydar Darici who conducted his PhD research on the YDG-H in Cizre between 2013 and 2015 explained in an interview that the urban wars were part of a specific strategy by the PKK to liberate not only the mountains but also the cities. The movement called this new process, which began around 2010, the 'process of construction', and was part of the bigger paradigm shift towards Democratic Autonomy:

Figure 2.2 Stencil graffiti of Abdullah Öcalan in Sur: For freedom of the leadership and freedom of Kurdistan, to the guerrilla ranks

I should note that it was the Kurdish youth and children who through a spatial politics prepared the ground upon which democratic autonomy could be constructed. From the late 1990s on, youth and children have conducted a radical street politics, clashing with the police almost every day, using stones and Molotov cocktails. Through this radical street politics, they turned streets into spaces of politics and made their neighbourhoods and even towns inaccessible to the Turkish police. (Darici 2015)

In order to fight the implementation of Democratic Autonomy, the state tried to enter neighbourhoods by force. In turn, the youths dug deep trenches and barricades and guarded them. After the general elections in

June 2015, the government declared the end of negotiations and started attacking the Kurdish towns where the resistance was best organised. Week-long curfews or sieges were declared. Snipers were located on high buildings and minarets, shooting those who did not observe the curfew. The infamous case of Taybet Inan is an example of how ruthless these operations were. Taybet, a fifty-seven-year-old mother of eleven children, was shot by a sniper while crossing the road on 19 December 2015 in Silopi. Her brother went outside to rescue the wounded women but was also shot and killed. Taybet was left to die on the street, where her body remained for a week. Only after the curfew ended could she be buried (Dicle 2016). Equally horrific is the story of Cemile Çağırga, a ten-year-old Kurdish girl from Cizre, who was shot while playing with her friends in front of her house. After being denied a proper burial, her family was forced to keep her body in a freezer until the curfew was lifted (Zengin 2015). Furthermore, the lawyers who went to Cizre on a fact-finding mission told me that around ten to fifteen women suffered miscarriages during that first curfew in September 2015 (fieldwork notes, 19 September 2015). These unprecedented levels of state violence unfortunately became the new norm with the curfews, peaking with the suppression of the resistance in Cizre, where more than 100 people were burned alive, while seeking shelter in a basement (Özarslan 2017).

Despite these inhumane measures, the 'security forces' were unable to enter the neighbourhoods for the first few months, also because the youth had dug deeper trenches and had received training and weapons from the PKK (interview with Agir, 1 September 2016). In order to protect themselves from snipers' bullets, they hung white sheets across the streets, blocking the snipers' view, a method they had learned during the war in Rojava (Figure 2.3, Darici 2015).

YDG-H fighters also broke down the walls between the houses in order to pass from one house to another without going outside to share food and assist the wounded (Figure 2.4).

Inside the 'liberated areas', women had built autonomous structures under the leadership and protection of the YPS-Jin. They had established 'purple squares', safe places for women, where they could seek assistance. The women in charge of running and protecting the 'purple squares' would intervene in family affairs such as arranged marriages, child marriages or other neighbourhood issues concerning women. The goal of these 'purple squares' was to already build the new way of life, while the conflict was still raging on (fieldwork notes, 23 March 2016).

The situation in the besieged towns and neighbourhoods was further complicated by the fact that, contrary to the 1990s, the boundaries between civilians and guerrillas became increasingly blurred (Shaw 2004; Sorkin

Figure 2.3 Barricades and sheets in Cizre, September 2015. Photo: Mahmut Bozarslan

Figure 2.4 In Sur, Diyarbakir, December 2015. Photo: Mahmut Bozarslan

2004). Civilians were arming themselves, no longer joining the formal ranks of the PKK but the more directly involved YDG-H. Furthermore, the mobility of fighters increased: from Rojava or Maxmûr to the hotspots in Bakur and back. Darici argued that in the process of the urban resistance, the youth became the main actors of the Kurdish movement, as it was they who defined the processes of politics and resistance (Darici 2015). However, it was the PKK who trained, armed and controlled the YDG-H, a former commander who had left the PKK after the city wars confirmed. 'The mayors were ordered by the mountains to declare Democratic Autonomy in certain places. They knew that this would mean war. After that, the mayors couldn't do anything anymore. It was the PKK who ordered it, who started it and who could stop it' (interview with former commander 5, 12 October 2019).

Critical Voices and Silences

Sometimes, when the siege was lifted for a few hours or a few days, certain journalists could go to Sur and other besieged areas. One of them was Mirza Ararat, who further elaborated on the PKK's strategy:

[The PKK] are trying to bring war and violence into the cities. There are two reasons for this. One reason is to put pressure on the government to turn back to the peace process. Secondly, they are fighting with IS in Rojava and some Western powers are supporting them there. They thought that with this support they can do something in Turkey, and they began to do this. [But] it is not working. It is the worst thing they ever did. Now people are angry with the PKK and the Kurdish movement. No one supports these ditches and barricades and the violence inside the city. [...] They are complaining about the fighters who are digging holes through the walls of their homes, they are complaining about the violence in their neighbourhoods. (Interview with Mirza Ararat, 1 February 2016)

This situation further divided an already polarised society, along the lines of state versus PKK, with many people continuing to show allegiance with the Kurdish Freedom Movement, despite their contested war strategy. Officially elected people would voice their criticism in private, and those working for the municipality only articulated their true feelings about the political situation on the condition that I would not use any of this information, being afraid that it would threaten their position within the community. A journalist who grew up on the frontline between the state and the PKK in the 1990s explained to me that the allegiance with the PKK was, not exclusively, but also a matter of the (broken) heart:

At first everyone was afraid, of both groups [PKK and Turkish army]. But after many years some of their children, brothers, and sisters joined the PKK and were killed. Now they feel close to the PKK because they lost their beloved children in the PKK. Maybe it is a good choice or a bad choice, that's not important for them. They feel close to them because it is linked to their people. And if one of your people is killed you cannot think about them negatively [...]. I don't know any family in my village and city who didn't lose a member of their family in the PKK. And this is the best support for PKK. I lost I don't know how many cousins in the PKK. It is not about the mind, it is about the heart [...]. In my neighbourhood my people cannot think [rationally], because they remember their loved ones. (Interview with Herekol, 12 December 2015)

Someone who was very vocal in his criticism was journalist Serdar. He spent four months in Suruç at the Turkish/Syrian border, when IS was attacking Kobanî just on the other side. This experience of the silence of the so-called Turkish brothers destroyed his hope of ever being able to live with Turks. He was a supporter of both independence and the PKK and HDP. He was however resolutely against the YDG-H, saying they were to blame for the destruction of the cities. Serdar often voiced his outrage over the fact that they had elected eighty HDP MPs and still they were unable to prevent the war in Cizre and other besieged towns. He elaborated:

It [urban wars for self-rule] is not working for the Kurds. The Turkish state is really successful, they have an army, soldiers and power. And after a while if you don't have language or culture, what do you want? For what? It is hard to answer these questions. I am confused too you know. I am sure a lot of Kurdish people who support these parties are asking questions, but there are no answers and many are scared to ask the questions too [...]. And we talked about intellectuals, if they exist or not. They are scared of both sides; of PKK and Turkish state. If you live in Diyarbakir, the de facto capital, you are scared of both sides. So where are the questions? Where are the answers? (Interview with Serdar, 9 October 2015)

This sentiment resonates with many other opinions I heard during my time in Diyarbakir, a mix between emotional allegiance to the PKK and the HDP, combined with real doubts about the capacity of the former to control YDG-H, and that the latter could find a political solution. Those were also the people who called the movement's claim of resistance mere slogans, hallucinations. 'What good is it if our MPs stands at the barricades and at the front of demonstrations? They should be in Ankara, finding a political solution for this,' I was often told. Ruken, a local businesswoman, also did not shy away from speaking her mind:

The PKK has done so much for people, the people are the PKK, everyone has someone in the mountains, dead or alive, and people will follow them uncondi-tionally. But right now [during the urban wars] they are really spreading that support thin. Kurdish people gave everything to this struggle, the PKK should be more careful with their supporters. (Interview with Ruken, 10 December 2015)

Ruken was also weary of the HDP's political power and abilities, emphasising how all the power lies with the PKK in the mountains, with the cadres in the cities and the prisons, which explains why no one said anything publicly during the curfews. She was very passionate in her critique for the HDP, saying that they lack leadership skills and use empty slogans. However, she acknowledged the importance of the women's movement:

The Kurdish women's movement is very effective and very strong. No one wants to get in their way or fight with them, they can do what they want. They brought freedom for women, they are very important. But their education needs to change. They cannot just teach Öcalan and talk about co-operatives. But they also need to educate the people about the bourgeois life. I tried to work with them many times, told them that us businesspeople could give them a list of our needs, we would train and employ them in our businesses. But so far nothing has happened. (Interview with Ruken, 10 December 2015)

I met Ruken a few times, and each time she was angrier and more nervous about the deteriorating political situation. 'It is such a tragedy that all our young people are dying, who will be held accountable for it?', she complained when I saw her for the last time during Newroz in March 2016. She was furiously chain-smoking: 'No one trusts our politicians anymore, everyone hates them.' Her tirade lashed out against politicians and mayors for being incapable of stopping this tragedy, for having failed to respond adequately to the needs of the displaced people; the YDG-H/ PKK for presenting the Turkish state with this opportunity to crush them and destroy the cities; the PKK for underestimating the Turkish state; KJA for only using slogans and creating a model of women that everyone has to abide by; and she was deeply upset about the effects of all this on the young people and on her businesses, saying it will take the region years to recover. 'People don't want to resist anymore, they just want to get on with their life!'. Ruken's anger reflects not only her outspoken nature, of which she was clearly proud, but also her different positioning within the struggle: being of a middle-upper class background, she had much to lose and very little to gain from this war.[7] Doing an ethnography in a war zone

---

[7] It is questionable whether the same people would articulate similar criticisms today, when the movement is under even more duress. From afar I observe that people have either unified behind the movement, have become even more polarised or have stopped voicing their political opinions all together. When checking back with my respondents in 2020, five years after our conversations, to double-check whether they want me to anonymise their names, which initially they did not request, most of them said yes, not wanting to draw attention to themselves.

also means developing a high tolerance for competing narratives, which on both sides resulted in fixed truths, polarised opinions and battle slogans. I contextualise some of them here to demonstrate that despite the strong backing of the Kurdish Freedom Movement in cities like Diyarbakir, not everyone was united behind party lines, and depending on personal histories of struggle and 'living-in-violence' (Moghnieh 2017), these shifted considerably as the human cost of the conflict increased.

Of Fear and Closing Spaces

With the escalating violence came fear: fear of more violence, fear of its unpredictability, and the knowledge that it will be unaccounted for. Especially during curfews, people living in non-besieged parts of Diyarbakir tried to be home by nightfall, which was around 4 p.m. in the autumn and winter months. Women in particular were advised not to be out alone after dark. Yet violence also found its way into the private sphere. Serdar put it as follows:

I don't even have a flirt you know. [...] The truth is that when you are making love with your darling you think about Nusaybin and Cizre. So it is a pleasure that you are making love but somebody dies there. You feel guilty in your bedroom. I talk with couples, married couples. Lots of people think like me. All the time we talk about politics and what is happening in Nusaybin, Cizre, Suruç, we think, we fight, everybody is angry. These things attack your bedroom. If you have no television and radio, it comes to your bedroom, the Turkish state comes to your bedroom. (Interview with Serdar, 9 October 2015)

I often encountered this sentiment of not being able to enjoy life anymore, combined with guilt for being safe, warm and alive. Life as a whole was being put on hold; people were no longer getting married or investing in future endeavours. 'You missed a great time,' I was often told, 'just before you came people were getting married in Sur, dancing in the streets of Sur, music was playing until the early morning hours!' The short-lived economic boom that started with the peace process and the neoliberal development agenda pushed by the Turkish state and facilitated by local businesses came to an abrupt halt in mid-2015. Tourists stopped coming and numerous general strikes in protest of Turkey's suppressive measures incapacitated the whole city on numerous occasions.[8] Since 2015, many

---

[8] Tourism, cross-border trade, investments and development all took a significant hit when the peace process came to a halt. Along with the bitter humanitarian and social repercussions, Al-Monitor reported in September 2015 that the termination of the peace process had produced an immediate bill of $55 billion for Turkey (Doğan 2015).

small businesses were forced to close, especially retailers, restaurants and hotels. According to the Diyarbakir Chamber of Commerce and Industry (DTSO), 3,000 businesses in the district of Sur have closed down while more than 10,000 people have lost their jobs between June 2015 and March 2016.[9]

The act of pushing people, especially women, into their homes and the movement out of the public sphere was a deliberate one. In its heyday, the DBP-run municipalities were criminalising domestic violence[10] and started to fight 'female suicides',[11] renamed streets, put up statues to remember state oppression (e.g. the Roboski massacre), rebuilt an Armenian church in Sur, took over a beautiful old city house to establish a women's academy, and used the city parks for conferences. Hazal Aras who in January 2016 was the co-mayor of Diyadin, a small district close to the Iranian border, told me during an interview that when she started getting involved as a female politician, she faced significant pushback and doubts about her capabilities from the community and that violence against women was and still is a huge issue:

Our main challenge is against the system that protects the perpetrator of violence against women. There is a saying in Turkish and Kurdish culture: 'keep your woman beaten and pregnant'. This is how bad it is to be a woman here. Because the state mentality is that women are purely there to become pregnant and to serve men. But with the Kurdish Freedom Movement this has changed. It was thanks to the movement that we learned to express this, it was due to the co-mayorships that we were able to address these issues. Years ago there was only one Leyla Zana, now there are dozens! (Interview with Hazal Aras, 31 January 2016)

Asked about her main efforts towards gender-based equality she told me of a large women's centre, where women can go to learn new skills and seek psychological support. 'Also we lit up our public parks, so for the first time, women can now go out after nightfall. Because there are a lot of places where men can go after seven in the evening to socialise. We wanted to create that for women' (Interview with Hazal Aras, 31 January 2016). Since

[9] Figures provided by the Migrants' Association for Social Cooperation and Culture (GÖÇ-DER) show that 200,000 people have emigrated from areas that have been put under curfew, 20,000 from Sur alone (Duran 2016).

[10] When the DBP started winning municipalities in 2007 and 2009, but mostly so in 2014, when the party increased its number of municipalities to 102, they started outlawing domestic violence by implementing a zero-tolerance policy: every municipality worker had to sign an agreement that he would not beat his wife. He would lose his job in case of a breach of contract (interview with Nurcan Baysal, 23 November 2015).

[11] Female suicides or 'honour suicides' were sadly common in Bakur, something the DBP-run municipalities tried to tackle. The high numbers of so-called honour crimes are due to poverty, the breaking of social ties as a result of rural-urban migration and the absence of a functioning justice system in the southeast (Birch 2006; Smith 2007).

the 1980s, the Kurdish women's movement had fought a long battle to gain visibility and audibility in social and political spheres, a battle that was fought against male comrades and 'male mentality', as the movement terms men's inclination to control, possess and oppress. Sabriye Orak, a female DTK member, told me: 'It is very important for us to be physically present [at DTK] everyday, also in case delegations come. We want to show that women are working here.' This shows the deep mistrust that women have in their menfolk, knowing that they have to constantly defend their spaces. 'I wish we could just leave men out and go away. But that wouldn't be democratic, so we try to change them' (interview with Sabriye Orak, 27 November 2018).

Getting women out of the house and organised along party lines has been one of the main goals and successes of the women's movement. This was possible due to the strong backing of the PKK in wider society, which meant that men could not stop women from working in the public sphere, organising a protest or working for the elections. The expectation, however, was that they would still fulfil the traditional roles expected by men – to look after the children, the husband and the household. 'The activist women started to get really tired because they were doing two things at the same time,' Gültan Kışanak, the co-mayor of Diyarbakir told me:

Now [January 2016] we have brought Kurdish men to an understanding that women have a right to be representative in Kurdish politics. But if a woman is not a political actor, if a woman is not working for the political party, they should fulfil the traditional expectations by patriarchal society. This is the thing that we need to dismantle right now, not only for activist women but for all women. [Women shouldn't just get] recognition because of our political activities but because we are women. (Interview with Gültan Kışanak, 5 January 2016)

Gültan Kışanak highlights the fact that just by organising women behind party lines and making them visible and audible representatives of the movement does not mean that the everyday reality at home and the wider society changes and that a much broader change of 'male mentality' is needed.

After a year of intense fighting and repeated curfews and sieges, the urban resistance was brutally crushed and those members of YDG-H who managed to escape either went home (if their home and city were not destroyed), went to fight in Rojava, joined the guerrillas in the mountains, or have found refuge in Maxmûr Camp, as I will further discuss in Chapter 5. In total, the security forces imposed eighty-five curfews in thirty-three Kurdish south-eastern districts between 2015 and 2016. Around 1,700 people were killed, and around 350,000 civilians were displaced due to the large-scale urban destruction.[12] All the municipalities in Bakur have been taken over by a 'trustee' from Ankara, the Roboski statue has been dismantled (Khalidi 2017), the Armenian church has been severely damaged and looted during the clashes (Bozarslan 2017), and the parks and other public spaces can no longer be used for the staging of events. Similar destruction and appropriation of the public spaces have been taking place across the Kurdish southeast; in Nusaybin, for example, a monument that honoured the martyrs of a particularly violent Newroz in 1992 has recently been replaced by a clock tower (Haber Erciş 2018).

For as long as physically possible, the women of KJA resisted this pushback into invisibility. I was advised after a certain point to no longer attend any demonstrations, not least because the police were using live ammunition and made a point of wounding or killing a few people during each demonstration. Yet the women were fearless, which among the many other occasions they illustrated during the women's march, which took place in January 2016. By approaching the besieged Botan province from different sides, the women were hoping to break through the police barricades and get to the city of Cizre. Apart from a sign of solidarity, this march was also a way to make visible KJA's protest against the twenty-four-hour curfews and all the human rights abuses that came with it. After two days, Sebahat Tuncel, a key figure in the pro-Kurdish political movement, made the following statement:

> In two days, we have been denied access to five different cities on the orders of the Ministry of the Interior. Our people have been resisting in Botan for 30 days. Their resistance is not for themselves; it is for us, for you, for the future of our children [. . .]. All we have in our hands is the flag of freedom, while they close off every road with bulletproof vests, snipers, and armored vehicles. We've seen how they fear our ululations. This march, by scaring them, has actually reached its goal. After this, this march needs to continue in all cities. (JINHA 2016)

These examples serve as an illustration that the Kurdish women's movement had a multi-pronged tactic to implement its liberation paradigm in Diyarbakir (and other cities): through legal party politics (DBP, a Kurdish local party and the HDP, at the national level), through the establishment of parallel networks of power (communes and assemblies), and through self-defence (solid women's ranks and YDG-H, guerrillas). First and foremost, this meant getting women out of the house, into the public sphere and organised along party lines.

---

[12] According to an open-source database compiled by International Crisis Group, between 20 July 2015 and 19 July 2016, 307 civilians, 582 security force members, 653 PKK members and 219 'youth of unknown affiliation' (YDG-H) were killed (Mandıracı 2016).

As part of my interviews I asked people, inside and outside the movement, what the women's movement had achieved in their four decades of struggle. Murad Akincilar, coordinator of the local NGO Diyarbakir Institute for Political and Social Research (DISA), responded that the main achievement was for women to gain the co-presidency and the women's quota in all positions. He also recounted a discussion he had witnessed between a female activist and some male comrades:

The man was saying that 'ok we accept and admit that you are a very important part of the struggle. We have no intention to exclude you in any procedure'. And the woman said 'comrade you know what you are not able to understand, we are not an important part but we are at the centre of the struggle!' (Interview with Murad Akincilar, 20 November 2015)

This anecdote resonates with a sentiment that I observed many times: women know that they are the backbone of the struggle, but that they also have to continuously prove their worth and defend their spaces. 'When we didn't pass the 10% in earlier elections, the men tried to blame it on us, accusing us of wanting to divide the party,' Ayşe Gökkan recounted. 'We fought a big battle internally [in the 2000s], in the family, in the party and against the state, it was very difficult' (interview with Ayşe Gökkan, 14 November 2015). Everyone I spoke to throughout my five months in Diyarbakir said, without a doubt, things have changed for women thanks to what the Kurdish women's movement has done. This was often followed by a 'but'. The late Tahir Elçi, a prominent human rights lawyer and head of the Diyarbakir bar association, told me:

Of course, the Kurdish Women's Movement is so strong, they are so visible in the society, in Silopi, Cizre, Diyarbakir. Women groups are more active than men, in protests, marches, and meetings. This is very important. [...] You cannot see the same with Iranian, Arabic and Turkish people. But it doesn't mean that the same developments take place in normal society. So the problem is still continuing. Politically you can see some new developments, but the traditional regional culture and religious culture is affecting society very harshly. And you cannot change this culture in a short time. So ok Kurdish women are so active, fighting IS, here in Turkey in the democratic struggle. Yes, this is important for the future of the Kurdish society. But it doesn't mean that the same developments are taking place in the other parts of life. (Interview with Tahir Elçi, 15 September 2015)

He named a lack of education and women's economic dependency as the main factors that keep Kurdish women in a subordinate position and emphasised that many women are illiterate and do not speak Turkish, so it is even more difficult for them to access legal support. Before we were interrupted by his colleagues he emphasised again: 'We need to achieve economic independence, create jobs, and education for women. These processes have to be in parallel with what the women's movement is doing, otherwise it is important but not enough' (Interview with Tahir Elçi, 15 September 2015).

The Murder of Tahir Elçi

On 28 November 2015, Tahir Elçi was shot while holding a press conference in front of the four-legged minaret in Sur, protesting the destruction of cultural heritage sites during the armed clashes between the state security forces and the YDG-H. To this day it is not entirely clear how his murder was set up, but all evidence points towards a planned assassination by the Turkish 'deep state'.[13] Elçi's killing was perceived by many as a warning, that the state would stop at nothing to quell the resistance, even the moderate voices, like his, who were trying to mediate between the warring factions. His murder was a huge shock to the whole region; thousands came to bid farewell to him the following day (Figure 2.5).

Despite all of the legal, political and social resistances discussed earlier, the murder of Tahir Elçi was a huge blow to the movement and people's morale. For days a grey veil hung over Diyarbakir, people barely left their houses and many shops remained closed. There was a sentiment in the air – that if 'they' would kill Tahir Elçi, who knows what else they were capable of. It was around that time that I perceived the women's movement to also become temporarily paralysed, as if they realised that they needed to prepare for a long fight for survival. The HDP was still calling for the spread of the uprising, away from Sur and into the middle- and upper-class neighbourhoods, but to no avail; fewer and fewer people turned up to these calls and those who did were always dispersed by the police within minutes (fieldwork notes, 18 December 2015).

At his last press conference Tahir Elçi was calling for an end to the conflict in Sur. Instead his assassination marked the beginning of its escalation (Forensic Architecture, 8 February 2019). On 15 December a new curfew was announced for Sur. Weeks of relentless shelling followed. On 27 December, the DTK held a meeting, where the DBP, HDP and DTK jointly announced their endorsement of the *Declaration of Political Resolution Regarding Self-Rule.* This was a show of unity and determination

---

[13] Forensic Architecture, a London-based research agency that undertakes spatial and media investigations into cases of human rights violations, published a frame-by-frame analysis that shows that the policemen present at the press conference are the most likely to have fired the fatal shot that killed Tahir Elçi. They conclude that 'despite the available evidence no policemen present at the scene were ever questioned as suspects' (Forensic Architecture 2019).

Figure 2.5 During the minute of silence at the cemetery, Diyarbakir

to implement this project of self-rule, no matter the costs of retaliation by the Turkish state. The declaration set out fourteen points that could solve the current political bottleneck: the formation of autonomous regions, the self-governance of the regions; the end of Ankara's tutelage; the establishment of the assembly structure; the advancement of democracy via these assemblies; equal representation of women; participation of youth; the provision of education, jobs and healthcare by the autonomous administrations; the rearrangement of the judicial system; administration of land, water and energy sources; the supervision of air, land and sea transport; the assignment of a budget to the autonomous administrations; and lastly the establishment of local security forces (ANF 2015). Seemingly as a result of this declaration, the AKP cancelled planned negotiations. Thereafter, I attended a press conference with Selahattin Demirtaş and Feleknas Uca, the HDP's co-president and a female MP, respectively. Uca did not say anything but looked stern and tired, wringing her hands. Demirtaş emphasised that the DTK announcement had been taken out of context and that the fourteen points were nothing new – that the HDP had already been advocating for devolution of power in its election campaign. This declaration was meant to be a call for dialogue about the devolution of power, not to polarise the camps further (fieldwork notes, 30 December 2015). The example of the DTK declaration aims to illustrate two things: how committed the political parties were (or were forced to be) to keep on pushing the project of self-rule, and how torn the political movement was between the East and the West. The consensus among the journalists I was with during both days was that the first declaration, which used a stronger language, was aimed at garnering support for the trenches and barricades from the local constituencies. The following press conference was intended to reassure people that the movement only uses democratic tools to make all of Turkey more democratic. However, Herekol, a local journalist's assessment, was bleaker: 'Us Kurdish people are like a chessboard for political powers to try something, erase, try something new, erase again. And in the process so many people die.' (fieldwork notes, 27–30 January 2018). After the breakdown of diplomatic relations between the HDP and AKP, the political space became noticeably narrower, not just between Diyarbakir and Ankara but also between Sur, Ofis and Dicle Kent, three of Diyarbakir's neighbourhoods. Squares were no longer accessible, more activists were being killed, and the state mercilessly continued its war in the cities. The state forces that entered the besieged towns mutilated women's bodies and left racist and sexist remarks on the walls of houses and schools, distinctly targeting women: 'Girls, we are here and penetrated your caves', implying that the repression of the Turkish state is a male act, a penetration of the Kurdish female (Burç 2018, 12; interview with Murad Akicilar, 20 January 2015).[14]

Conclusion

The structures built by the women's movement in the urban sphere before the attempted coup in 2016 were complex, multi-layered, and intertwined with the municipality and state system. Women organised under the umbrella of KJA have built a strong power base, a (from the outside) seemingly unified women's block. They influenced policy-making, educated women and youth, organised conferences and campaigns, and marched at the front of protests when their people and structures came under attack. Nevertheless or perhaps because of it, the women of the movement never tired of repeating how long they have been fighting, and that they were prepared to continue this struggle at any cost. Only in private would they admit how exhausted they were. Most women I spoke to portrayed men as the main nemesis, but I was always assured it

---

[14] A reference to a collection of photos documenting this form of psychological warfare can be found under multimedia in the bibliography (M4zlum 2016).

was not them personally, but their mentality and their systems. Women have fought hard to get women's equality enshrined in the written ideology and to translate that into actual political mechanisms. By 2016, there was little the men from within the movement could do to sabotage the women. One informant told me that at a DTK meeting, the co-chair and influential Kurdish politician Hatib Dicle warned one of his male peers: 'If you mess with the women, not even I can save you.' As the political situation deteriorated, people became more polarised and disheartened, but resistance continued: MPs marched and attempted to break through barricades; for a long time the press covered human rights abuses; law offices were gathering evidence; and as long as the politicians were still free they continued to advocate for the idea of peaceful self-administrations. However, for ordinary activists and civilians it was a different story. Whole neighbourhoods were destroyed, activists and lawyers got killed and the hope for peace was lost. The case of the Kurdish women's movement illustrates that a movement that is under constant attack and faced with so many obstacles needs a unified 'resistance ideology', clear goals and strict organisational structures in order to survive the attacks of the sovereign state power. The women I worked with in Diyarbakir operate within a continuum of violence, using a continuum of resistance to live up to their promise of militancy and sustainability. Women interfere and shape resistance at multiple fronts as they encounter the Turkish state, the family and the Kurdish Freedom Movement. In these matrices, audibility and visibility do not equal lasting emancipation, but it is an important tool in the struggle to achieve Democratic Modernity.

Since I left Diyarbakir in February 2016, the situation has become much worse. After the attempted coup in July 2016, most of the HDP politicians were arrested and face lengthy prison sentences. The prosecution has asked for 230 years for Gültan Kışanak and 145 years for Sebahat Tuncel, on fabricated charges accusing them of being members of a terrorist organisation and spreading terrorist propaganda. In early 2019, they were sentenced to fourteen- and fifteen-year prison sentences, respectively. All of the 102 municipalities have been taken over by 'state trustees'. Dissent has been silenced but arrests continue on a daily basis. Public resistance has largely stopped. However, the women's movement proves to be resilient: KJA was forced to close its doors in late 2016 but re-emerged as TJA a few months later.

In their glory days, the Kurdish women's movement reinvented politics and created new imaginaries of what gender-based equality and justice could look like. Now, during the darkest days in the history of the Kurdish women's movement in Turkey, among the militants a memory and sentiment lives on of 'we did it once, we can do it again'. This spirit of resistance proved its power yet again during the elections in June 2018, when despite huge political oppression, the HDP managed to surpass the 10 per cent parliament threshold. However, in August 2019, in another cycle of state repression, the Turkish interior ministry removed the Kurdish mayors in Mardin, Diyarbakir and Van, accusing them of terrorism and replacing them with government-appointed 'trustees'. In May 2020, eighteen members of TJA and the Rosa Women's Association were detained – among them Ayla Akat – and eight of them arrested thereafter.

Many women leave the civilian sphere, where the Kurdish population is under constant pressure, not only in Turkey but also in Iran, Syria and Iraq. Instead of political activism they choose the armed resistance, a life as a freedom fighter. Chapter 3 will discuss how militant femininities are learned and lived by the guerrillas in the mountains.

3   The Mountain Life: On Learning to Become Free

Introduction

'What makes a good woman fighter?' I asked Viyan, the commander of the military training camp of the Women's Defence Forces (HPJ, *Hêzên Parastina Jin*). 'Women of the PKK love to fight and they love to be good fighters,' she replied. 'The best fighters were Şehîd Zîlan and Şehîd Bêrîtan.' But, she emphasised, to become like them you have to understand the essence of Öcalan's teachings and you have to combine it with your practice, 'if you only have weapon skills and lack *îrade*, you will not be successful'. We were sitting under a tree, a few metres away from the training grounds in the boiling mid-day heat, when Viyan told me about the importance of both the mental and physical elements in the training the young women at the camp undergo. At this HPJ camp on the Iraqi-Iranian border, young women from all four parts of Kurdistan were training to become guerrillas, some of whom would later go and fight for the liberation of Kurds in Rojhelat or Iranian Kurdistan. I visited 'the mountains' after I had observed how the Kurdish Freedom Movement's liberation ideology was being put into practice in Diyarbakir, Rojava, Maxmûr, and to a lesser extent in the cities of Iraqi Kurdistan. The mountains are different though, I had been told on numerous occasions; 'mountain life is difficult but beautiful!' I had come here to gain a more nuanced understanding of how the women 'got there' and what enables them to stand these contested grounds so firmly. In order to do that, I spent two weeks in different guerrilla education camps, where apart from participant observation I conducted fifteen interviews with trainee guerrillas and their commanders, asking a simple set of questions about personal trajectories, everyday routines and visions of the future. While the journey of the women to the armed wing of the movement is crucial, this chapter shifts the focus onto the everyday and gendered process of living, learning and transforming within the movement, looking at the tools and mechanisms that enable them in the process of becoming a female freedom fighter. I was particularly interested in how meaning and longevity are given to the struggle and the continuum of violence and resistance the Kurdish Women's

Freedom Movement operates on across the region. Conceptually, this analysis moves away from the binary of victimisation (women as pawns in a masculine order) and emancipation (idealisation of Kurdish female fighters), and instead analyses on the one hand how the movement itself defines freedom, empowerment and the role of women within the larger quest of liberation. On the other hand, I examine how the female guerrillas translate 'liberation' for themselves in communal life, at work, and in the moments 'in-between'. As women join the 'mountain life', in order to become 'free', they first and foremost have to overcome the old ways of life, including individualism, and learn the new, a process that can be understood as 'the radical remaking of the decolonized personhood in dual acts of "unbecoming" and "becoming"' (Duzel 2018, 3). I argue that this process of 'overcoming' and subscribing to a particular form of institutionalised militant femininities constitutes a framework within which agency is to be located. Looking at militant femininities is a useful framework to understand the ideal, and the highly disciplined and often painful process individuals go through to become or live up to that ideal, as well as the inherent contradictions faced by members of this party on their path to liberation. After a conceptual discussion, this chapter is divided into three parts, which address the trajectories of female fighters, their education and their everyday lives in the mountains. The chapter also highlights some central conundrums that have puzzled me along the way: the discrepancy and disconnect between mountains and cities; the essentialist notion of the 'free woman'; the seemingly wide horizon of the fighters and commanders, mirrored with the advocacy for one 'truth'; and lastly the normalisation of violence and death, versus the quest for freedom and peace.

Becoming a Militant, in Theory

I locate the conceptual discussion that frames the ethnographic data of this chapter at the intersections of the themes that make up militant femininities: nationalism and feminism, militarism, subjectivation and agency, and the continuum of violence and resistance. Particularly important in this chapter is the process of subjectivation, of becoming a disciplined soldier and 'free woman' at the same time. Historically and cross-culturally revolutionary and post-colonial liberation movements have recruited women in large numbers, promising profound social transformation, including that of gender norms and relations (Alison 2003; Lanzona 2009; Moghadam 1994; Parashar 2014; Viterna 2013; Yuval-Davis 1997). Yet, as observed in many post-colonial settings, such as Eritrea (Bernal 2000; Hale 2001), Palestine (Hasso 2005), Sri Lanka (Alison 2003) and Algeria (Amrane-Mine & Abu-Haidar 1999; Salhi

2010), women who actively participated in armed liberation movements faced varying degrees of male backlash and were often pushed back into the domestic sphere 'post'-liberation (Al-Ali & Tas 2018, 2; White 2007). Cynthia Enloe considers violence in war and conflict as a continuation of masculine orders, despite women's participation and '[o]nce the war was over, women were demobilised as quickly as possible. Any Amazons were pushed back across the frontier of social imagination. The world was put right once more. War and peace were portrayed as distinct – war abnormal, peace normal. In 'normal' times women do not soldier' (Enloe 1988, 123). Enloe's quote sums up the master narrative about women and armed conflict: women engaged in paramilitary or guerrilla activity are still seen as exceptional and temporal, despite women having played key roles in national liberation wars (Gentry & Sjoberg 2015). The Kurdish women's movement argues to be different not only because it claims to institutionalise and safeguard gender-based equality and justice during and 'post'-war, but also because women do not fight in a men's war. Instead, they have created, under the leadership of a male ideologue, their own epistemology and autonomous ranks in the armed and political spheres, while building a new gender-equal system in those societies it seeks to revolutionise.

Existing literature on nationalism and feminism has shown that women often serve as markers of the (post-)colonial nation state, having been assigned clear roles and symbols to represent the 'modern' nation (Jayawardena 1986; Kandiyoti 1991; Yuval-Davis & Anthias 1989, 1997). However, nationalism as a project emerging from masculinist hope, memory or humiliation (Enloe 2014) and feminism are not mutually exclusive per se; instead, nationalist movements can simultaneously open spaces for women (Al-Ali & Pratt 2011) and women often use these spaces to change the movements from within (O'Keefe 2013). To understand the potential of these spaces it is crucial to ask what kind of feminism and what kind of nationalism are being practised, to examine at what point nationalist or liberation struggles open spaces for women and for which women, how those spaces are used, and how claims of gender-based equality and justice are articulated.

When women and men enter this grand complex that is the Kurdish Freedom Movement, they give their life to the struggle. This life-long commitment is a central part of the subject formation. The process of becoming 'PKK'cised' is obtained through the studying of Öcalan's teachings (Çözümlemeler, analysis) and his prison defence writings (savunma, defence), the striving towards perfection and personal responsibility, as well as the spirit of self-sacrifice. 'Personal responsibility itself was not understood in a positive, self-improving manner but required that one accept the complete destruction of his or her personality in order to fuse with the abstract collective personality of the PKK' (Bozarslan 2004, 54). The party can be seen as a matrix of domination (Collins 2000), within which the concepts of freedom, truth and militancy operate, and the desired femininities and masculinities are fashioned within a new set of gender norms and relations. This act of becoming is linked to a specific performance, 'an identity tenuously constituted in time – an identity instituted through as stylized repletion of acts' (Butler 1988, 519). It is in education where the young recruits learn to perform a new femininity, and, while hinged on practice and repetition they are told that there is an ideal type of woman, a female essence that has been buried under millennia of patriarchal rule and that needs to be reclaimed. This happens through the adherence to the 'goddess image' (*Îştar*), which gives meaning to a life of struggle and timely deaths (Duzel 2018).

In this process of finding their place in this new matrix of domination, how are revolutionary subjects formed, other than through the repetition of certain revolutionary performances? And how does one become a revolutionary who then goes off to commit spectacular acts of resistance and self-defence at the many front lines of the four parts of Kurdistan? I argue that this particular women's movement demands us to steer away from the binary of structure and agency and develop a more geographically, temporally and bodily grounded framework of analysis that takes into consideration the militarised spaces these women operate in, the emancipatory power the party holds, and the moments 'in-between' war, training and education, in which communal life creates meaning for the individual sacrifice. Creating what Foucault calls 'docile bodies', formed by specific modes of discipline, is certainly one of the principles of mountain life, as the Kurdish Freedom Movement, among other things, needs subjected and practised bodies it can mobilise and deploy (Foucault 1991, 138).

In party education, recruits learn to obtain what is called *îrade*, the will to resist, part of which is learning the art of self-control (*oto-kontrol*). In her analysis of piety and ethical self-making, the late Saba Mahmood calls this *habitus*: 'the conscious effort at reorienting desires, brought about by the concordance of inward motives, outward actions, inclinations, and emotional states through the repeated practice of virtuous deeds' (Mahmood 2001, 215). This process of disciplining the mind and the body through education leads to the subject formation and subordination to the leadership and party hierarchy. Yet rather than thinking of the women in the movement as only acted upon, it is exactly this subordination that Mahmood, building on Judith Butler's notion of *subjectivation* (Butler 1997), calls agency – the process in which a subject becomes self-conscious agent by subordinating herself. 'Such a conceptualization of power and subject formation also encourages us to understand agency not simply as a synonym for resistance to relations of domination, but as a capacity for action that specific relations of subordination create and enable' (ibid., 210). However, Lois McNay argues that the theory of subjectivity fails to recognise generative human agency because, from its perspective, 'the process of subjectification is understood as a dialectic of freedom and constraint' (McNay 2000, 2). Thus, the making of selfhood remains negative, passive, linked to discursive practices and agency, and is seen as limited. 'The idea that the individual emerges from constraint does not offer a broad enough understanding of the dynamics of subjectification and, as a consequence, offers an etiolated understanding of agency' (ibid., 3). Building on McNay, among others, Sertaç Sehlikoglu urges feminist ethnographers not to limit their quest to locating agency to visible forms of 'ethical self-making' within clearly defined power structures, but instead shift the scholarly gaze to unpack moments of pleasure, desire, joy and ordinary daily life (Sehlikoglu 2018; Joseph 2005). Given that the Kurdish women's movement needs to operate in war and conflict and its armed wing is embedded in a hierarchical military structure, this chapter discusses how the disciplined process of 'subjectivation' unfolds in education and how that process is filled with moments of compassion, silliness and joy, but also with loss, pain and hardship.

Learning to Be Free, in Practice

Getting invited to spend time in the mountainous training camps took time and patience. After leaving Turkey in early April 2016, I initially resettled in Erbil. From there I went on a first trip to Sulaymaniyah, where I met the female party cadre responsible for the area. She urged me to spend time in Maxmûr and Sulaymaniyah and improve my Kurmancî, before they would take me to the mountains. I did, and eventually the female cadre of KJAR working in Sulaymaniyah told me they wanted me to visit their camps and spend some time in education.[1] After a few more weeks' delay on their side, and gentle reminders from my side, on a hot August morning it was finally time to go.

   After a few hours of climbing the dusty hills in one of the party's big white Toyotas, we reached the KJAR camp, where the end of one road marked the

---

[1] Education (*perwerde*) refers to the ideological, political and military training courses that each party member undertakes and often goes back to after a few years in 'practice'.

beginning of party territory. The parties working in Rojhelat are organised under the Eastern Kurdistan Free and Democratic Society (KODAR, *Komalgeya Demokratîk û Azad a Rojhilatê Kurdistanê*), which has a parallel women's structure called KJAR. The Kurdistan Free Life Party (PJAK, *Partiya Jiyana Azad a Kurdistanê*) is the ideological party, and there are two armed wings: HPJ, and the Eastern Kurdistan Defence Units (YRK, *Yekîneyên Parastina Rojhilatê Kurdistanê*), the mixed forces. All parties are working towards implementing Democratic Confederalism in Rojhelat and are under the direct control of the KCK/KJK.

Upon arrival, we were greeted warmly and instantly ushered through welcome shade into a circle of plastic chairs where we met the commanders of the camp: Leyla Agirî, Zîlan Vejîn, Newroz Cizre and Nurhak. We introduced ourselves and had a simple lunch of bread, eggs and cheese. Sometime between that and tea, it was decided that I would go to a guerrilla training camp first and do a week of ideological training later. Immediately a note was written to inform the commander in the next camp about this plan. Shortly after, I was told to grab my bags and turn off my phone before another car signalled our departure.

The four-hour drive from one camp to the other was an eventful one. In order to avoid the Iraqi Kurdish checkpoints (*Asayîş*), we only took bumpy and dusty back roads. Two male guerrillas sat in the front, Bêrîtan, the companion entrusted with my safe delivery and I sat in the back. It was all blaring revolution music, laughter and ice cream on the way: they showed us where they almost drove off a cliff the last time they came this way, and we stopped at numerous small shops to buy water for the camps and a lot of ice cream, crisps and soda for the group in the car. It seemed that the worldly pleasures party members miss most about 'system life' are ice cream and sweet drinks. We munched and jolted on.

We arrived at the camp at around 11 p.m., honked once into the dark, and Tekoşin, who was on night-guard duty, stepped out of the dark and quickly took us up a narrow path. In the dark she led us to the commander tent (*manga*). Commander Eyrehan did not know I was coming, as this camp is only reachable by radio during certain hours each day. They communicate with each other through personal meetings or handwritten notes that get passed on. Bêrîtan handed the commander the note dictated by Leyla Agirî earlier. It presumably said: 'This is Isabel, she is doing research for her doctoral thesis, take care of her for a few days, send her to a training camp and then send her back.' Eyrehan greeted us but said that she was busy and that we would speak tomorrow, telling Tekoşin to give us food and show us where we could sleep. We were led to another *manga* and given a plate of *dolma* (stuffed vine leaves), which we ate in the light of a small electric lamp. Shortly afterwards a few blankets were rolled out and I, for the last time, went through the civilian notion of changing into some form of pyjama, highly impractical in the dark, not to mention removing my contact lenses. The next day I would be given a guerrilla uniform, which I would not take off for a week.

I barely slept, as my flimsy T-shirt did not protect me from the mosquitos in full attack mode. In the night, I heard the change of guards and at 4.30 a.m. and the morning ritual 'Rojbaş Gerîla!' (good morning guerrilla!), before everyone gets up for breakfast at 6.00 a.m. I stumbled out, disoriented from a lack of sleep, but was with five new friends, who all welcomed me warmly and quizzed me about who I am and what I am doing here. Some of the women were used to foreign visitors since the PKK frequently opens its doors to sympathisers, journalists and academics, particularly during more peaceful periods. The women who had previously fought in Rojava were particularly aware of how glorified they are in Western eyes. Other younger recruits from more rural areas found it very exciting that I was writing about their struggle. At the end of the week, when we promised not to forget each other, Zemyan, my companion for the week said, 'How nice to think that someone in Europe will notice when I become şehîd (martyr).'

After breakfast, I met Eyrehan to properly introduce myself and tell her why I was here. She planned to send me to *Akademiya Şehîd Şirîn Elemholî*, a combat training camp for women, located another few kilometres up the mountain. At first glance, Eyrehan was kind but reserved and strict about time; after I finished my tea, I was asked to leave again and join the others in the communal tent. Before lunch two guerrillas asked me for some civilian clothes, as they had to go back to the KJAR camp in a shared taxi instead of a party car. They could keep on their uniform trousers because no one would see anything but their upper body. When they put on my loosely fitting T-shirts and blouses, wearing civilian clothes for the first time in a few years, they were all giggling in embarrassment about the way it showed their curves and arms, 'Şerm e!' (shameful!) they laughed. In a similar way, I went through my own transformation; civilian clothes off, uniform on; it was heavy and hot, and the belt (*şûtik*) alone felt like it added another five degrees at least. The uniform plays a key role in every fighter's process of becoming a militant, as a visible signifier of having shed 'system life' clothes and putting on the desexualised guerrilla uniform. This uniform is inspired by traditional Kurdish male clothing: wide trousers (*şalwar*), a uniform jacket and vest, completed with a colourful belt, and worn by women and men alike. Shortly after I was dressed, I was told to grab my bags, as my car would arrive soon. I would learn a few days later that 'soon' means nothing and everything here; it could be in the next hour as it did on that day, or it could mean four days later (as it did later that week); patience is key in a guerrilla's life. I climbed a steep slope to the dust path, where my jeep was waiting. Then Zemyan, my companion for the next three days, climbed in. She was sincere and alert and we took to each other instantly.

The Academy

We arrived at the *Akademiya Şehîd Şirîn Elemholî* mid-afternoon. It was located on a mountain slope; the *mangas* were well camouflaged with branches or hidden under trees. Around twenty young trainees were undergoing the four-month training at the academy. A guerrilla's day starts early and ends when the light goes down. At 5.30 p.m. their training finishes; at 6 p.m. dinner is served – a combination of potatoes, rice and bread and a few grilled onions for vitamins (Figure 3.1). I ate in the commander's 'hut', where we discussed their and my work, politics and the destruction of cities in Bakur. Interestingly, commander Sewa, one of the commanders, thought that the urban war tactics in Bakur were correct. 'Yes, now people are angry because they lost everything but our comrades

Figure 3.1 The commanders during dinner

are in these destroyed places, organising, giving education. With enough education people will come to see and understand why this was necessary,' she argued. I disagreed.

We went to sleep around 9 p.m.; a few blankets were rolled out on the floor as mattresses and pillows, and we only took off our shoes and our belts. My belt (made out of a long piece of fabric) became a net, wrapped around my face, to protect me from the merciless mosquitos. To no avail, I woke up at 4.30 a.m. with a swollen face. On with the shoes and up the hill for the morning ritual and morning sport, which was an amazingly romantic scene that would make any revolutionary heart beat faster; all the fighters lined up in the half light, pledging allegiance to the struggle and the leadership. I had agreed to participate in the day's training, so I ran, jumped, stretched and bent for an hour. Some of the recruits were young girls with barely any body awareness at all; they still had to be trained to walk, talk, sit and fight like party militants. Others had already gained first battle experiences in Rojava and were physically strong and disciplined. However, this education unit was not only about obtaining a soldier's body, as commander Eyrehan explained to me later: 'A part of what we are trying to teach them here is to get to know and like their bodies. Many of them have never done sports in their life and see their bodies as shameful.' Here, among other things, Eyrehan speaks to the difficulty of women to take ownership over their bodies by exercising in public in Islamicated contexts, which set clear boundaries around women's public and private sexualities (Sehlikoglu 2016). And so, during this particular morning sport unit, it was mainly awkward teenage girls feeling insecure, giggling when someone did the exercises wrong. We ate breakfast at 6.00 a.m.: bread, cream cheese mixed with oil and dried herbs, and natural chewing gum they had cooked the night before, which apparently helps the digestive system. I learned that most long-term guerrillas have stomach problems, having to eat whatever is available for many years (which is often very little) or just carbohydrates such as potatoes, lentils, rice and pasta. Depending where they are based they may also have chronic iron and vitamin deficiencies.

Shortly after breakfast (eating is a quick affair here, 'we are soldiers' after all), they packed their weapons and the teapot, and off we hiked to the training ground. Here they put down their ammunition and stood in line for their exercises, set up the radio station to communicate (in code) and listened in on inter-party radio, and prepared the sniper training spot. For the next three hours the guerrillas repeated different positions with their Kalashnikovs, including pulling the trigger, over and over again. The more experienced ones who were training on the big weapons to become snipers or rocket launchers were called one by one to practise on the other side of the slope.

Figure 3.2 Two trainee guerrillas at Akademiya Şehîd Şirîn Elemholî

I sat on a stone, observing the training, and after a while I started my interviews a few metres away. These are perhaps my favourite interviews because of the content but also the setting: high up on the mountain, the background noises (sniper shots), and the simple absurdity of the situation – me sitting there with my swollen face and my uniform in at least 45 degrees heat. The commanders left it to the trainees themselves as to whether they wanted to talk to me; those who did came over and sat with me one after the other. They told me their age, where they came from, what brought them there, how they saw their roles as revolutionaries, and what they wanted to do for Rojhelat – both heartbreakingly sad and hopeful stories, all transnational and ideological in their nature. I kept most of these interviews short, as they had training to do (Figure 3.2).

Women's Trajectories: From 'System Life' to 'Mountain Life'

Most fighters I spoke to were in their late teens and came from a strictly patriarchal family or violent political context. Many of those coming from

Rojhelat had been married off to an older man at a young age, one bearing scars of self-immolation all over her body. More than one had left her child with her family to join the struggle. One fighter had been a university student in Iran and worked as a chemist before she realised that 'system life' was not for her. Two others stated that they were poor villagers before but having seen how Iranian soldiers treated the bodies of HPJ martyrs (they brought a mutilated corpse to the village), they learned about the work of the party and joined. Two came from Rojava and had previously fought in the ranks of the YPJ, two others hailed from Bakur, one from Maxmûr, and one from Erbil. Instead of a common pattern as to why women joined the party, I recorded as many different traumatic and violent stories of state and family oppression as women I talked to. People of Kurdistan (and others in the region) are embedded in a continuum of violence that fluctuates in scale and location depending on time and space – from massacres to domestic violence, and political repression to genocide. I found that it was rather the rupture points in this continuum, such as heightened (state) violence against the Kurds, and the accumulation of these rupture points that eventually led my informants to join the party. The rupture points differ from generation to generation. Witnessing the attack of the Islamic State on Şengal and Kobanî in 2014, and female fighters resisting and fighting back *deash* in both those places were important rupture points for the younger fighters. For the older generation it was the uprisings in the early 1990s (*Serhildan*) and the resistance of Bêrîtan and Zîlan that woke them up to the struggle. Across the decades it was the accumulation of witnessing state brutality, losing loved ones in the war, the treatment of martyrs, or personal experiences of police brutality and racism against Kurds that motivated them to join. There are also many different stories of how the young recruits heard and learned about the PKK. Some grew up in a sympathiser family; some got hold of one of Öcalan's books; others heard about the struggle from guerrillas who were recruiting in the villages; others again watched Öcalan's arrest (1999), the Kobanî resistance (2014–2015) or the defence of Şengal (2014) on television. For many, joining the party was an option at the back of their mind for a while before they actually did. I have found that deciding to join this armed struggle, leaving your life behind and living the harsh life of a guerrilla in the mountains can be a snap decision, a gradual process, or what feels to some women as the most natural trajectory.

What became obvious to me is that the PKK, or in this instance KJAR and its armed wing HPJ, offers an alternative for women. Many join out of necessity and desperation, seeking a physical or geographical escape, but also an ideological, political and intellectual alternative to narratives, realities and systems lived in all parts of Kurdistan. This alternative and its appeal cut across gender, class, religion, rural/urban and other power structures. Rather than trying to determine exact patterns of mobilisation (Tank 2017), I will discuss and unpack this alternative. While stories of life before the party and journeys to the mountains are rich and telling about the respective context, it is more revealing to ask what women find in Abdullah Öcalan's liberation ideology that keeps them there and gives them will and strength to resist. It is important to note that even though everyone has to learn and internalise this liberation ideology, not all fighters are equality militant, nor do they all become the 'same'. It is rather the ideology, and the hierarchical military structures it is inter-twined with, that offers a blueprint for the militant femininities[2] and how one can live up to that personality. Upon joining the PKK, the party members leave behind their old societal ties and at least for a few years cut all contact with their family.[3] Instead, all mothers of Kurdistan are their mothers, and they gain thousands of new brothers and sisters in the other guerrillas (interview with Bêrîtan Rojhelat and Zemyan, 1 August 2016). From now on, they are subjects of the party, which decides who trains and works where and for how long, who is sent to war and who works behind the front lines. Most of the cadres I spoke to did not know for how much longer they would be working in their current position, 'The party knows,' they simply said.[4]

Curriculum of Liberation

The PKK sees itself as an educational party, which transforms each member into a militant who then has the capacity to fight for revolution-ary change (Westrheim 2010). Kariane Westrheim quotes a cadre who described the process as follows:

The life of a guerrilla is like a re-birth. You have to give up everything for the love of the struggle. Attending [PKK] means forgetting the past, struggle means struggling with yourself. You have to change your personality totally. It is impossible to describe this process when you don't live there, when you are not a part of it. The guerrillas

---

[2] The party has a gender-neutral concept for militant femininities, which is the 'militant personality' (*militan kişilik*). Öcalan has written at length about how the militant personal-ity should be developed (e.g. Apcu Militan Kişilik Cilt II; Flach 2007, 86).

[3] For the first few years, most recruits are not allowed to have contact with their families. After that, families are sometimes allowed to visit their children in the mountains or in Maxmûr Camp. The frequency of these visits depends on the power and influence of their family or the rank of their child or relative within the party.

[4] Guerrillas could ask to be moved elsewhere via written requests or refuse to be sent to a certain place (e.g. Europe, which is unpopular for those who want to be involved in a more direct struggle), but the party always has the last word.

have a different life than others and it affects you deeply. All these difficulties change your life and you become a new person. (A. quoted in Westrheim 2010, 115)

This process of being reborn, of obtaining a militant personality, is a long process that starts off with an initial three-month 'new fighter' (*şervanê nû*) training, where they cover basic weapons and physical training, receive the first ideological lessons, and learn about the importance of friendship (*hevalti*) and the communal life. Most young women came to *Akademiya Şehîd Şirîn Elemholî* after having finished that first training. Others came from Rojava where they only had one-month training before being sent to the front line. Here they were training to become PKK cadres that could then be deployed anywhere in the region. Apart from being physically disciplined during this first education period, the recruits learn about Öcalan's concept of freedom and how struggling for that makes you free. But in order to fight, female recruits first have to learn to believe in themselves, in their strength as women, and in a better world, according to Apoism, the party's cosmology of liberation. There is a clearly laid-out curriculum for the four months at the academy, which structures education as follows:

Ideological Lessons[5]

1. Importance and meaning of education
2. History of society
3. Concept and conceptualising
4. History of Kurdistan
5. Reality of leadership: the history of PKK, joining the PKK
6. History of women and Jineolojî
7. Building a democratic nation; the system of KCK-KJK
8. Special war
9. Culture, life and morality of the party
10. Building the army and the party, system of organising

Theoretical Lessons for Soldiers

1. Art of war
2. The experience of war in Kurdistan, the history of PKK's war, and in the PKK the experience of war of revolutionary people
3. To reinvent yourself in the YRK-HPJ
4. The current situation of female commanders and guerrillas; is there an absence or shortcoming in this regard?

[5] Prior to these lessons, Öcalan's books (*Savunmalar*, defence writings) are read for a week or ten days.

Practical Lessons for Soldiers

1. Methods, tactics and the techniques of the enemy
2. Our technical instruments and methods of using those (weapons)
3. Basic principles of guerrillas and their methods[6]

Women's roles and positions are part of every lesson, but this education does not go into intellectual depth. However, the key aspects of the party's self-understanding as a women's liberation movement are covered. Analysing this curriculum, the building blocks of a guerrilla's identity become apparent: knowing one's history of oppression but also the tools of resistance, gaining a voice to talk about this oppression, a belief in yourself, and self-confidence in your practice through education. Another aspect of this identity construct was added in my interview with Eyrehan: 'We are people first and foremost. To build a new society we have to strengthen each person's good side and weaken their bad side, one person is never just one or the other.' This strengthening and weakening is achieved through adhering to strict rules of communal living, close observation of each other, and the regular criticism and self-criticism sessions (Duzel 2018; Flach 2007; Grojean 2014). All these methods are tools to create the desired subjects who adhere to the specific ideal of the militant personality. However, I concur with Westrheim who observed that the party encourages a respectful and kind behaviour and personality that can inspire social change and potentially encourage others to join (Westrheim 2010, 118).

This ideology is memorable, coherent and often repeated. To the extent that every guerrilla can recite the oppression of Kurdish women, and how Öcalan's paradigm and the party offer an alternative, and how this fight is important, potentially for the whole world, because in the West also women are not free. The fluency of this recitation depends on personal background and the length of membership. For example, Berwar Şiyar, a trainee at the camp and the daughter of a political family in Maxmûr, talked for seventeen minutes without interruption, after I posed the first question to her. Other interviews with shyer and less-experienced recruits only lasted six minutes. I found that the repetition and ability to recite the ideology have a strong performative aspect (Butler 1988), something that the younger, less-experienced recruits were yet to learn.

---

[6] This handwritten plan ends with the following general 'Internal Rules for the Academy': watch recordings of the Leadership (Öcalan or Apo) twice a week in the evening; study Kurdish twice a week in the evening; go on a night march twice a week; one day theoretical education, the other day practical education; ideological education 7.00–12.00; break 12.00–14.00, practise 14.00–17.30; one day commando training, one day karate training; home/evening work 19.00–21.00; break once every fifteen days.

At noon, the weapons training finished, we all lined up and walked down the hill, the recruits singing party songs in admiration of the leader Öcalan, until the commander told them to be quiet. Lunch was eaten at 12.00 p.m., food being a quick but lovingly prepared affair that breaks up the day in its blocks. In this high altitude nothing grew so everything was delivered from the base camp. Each day a different group is responsible for cooking and getting water; every ten days or so they make fresh bread, which is a whole day's work. The food is simple: fried potatoes, rice, bread, some olives, always onions. The commanders taught me how to get the right vitamins and that garlic makes you drowsy because in high quantity it has the same effect as antibiotics. One day Sewa prepared '*xwarina şoreşê*', the 'revolution food' for me: flour, oil and some onion stirred into a mush and quickly fried. She explained: 'Our friends learned this in the early years of the struggle from the poor villagers who gave them shelter sometimes. These women would have nothing else to feed their children, so our friends started making it in the mountains when food was sparse.'

Talking about the difficulty of finding food and the harshness or beauty of their surroundings is an integral part of everyday conversation – how stunning the nature was; how fresh and plentiful the water was where they were previously stationed; how they fish (throwing a hand grenade into the water), hunt (if there is time and animals); all the things they would eat when on a long and difficult operation (everything); how long they could not shower (months); how many kilos they carry (20–50), always emphasising how mountain life is difficult but beautiful. Because once you know what you are fighting for, you learn how to handle the hard parts. The latter resonated in another discussion I had about the hardship of the mountain life. I asked about the winters, about being snowed in, spending three to four months in a cave or an underground construction. A male commander told me:

We woke up early and ate breakfast, usually I spent my time reading until I cooked lunch for my group. I liked cooking then, we had all our supplies neatly prepared. Sometimes in the afternoon we would have electricity so we could watch TV. The rest of the day would be spent studying or watching movies. Sometimes we would open the door a little bit, for fresh air. It is all about education. Once you know what you are doing this for you can do anything. But you can't do it without education, because the mountains can make you free, but they can also make you wild. (Interview with Sipan, 15 August 2016)

Having strong *îrade*, the will to live and die for the struggle, is a big part of each fighter's identity. *Îrade* is also tied to the land – a love for nature, the mountains, the water and their beauty. Romantic love is for civilians; in the mountains, you officially only love your comrades as friends, Kurdistan, its people, the struggle, and most importantly, the martyrs and Apo. The following anecdote, recounted to me by Sipan who had spent three years working in Rojava as a high-ranking YPG commander, aims to illustrate what *îrade* means in the day-to-day work of a revolutionary.

One day me and two other YPG commanders were called to a meeting in Aleppo with the Free Syrian Army, *daesh* and other opposition groups. The second highest *daesh* commander was also there. We had just captured a few tanks from the Syrian regime and the *daesh* commander wanted our tanks. We were all in a room together when he told us that if we don't hand over the tanks, they will kill us. I took out my hand grenade, pulled out the pin and said, 'If we don't leave here alive, we all go to paradise together!' They got scared and told us we misunderstood. I put the pin back in and we left.

IK: You would have killed yourself and your friends in that moment?
Of course! In that moment you don't think, you just do it. And it would have been a successful operation with thirty of them dead, and only three of us martyred. I used that hand grenade trick a lot when I was travelling around Syria, going through checkpoints. It always worked! *[laughs]* (Ibid.)

This sort of recklessness and dedication was something the young recruits of the camp were yet to learn. It comes with years of battle experience, having lost countless comrades in the war, and being truly indifferent to your own death, because it would be for a bigger worthwhile cause.

At the camp, every day after lunch there was an educational activity, in the library-classroom tent. The first day commander Sewa read out a KJAR statement, an eight-page-long summary about a meeting held recently, assessing the current local, regional and international situation, positioning the work of the party within that, and condemning Apo's solitary confinement. As I had observed many times before, women's demands and women's work are always tied to the request of freedom for Abdullah Öcalan. Accordingly, the title of that particular document was '[i]n line with the free women's resistance we are leading a radical fight, to realise a meeting with our leader Apo in freedom'.[7] During another afternoon session, Zemyan translated three letters from Turkish into Kurdish, written by new martyrs, who had sacrificed themselves in the fight against the Turkish state a few weeks earlier, as part of the PKK's intensified struggle against the Turkish army after the attempted coup on 15 July 2016. Those who plan and carry out these attacks and know that they are very likely going to die write down their life story, motivations, convictions and hopes for the future before they undertake the operation. These statements are then distributed among the camps and serve as an

[7] In Kurdish: *Di xeta berwedana jina azad de em tekoşînê radîkal bikin, bi Rêber Apo re hevdîtina azad bikin rastî* (KJAR Leadership Council, 2 June 2016).

ideological and educational tool to talk through shared notions of commitment and determination. Everything starts and ends with '*Bijî Serok Apo!*', long live leader Apo!

During both afternoon sessions, the trainee guerrillas were sitting in the boiling mid-day heat, listening to what felt like hours of lectures. The party always claims that their education does not follow the frontal structure and learning is a dynamic affair between teacher and students or commander and guerrillas. This might be true in the sense that students are asked to give their opinion and take over an activity, especially during morning sports or weapons training; the commander would ask a trainee to stand at the front and shout the commands. However, the classroom procedures are an organised and hierarchal affair; this is a military setting after all. When the commander, as teacher, enters the tent, all students spring up and stand at attention. There is a certain sequence of slogans they shout before and after studying; '*xebat xweş!*' (good work!) is one of them. Those who want to say something stand up before speaking and they only speak if spoken to.

During this particular afternoon session, we were all suffering from the heat. I tried to learn from their discipline and not pant too much or look too weak. I sat there and observed: how the trainees completely seemed switched off but pretended to listen; how they struggled with the heat too (*ez mirim* – I am dying, one muttered); and how they were doodling in their notebooks during these extended lessons. A former commander later assured me: 'Many are sleeping or thinking about something else. You drift off, maybe you have a crush on someone, so you think about him, your hopes and dreams. Because you can't stand hearing the same thing every day!' (former commander 3, 11 May 2018). However, as soon as the lesson was over, they were back to their ritualised standing at attention and shouting the slogans. I was struck by how they switched between normal bored teenagers and always at the ready soldiers. At one point I crossed my legs and was instantly scolded by a young guerrilla: 'We guerrillas, we never sit like that,' she hissed, reminding me of my duties, even as a participant observer.

Getting to Work

Once the new guerrillas have that will to resist (*îrade*), officially they can do anything: control their body (*oto-kontrol*); go on dangerous operations; kill the enemy; and endure pain, loss, physical strain, and the cold harsh winters or the excruciatingly hot summers. I say 'officially' because unofficially of course the reality is different, and the fighters suffer greatly from losing their friends, witnessing violence, or leaving behind their families and children. Many young recruits miss their mothers, cannot sleep, have bad dreams or show sudden outbursts of emotions. One of the trainees at the camp developed a stutter after her brother was martyred. Shedding 'system life' and becoming a subject of the party is a liberating experience for some and a painful one for others, who struggle to live up to the expectations of women as goddess image (Çağlayan 2012; Duzel 2018). I found that many party members try to deal with the violence and contradictions of becoming a revolutionary quietly, in order to be part of this greater whole, and have the means to resist, even if they do not agree with or obey every rule set by the party.[8]

Upon completing training and obtaining these physical, mental and social skills (after six to twelve months of education),[9] the guerrillas are either sent to one of the many front lines in Kurdistan, or in the case of Rojhelat, some of them go back to society and organise their fellow citizens. Organising is key, since you can only be free together. The party has cadres in certain cities and villages in Rojhelat, who under great danger go to people's houses and hold education courses, for women, men, adolescents and children. Education is gendered in the sense that they try to organise women in particular but not exclusively. Refusing to work with 'classical feminist' organisational tools as they call it, meaning only focusing on women, everyone is addressed. Meetings are held for everyone but always with a 'women's perspective'. This means making people aware that women are those most oppressed by the state and patriarchy as a whole, but also the bearers of the old knowledge and culture, the backbone of society. Freeing them means freeing everyone (interview with Eyrehan, 2 August 2016). The goal is to mobilise as many people to join the party as possible, to go for education in the mountains and then return again to organise. Not everyone working for the party does so as a guerrilla in uniform – just as many people are needed in the civilian sphere to build the political base. So that when the political opportunity arises, the party would have a social base to activate. KODAR, the umbrella organisation for all political and armed branches working in Rojhelat currently, wants to find a diplomatic solution for the problems in Iran and is not interested in

---

[8] This room for manoeuvre is only partly visible to the outside observer, as demonstrating militancy to a European academic is part of their labour. Only in personal encounters outside of the set framework of an interview did I meet cadres who managed to bend the rules slightly, however, usually under the watchful eyes of their comrades.

[9] The amount of education each person undergoes varies from case to case. The basic training lasts three months, followed by another four to six months of consolidation training. Many people join before the age of eighteen. The party officially educates and trains them until they reach legal age, when they can be sent to the frontline. Every few years the cadre are called back to do more education, to deepen and refresh the ideological knowledge.

a fully fledged confrontation with the Iranian regime. If attacked in this process, or to take revenge for previously fallen guerrillas, the YRK and HPJ fighters will engage in 'legitimate self-defence' as the movement calls it. There are reoccurring clashes between them and the Iranian regime, and many guerrillas fall, but at this stage a mutually agreed ceasefire is still in place. Due to security concerns I did not do research in Rojhelat itself. So this chapter does not speak to the extent to which people in Rojhelat are organised and mobilised along party lines. The protests that took place across Iran in December 2017 and January 2018, however, suggest that the time for activating that base has not yet come. Despite repeated calls for a widespread uprising, protests in Rojhelat remained small (ANF 2018a, 2018b). During the renewed wave of protests during the summer of 2018, KODAR tried to position itself as the only opposition force with the necessary military power and a feasible plan to stabilise and democratise Iran. In a declaration published in August 2018, they proposed Democratic Confederalism as a viable alternative for all of Iran, stressing the important role of women in the democratisation process (ANF 2018c, 2018d).

The party withholds exact numbers of how many recruits join the movement each month. 'It all depends how well the cadres do their work, sometimes one, sometimes fifty,' I was told. The goal is to create an educated base, that agrees with the party's ideology, which could carry the party's aspirations, in case a political opportunity arises, similarly to what happened in Rojava in 2012, when Assad's troops retreated and the PYD was able to take control. For almost ten years, the PYD had been following a similar strategy there: go to the grassroots, educate people about Öcalan's liberation ideology, visiting martyr families, and thus maintaining and expanding the party's base.[10] A cadre who had previously worked in Rojava and was now coordinating YRK work in Rojhelat told me about the difference between what they did in Rojava and what they are planning to do in Rojhelat:

Rojava is different from Rojhelat. Rojava is simple, but Rojhelat is not simple. For example, in Rojava there is only Kurmancî, in Rojhelat you can see Kurmancî, Sorani, Haurami, Kelhor, Lor. And for religion you can see Sunni, Alawi, Yarsan, Kalkan, al-Haq, everything. So it's not simple. And it means that there are a lot of different mentalities. Not just in terms of ideology, but everything, for life. Maybe in Rojava people also had different ideologies. But their mentality was similar. And the Syrian system is not like the Iranian system. Iran has a long history of the state. Arabs don't have that. (Interview with Sipan, 5 September 2016)

---

[10] Abdullah Öcalan lived in Syria for twenty years from 1979 to 1999. Many Kurds from Rojava joined the party during that time and returned to help with the revolution post-2012 (Flach et al. 2016, 105ff).

So Rojhelat is different, but the party's ideology remains the same and so does the party's strategy to mobilise and educate people. Convinced that the women's liberation ideology can also work for women in Rojhelat, Leyla Agirî, the commander of KJAR, the women's umbrella uniting the political and armed branches of Rojhelat, told me:

> For me it doesn't matter where I work. Today I am working on Rojhelat, tomorrow Başûr, the day after tomorrow Rojava, and after Bakur, it is unclear. What is important for me is that wherever we are we can develop women's work, we can advance our revolutionary work. I have been in the organisation for twenty-four years and women's work is my first priority. (Interview with Leyla Agirî, 25 August 2015)

When asked about the specifics of the Rojhelat context, compared to other Kurdish regions, the women I interviewed emphasised its rich and long-standing culture, but also the acute pressure to assimilate to the dominant Persian culture. Kurds in Rojhelat have a certain degree of cultural rights; for example the Kurdish languages are not forbidden (Yildiz 2007). However, I was told that Rojhelat is kept impoverished and drugs to the area flow freely in order to diminish people's aspirations to organise and demand rights of self-determination. The state targets women especially, including Persian women, being worried about their potential to challenge the Islamic Republic. In return, the regime is especially wary of the movement's ability to give women and therefore wider society hope, when it is trying to create a sense of hopelessness in Rojhelat. Each party member I spoke to about why they are fighting for Rojhelat also emphasised the disproportionally high numbers in child marriages and self-immolation. Commander Viyan stressed that Öcalan's ideology is applicable to all four parts of Kurdistan, but that Rojhelati women are especially oppressed due to the nature of the Islamic Republic, putting great pressure on both women and Kurds. 'They have this ideology that women cannot do anything, that they should just stay in the house. We teach them about their history and their power' (interview with Viyan, 1 August 2016).

Life and Death, or How Death Constitutes Life

Life in the camps was hard work and tough training but also a lot of laughter and genuine fun. The fine line between life and death, however, between sadness and laughter, destruction and beauty became apparent in many encounters, stories or activities. One day during a tea break under a tree, Zemyan was invited to share the story of her first operation in Rojhelat with the young trainees. As she was telling it like an adventure story, we were hanging on her every word, laughing as she insulted the Iranian soldiers for their cowardliness. Suddenly though, as she started talking about her friends dying (four of them went, two survived) and her getting lost for many days, she started crying, jumped to her feet and disappeared for a few minutes to regain her composure. Another recruit ran to console her, and when they came back after a while she finished her story. This episode demonstrates two things: first, the heroic packaging of a guerrilla life also includes many layers of suffering and hardship. And second, emotions and controlling or re-directing them are very much part of a young fighter's education. Losing your friends never gets easier, older commanders told me, but you learn to deal with it.

One afternoon, the recruits trained with balloons as targets. Dozens of colourful balloons were inflated and hung in the trees (Figure 3.3). This brought much joy and laughter to the training, especially when later on the balloons were arranged as a *parcours*: they had to shoot from afar, then run and roll to the next target, shoot sitting down, crawl onwards, and shoot the last one standing up. The group cheered every time someone hit

Figure 3.3 Balloon backdrop

Figure 3.4 'Long live the leader!', they shouted as they set his name on fire

a target and ran on. The rest of the group sat under a tree, playing with the remaining balloons, or writing Apo's name with gunpowder and lighting it on fire (Figure 3.4).

At the end of the day, the tally of who hit how many targets was read out, and the daily feedback session (*tekmîl*) was held. Since it was my last day, the group held a *moral*, an hour of singing and dancing. As the sun went down behind the mountains, they sang their sad songs of far away and brave friends, of loved ones who will never return. At the end, they danced battle dances, of horses and eagles, with music blasting from a small portable radio. Before Zemyan and I left, I was encouraged to give my criticism (*rexne*), while they were all lined up in front of me. I did not feel like criticising anyone; instead I praised and thanked them. I suspected that this moral session was performed especially because of my presence, but nevertheless is an integral and regular part of communal life. It is intended to lift people's spirits and is an aspect of the everyday performance of resistance for a people whose cultural expressions, such as language, music and poetry, have been severely oppressed for almost a hundred years (Zeydanlıoğlu 2012).

As Zemyan and I hiked back to the base camp in the dark, we talked about her history and her ties to the mountains. I asked her if she missed anything about 'system life'. Laughing, she replied: 'No of course not, the mountains are my home, the mountains protect me. Serokatî (Öcalan) has this idea that even if Kurdistan is liberated, a group of women will stay in the mountains to guard that freedom. I want to be one of them, if I don't die.' I also asked her about the clarity in the eyes of women from the movement, something I had noticed distinctly everywhere I had been so far, from Diyarbakir to Istanbul, Maxmûr to Rojava:

What a beautiful question Heval Isabel. That's because of Serokatî's ideology! He always wants us women to be free, and for that he wrote something very special, and this beauty is in people's heart. And because our heart is clean, this beauty shows in our faces. This is because of Serokatî's ideology and because of the ideology of the şehîd. This is always alive in our eyes. If you believe in something, it will always be with you [...]. If Serokatî didn't exist, if our şehîd didn't exist, we couldn't do this. Without this friendship, we couldn't live. (Interview Zemyan, 1 August 2016)

This quote is full of official and almost cultish slogans, of giving meaning to death and losing your friends. However, Öcalan and his writings on women's liberation and the way women themselves have pushed for and implemented his writings are the main meaning-giver for guerrillas. And it works because this meaning not only constitutes the community now, but also gives the fighters hope for the future. No matter how bad things are, no matter how brutal the regimes they fight, there is friendship on the way and freedom at the end. And even if they will not witness it themselves, their deaths will make others stronger, who will continue their struggle.

One key aspect of a guerrilla's identity, lust for life and indifference towards death, is the martyr culture. Throughout the two weeks I spent in the mountains, and the four weeks I spent in Maxmûr, I heard many adventurous battle stories, retelling the heroic deeds of the guerrillas or the martyrs – about how six guerrillas could stop an army of 4,000 Iranian soldiers for hours; how the Iranian soldiers are cowardly and dirty, and how easy it is to kill them; how many enemy soldiers were taken out by Şehîd Zîlan, who bravely sacrificed herself using her and her friends' hand grenades, after being fatally wounded (Figure 3.5).

These battle stories are used as educational tools, but also as a form of oral history and for remembering fallen friends. 'My heart hurts every time

Figure 3.5 Photo of small laminated card of Şehîd Zîlan, given to me by
Zemyan before my departure

I lose a friend. But remembering their bravery and strength helps me to be
a better person, also for them' (interview with Zemyan, 2 August 2016).
What struck me most about the martyr culture is its position between life
and death and it its meaning-giving power. From the moment you enter the
party you become a revolutionary (şoreşger) and therewith agree to live, fight
and die for the struggle. Death becomes a permanent possibility and
presence in a guerrilla's life, which manifests itself in many different physical and metaphysical ways, most strikingly so in people's behaviour
towards themselves and each other. If a good friend falls in battle, you
mourn them but only within a set time frame. A mechanism is immediately
switched on of diverting the sadness into strength. Of course, the feeling of
sadness can come back over the months and years, but the same mechanisms apply: remember what they stood for, remember what they died for.

Loss and hardship are made bearable through their ritualisation: the
preserving of photos, the telling of stories, the taking on of their best
abilities. With that also comes a big responsibility; if you are still alive you
have to pick up the weapon of your martyred friend and make the struggle
bigger and better. And you can never give up. Contrary to Maxmûr, subject

of Chapter 4, sadness was less omnipresent in the mountains. 'It is hard for us to see our people grieve, when we are in Maxmûr for example,' one guerrilla told me. Here in the mountains there were no prolonged wakes, no lamenting mothers, but a clear path of action to snap back into. You honour the martyrs and their sacrifice by never forgetting them, their heroic deeds and their good qualities. These memories are written in journals kept by most guerrillas and are shared around the fire, over tea, or during the *moral* sessions, when songs remind everyone of their comrades. Party members also carried with them, among their sparse personal belongings, some laminated martyr photos, usually in their uniform chest pocket or in the back of a notebook. Sometimes they pulled them out and told their story, 'Did you know *şehîd* so and so? We were there and there together!' Or over tea they would share anecdotes: 'Do you remember how much sugar Şehîd Zîlan put in her tea? With every sip she took a sugar cube!.' Zemyan also showed me a small note she kept from the famous Zîlan, a hand-written night guard itinerary, and told me: 'The possibility of death is great for us, we never know what will happen tomorrow, so we try to be the best version of ourselves today, and our *şehîd* help us with this'. This is again a party slogan, just like many things they told me. However, ideology is life here, and life is lived according to ideology.

One day I spoke to a commander who had been in the party for more than ten years, asking about his well-being: 'I am sad today. I lost my best friend. Off, what a difficult life we have. I wish I was dead too,' he replied. After a few days I called him again to check up on him; 'I am OK now, I am listening to his music.' He sounded like his old self already, listening to the recording of his fallen friend, a talented musician. It did not take him long to seemingly normalise this loss in his head, put labels on emotions and place them into certain drawers, or so I imagine. Only later did I learn that the mourning happens in private and takes much longer than is apparent. And while killing the dehumanised enemy apparently does not faze the guerrillas much, the loss of friends lingers forever, often keeping them up at night or haunting them in their dreams. A former guerrilla told me that sadness is also curbed with self-control (*oto-kontrol*): 'I was very sad. Sometimes I was so sad I couldn't eat or sleep for a week. But I didn't break. You always have to be strong. I was like a bomb that didn't explode. For twenty-two years I didn't cry. Now if you give me your hand I will cry' (interview with former commander 2, 20 July 2018).

The Wait

Following the three days in the training camp, I waited for four days for the car to take me back to the KJAR headquarters. 'It might come tonight, or tomorrow, we don't know,' I was told repeatedly. This waiting period meant that I had a lot of time to think, write, talk to the guerrillas, participate in their daily routine, and observe the comings and goings of the camp.

Despite harsh realities of a guerrilla's life, I was often surprised by the silliness of the guerrillas, the things they laughed about, the repetitiveness of their jokes. Two of their favourite jokes were to call each other fatso (şişko) and throw stones into each other's cleavage, which is of course not the actual cleavage because under the uniform they wear a tight T-shirt, but the gap between the jacket and the vest they wear over it. Calling each other şişko also hints at someone's laziness or indulgence (kêyfiyet), when guerrillas' bodies should be active, strong and always at the ready (fieldwork notes, August 2016). While watching TV with the group one evening, one guerrilla swore at every single Turkish politician, before we stopped flicking through the channels and ended up watching the Smurfs on Zarok TV.[11] Again I was struck how easily entertained they were, giggling at children's cartoons. Perhaps I was expecting serious, battle-hardened fighters, talking about political philosophy, referencing Adorno, Rosa Luxemburg, Marx or Bookchin, even in their free time.

The şişko joke also illustrates that a healthy and strong physique is key in a guerrilla's life. Female guerrillas are very conscious of their bodies, and comments about skin, menstruation, or body hair and body weight are frequent. For example, one evening I had a whole informal conversation off the back of my interview with commander Eyrehan about how Apo taught women not to be ashamed of their menstruation, which many are because in Kurdish culture it is called 'illness' (naxweşî). If you appreciate this time and move during your period it can give you energy instead. Generally, I observed a mix of societal bodily and beauty standards (Düzel 2020), combined with personal preference and 'what Serokatî [the leadership] said'. I have been told that he stated at a certain point that he prefers women with long hair, who take care of their appearance and pluck their eyebrows.[12] Older commanders in particular are extremely poised, very aware of germs and cleanliness of their clothes, nails, and hair; their whole appearance is elegant and composed (Figure 3.6).

One of the many chores in the camp was laundry and bathing (hammam), if there was time and water. During military operations fighters endure

[11] Zarok TV is a popular Kurdish children's TV channel that was shut down by Turkish authorities in September 2016, as part of the state of emergency rule after the attempted coup in July 2016. It can still be watched online.
[12] As further discussed in Chapter 5, there was a shift from what a revolutionary woman looked like in the early 2000s. In the 1980s and 1990s, the more 'tomboyish' or unfeminine a woman was, the more she was considered to be a true revolutionary.

Figure 3.6 Two commanders letting their hair down.

weeks, sometimes months without being able to take a shower. But in the camp in the hinterlands with enough water supplies, doing *hammam* and washing your uniform is a frequent activity with clear rules. 'Heval Isabel, do you know how to wash by hand?' I was asked after I came back from my excursion to a higher camp, where I could not wash. 'Yes, of course,' I said, thinking of my wools and silks that I wash by hand in my other life. 'Really?' Deniz, an older guerrilla asked me doubtingly. To be sure she accompanied me to the outdoor *hammam* and prepared the bucket and watched me as I started to wash my first piece of the uniform. 'You weak Europeans, you don't even know how to wash! Give me that,' she laughed and took the item out of my hand. I protested to no avail. 'You don't know how, watch,' she said and started pounding the uniform. 'Yes, really I guess I can't do it like that.' I said, as I watched her for the rest of the process. 'Now I will wash you, because you probably also don't know how to properly wash your hair,' she insisted. Gone were my twenty minutes of potential silence and solitude that the 'weak European' in me was yearning for; already after four days of 24/7 companionship, I longed for a minute to breathe. But that was not to be. The lack of privacy, except when reading or sleeping, was something I would have needed longer to get used to. Yet the absurdity of these situations never failed to amaze me either. Here I stood in front of this fighter, who was scrubbing my head and back. For days after Deniz made fun of my lack of practical skills in front of the others, amusing the whole group. Teasing the weak European and feminist, both considered robots in an inhumane system and slaves of capitalism, was another repeated joke. 'Can you defend yourself?', commander Eyrehan asked me one day, as we were waiting for lunch outside the communal *manga*. 'No, not really,' I replied and jokingly added: 'but I can run really fast!'. Eyrehan shook head in disapproval: 'Women who run away [from the enemy] are only half women, women who know how to defend themselves are real women.'

During the two weeks I spent in the mountains, I only gained an outsider's perspective. Those who left the party also tell of instances of backstabbing, sabotage and ruthless power games among women. However, aside of continuously making fun of each other, I only noticed brief moments of frictions between the guerrillas, short instances of bickering or talking behind each other's backs about the lazy one, poking fun at the one with the lesser mental capabilities or teasing the 'nerdy' guerrilla for being the commander's favourite. However, these were rare, considering the tightly knit community they lived in. Or perhaps it was precisely due to this controlled communal living that none of these tensions got out of hand: a few times a week the group would sit down and hold a meeting (*tekmîl*), during which they reported or criticised anything they disliked or disagreed with during the past few days.

Communal life is clearly structured, from the time you get up, to how much time you get to eat, to how you sit and when, how you speak to each other and what you do and do not say. For example, swearing or shouting at each other is forbidden, never mind using violence against one another. The togetherness in the camp is relatively relaxed, full of chatter and laughter, and there is a feeling of equality between younger and more experienced guerrillas. Still, you never question who is in charge, who the commander is, in this case Eyrehan. She had her own tent to start with, plus has a commander *manga*. We often rested during the very hot midday hours in the communal *manga*, but if we saw Eyrehan coming, everyone sat up and talked slightly differently. Chatting with her was also relaxed but more composed. Normal conversation during lunch and dinner breaks evolved around the hot weather, battle anecdotes, politics or martyrs. One day, Eyrehan told us that she always used to have cats in the camps and particularly loved the one that would lie on fighters' bodies, exactly where it hurt. A different cat gave birth to kittens, whom she later mauled to death. Coming back from an operation, they found the mother cat dead, hung in a tree. Horrified, they asked the guerrilla who killed her: 'Are you the Iranian regime or what?' He replied, 'This is the third year in a row she has done this, the world is a better place without that cat' (fieldwork notes, 3 August 2016).

Animal love stories are a reoccurring conversational topic. Party members keep horses, cats, dogs and eagles. There are images and videos of guerrillas training mountain gazelles,[13] and in one camp I was at they were taking care of a wounded falcon. One commander told me a heart-breaking story about him and his eagle. He had spent weeks training it, so that it would go and come back on his command. It hunted and brought the prey back to the camp. One day he had to go on an operation and when he came back three days later he was furious and frustrated with what had happened during that particular operation. 'I came back to the camp and didn't acknowledge the eagle, I walked straight past him and went into my tent, I ignored him while I was calming down.' When he felt better he went to see his bird but could not find him anywhere. They found him a few days later dead in the forest. Apparently, the bird had committed suicide by flying straight into a tree trunk. 'Eagles do that if they feel like they have done something wrong you know. I was very sad after that, I never had a pet again.' To me these pet stories demonstrate instances of attachment and loss. A guerrilla (officially) has no private life, no personal belongings or intimate relationships, beyond platonic friend-ships. It always struck me how dearly they hold onto things and how seemingly easily they let them go; how much they love their friends and how quickly they have to get over their deaths. All ideas of possession, time and mortality have a different meaning and move on a different spectrum.

'And what about men?' is a question I frequently asked the guerrillas I had a good rapport with. 'You can't trust them. We can educate men all we want, they pretend they have understood and are democratic but especially at home they don't want to let go of their power,' a commander told me over dinner. A few days later a group of us were standing around the fire, smoking, waiting for the pasta to cook, when we started talking about men. They asked me if I was single; I nodded and added that some good men had crossed my path. 'Really? Do democratic men exist in Europe?' Dilpak asked. 'I think it's better you stay single, because relationships always end in violence,' she said as she playfully punched me in the stomach. 'Not only that, you should also never have children,' reiterated Ruken, stirring the pot. 'They will tie you down, you will never be free again after that!' It dawned on me then that Abdullah Öcalan is the only men these women

---

[13] Guerrillas frequently train wild animals such as eagles and gazelles; see clip (Xezal û Gerila) in multimedia.

trust, the only one who will never hurt them or let them down. The PKK is a revolutionary movement that lifts women out of society and disciplines them according to a new set of rules. Women do not have full control over their own bodies in the party, since the party decides where and how they should live, fight and potentially die. But the party gives them a raison d'être in the meantime; if they get killed they die for a worthwhile cause. This they learn in education: to believe, to defend, to sacrifice. Guerrillas obtain an almost sacred status in society; their quest of liberation is a holy one (Bozarslan 2004). That also means that sexual activities are seen as something menial. Commander Viyan told me that yes, of course, she still thought about sex and men in the beginning, when she had not yet properly internalised the ideology. But that once you realise how big and important your task is, how much responsibility you have for your friends and your people, you simply forget about sex; it becomes negligible (interview Viyan, 1 August 2016). That is certainly true for many people in the party, who give it their all to be the ideal militant. The logical next question would be whether more women instead engage in same-sex intimacy? I do not have any conclusive data on this issue, as this topic is taboo, and I did not broach it during my interviews with active cadres. From the interviews I conducted with former commanders who spent many years in the party, I conclude that yes, of course, 'it happens' but rarely, a subject that I will come back to in Chapter 5.

How dogmatic is the party ideology really? How do you measure freedom? Does the notion of freedom change because you come from a more violent context? Can what works for the mountains work in a civilian context? Or are these meaningless questions because this is a long-term process, with the party fully aware that the world order as we know it is coming to an end and that someday it just might rise like a phoenix out of the ashes of regional wars? These are questions I asked myself as we drove back to the city after a week in the mountains, longing for some aspects of 'system life'; the door to my house and bathroom, a cold beer, and some physical intimacy. One thing I had understood though is that these female fighters know that they are onto something, their bodies, faces and eyes speaking of years of internal and external struggle, many winters of reading, and a deep unfaltering conviction that their struggle is just. Many aspects of their quest for Democratic Confederalism are utopic, they often say so themselves, but they are all in for the long haul. 'How is the revolution going?', I asked a commander who works in Rojhelat, after I was back in London. He chuckled and said: 'I have to think about it over the winter, I think it will be difficult.'

Conclusion

During a weapons training break, commander Viyan sat down with me and discussed the process of becoming a female fighter. She emphasised the importance of *îrade*, and of role models, such as Bêrîtan and Zîlan. She assured me that if you only have weapon skills and no *îrade*, you will not be successful:

[I]f you know and love your weapons and your friends well, you know everything that Serokatî said, you love your people, defend your people, and educate your people, then you are a good fighter. You also have to have big *îrade*, a big belief in yourself, and you have to be willing to defend your friends, that's a good fighter. (Interview with Viyan, 1 August 2016)

With these ideological tropes, the commander of the training camp summarised the identity that is being taught and learned in education. The self-sacrifice and martyr references are key in her explanation, because the women can only truly become like the models of Bêrîtan and Zîlan if they die. Only in martyrdom can they become the goddesses they so admire (Bozarslan 2004; Çağlayan 2012; Duzel 2018). I left the mountains and shorty after left Iraqi Kurdistan, wondering how to do justice to these women, who are giving their lives for this cause? How do I tell their stories, staying true to their voice? The challenge of situating my ethnographic data within a conceptual debate, among others, is to acknowledge the importance of what these women do in wartime, without reproducing the exceptionalism of female militancy (Gentry & Sjoberg 2015), treating women's political violence as a necessity in a conflict landscape that often leaves them no other choice than to pick up arms, but without situating them in a false structure-agency dichotomy (Sehlikoglu 2017). The only way I knew how was by taking their trajectories, stories of resistance and everyday tools of liberation as a departure point, to eventually understand how such a powerful women's movement came to be and what women do to sustain it.

Who are these women, how did they get here and what are they doing here? These were helpful questions in acknowledging the fluidity and complexity of personal trajectories and stories of continuous violence and resistance. The pattern of why women join the party is shaped by violence, which is case and life story specific. This party, with its multiple branches in all four parts of Kurdistan, creates hope and offers an alternative for women, coming from many different contexts. Here they can become 'free' by being outside the arenas of political and domestic violence and working against the very source of reactionary forces that brought them to the party in the first place. And they become militants by the repeated acts of physical exercise, military training, ideological education and the introduction into communal life. It is here where the emancipatory moment takes place. I have demonstrated that once women (and men) go through education, it is the recognition and meaning-giving that keeps them there. They learn how to defend themselves against Capitalist Modernity and its many tools of oppression and gain an identity built on the rediscovery of women's history, power and voice. This also clearly lays out the path ahead: to go and fight, or to go back to society in order to educate and liberate others. It is in these mountain camps that the separate women's structures are built and lived, and it is these autonomous structures that allow us to complicate existing literature on female militancy and male backlashes post-independence. Not because they will necessarily protect women in a 'post-conflict' setting, but because men cannot interfere into how women run their business, as long as that business adheres to the framework set out by the KCK/KJK.[14] However, despite the women's movement's claim of difference from previous revolutionary struggles and sustainability in terms of women's centrality, the project of Democratic Confederalism and its liberation ideology remain deeply gendered, with the 'free women' being an important but strictly disciplined, policed and essentialised marker of the aspired 'non-state nation'.

In education, the recruits learn to be self-controlled and desexualised revolutionaries. They carry different experiences of violence and gender norms into the movement and learn to turn that into specific forms of resistance and the struggle for freedom. This process of becoming a revolutionary also entails much disciplining of each individual body; teaching them *oto-kontrol*, for example: learning to control all physical urges such as hunger, thirst, tiredness and sexual desires, because it is the struggle that comes first and needs the entire focus. If a person does not follow the rules set out by the parameters around a militant they are labelled '*düşkün*', or 'fallen', or fallen from grace, not having enough *îrade* for life as a revolutionary. Certain individual character traits such as resourcefulness, humour or artistic talent are valued and appreciated. Unwanted or unsuitable 'capitalist' or 'petite bourgeoisie' behaviour, traumatising experiences of violence, lack of physical strength or insufficient love for Apo are shaped into one form of militancy, using the tool of education. This process of subjectivation is often an uncomfortable and sometimes violent one, and the unlearning of past truths or enduring desires is a difficult feat to achieve (interview with Zîn, 27 August 2016). Even those who do not fully believe

---

[14] The women's movement operates autonomously in terms of ideological production (PAJK) and social and political affairs (YJA); however, the armed branch (YJA-Star) is under the control of the mixed and male-led People's Defence Forces (HPG, *Hêzên Parastina Gel*).

in what the framework of militant femininities set out for them have to at least perform it, if they want to get through the criticism and self-criticism sessions and make sense of life in the party. This links back to the initial conceptual discussion of needing more complex and nuanced analyses of agency. The case of the Kurdish women's movement and their training to become fighters has shown that it is possible to do both – acknowledging the hierarchal and militarised framework these women have to learn to operate in, in order to be able to resist, while acknowledging that spaces for humour and silliness, but also pain and loss are possible. Most importantly, in communal life, fostering friendships, respect, integrity and loyalty gives meaning to their losses and their own sacrifice.

During my time in the mountains, I only got a glimpse into the everyday reality of the women who are building and defending a 'new life'. In a daily routine structured around military training and ideological education, I was grateful for all 'in-between' moments, when I was able to just spend time with my interlocutors, stop the formal interviews, and listen, talk, laugh and smoke with them. It was during meals or the moments of drinking tea, cooking or sleeping next to each other, or just sitting around for hours and sometimes days, when I saw what the party members mean when they say that 'mountain life is difficult but beautiful', and how creating closed ranks, enduring friendships and a strong community is a key prerequisite in order to fight for freedom, or the PKK's version of it.

Another place where the liberation ideology is being implemented is Maxmûr Camp. Situated in the middle of the desert, far from the protective shield of the mountains, the camp residents are tasked with building a revolutionary society, amidst repeated attacks by *daesh* and the Turkish army. Together with the guerrillas who protect the camp, it is the women who keep it all afloat, as I will demonstrate in Chapter 4.

4   Mothers and Martyrs: The Struggle for Life and the Commemoration of Death in Maxmûr Camp

Introduction

'All slavery is based on housewifization,' Abdullah Öcalan writes in his freedom manifesto for women, and states:

> Gender discrimination has had a twofold destructive effect on society. Firstly, it has opened society to slavery; secondly, all other forms of enslavement have been implemented on the basis of housewifisation. Housewifisation does not only aim to recreate an individual as a sex object; it is not a result of a biological character-istic. Housewifisation is an intrinsically social process and targets the whole of society. Slavery, subjugation, subjection to insults, weeping, habitual lying, unassertiveness and flaunting oneself are all recognised aspects of housewifisation and must be rejected by the freedom-morality. (Öcalan 2013a, 26–27)

In this excerpt, Abdullah Öcalan describes what he sees as one of the fundamental ills of societies far beyond the Middle East: the confinement of women to 'traditional gender roles', and domestic spaces, being bur-dened by never ending house chores, childrearing and often trapped in dependent and unequal relationships with men.[1] A large part of the efforts of the Kurdish women's movement is to break these ties, as well as male dominance and women's confinement to the house. Ideally this would result in what he calls the 'sisterhood of women', separate spheres of life defined and shaped by women (ibid., 52).

Democratic Confederalism, of which gender equality is a core pillar, has been put into practice in the mountain camps of the guerrillas, but also in Rojava since 2012, in places like Şengal since 2015, and in Maxmûr Camp (*Wargeha Şehîd Rûstem Cûdî ya Maxmûr*) in Iraq since 1998. Between April and August 2016, I spent one month in the Maxmûr refugee camp, which is home to around 15,000 Kurds from Turkey and is located one-hour south of Erbil. The camp is one of the few easily accessible places where these intended power shifts can be observed.

---

[1] Öcalan was inspired and influenced by Maria Mies, who in her book *Patriarchy and Accumulation on a World Scale* (1986) traced the links between colonialisation and housewifisation.

Maxmûr is highly militarised and a hybrid form of old and new gender norms and relations, full of contradictions, challenges and possibilities for women. First and foremost, it is the history of this place that makes the deep anchoring of the PKK ideology possible. The strong web of political and emotional ties between the individuals, the family and the party is due to the uprooting of the around 17,000 refugees[2] from Bakur (Botan region, mainly Şirnak and Hakkari) in the early 1990s, and their perilous journey through different camps in Northern Iraq, until they finally settled in Maxmûr in 1998, all the while supported by cadres of the PKK (Yılmaz 2016). In addition, every family has a deep personal connection with the party through their martyrs.

Since the early years of the party, Öcalan has carefully included mothers into the everyday workings and ideological production of the PKK. Mothers are asked to make great sacrifices for the cause by letting their children join the struggle and as such are held in high esteem in party ideology and practice: 'The Kurdish movement portrays mothers as procreators of a revolution-to-be; as "matriarchs" of the family; and as the most visible, dramatic face of the suffering of Kurdish women' (Göksel 2018, 2). Mothers of guerrillas and martyrs are presented as mothers of the nation, while the guerrillas are considered sons and daughters of the nation (Weiss 2010, 59). This chapter is based on an ethnographic analysis of three key sites for mothers in Maxmûr: first, the martyr house and the death wakes for the newly fallen; second, committee, commune and assembly work in the autonomous women's organisational structures; and third, the family home, the 'not so private' private sphere. I ask how women, in particular martyr mothers, organise and perform rituals of resistance and remembrance in the everyday and use the liberation paradigm of Abdullah Öcalan to continue their lives amidst violence, loss and continuing regional conflicts. Leading on from that I investigate how gender norms and relations have shifted and how the gendering of remembrance helps to understand how the non-state nation is performed on a daily basis.

Conceptually, this chapter ties into my overarching concept of militant femininities, showing how mothers also have distinct roles to perform in the transnational division of labour within the party. Analytically, I want to break through the 'martyr mother as icons of the nation in the making trope' (Peteet 1997), as well as the binary of the oppressed or liberated women, knowing that the women are everything – victims and agents,

---

[2] The exact number of refugees is debated, according to UNHCR records the number was around 15,000, Arzu Yılmaz in her research in the Duhok Governorate Archive found it to be closer to 30,000 (Yilmaz 2016).

icons, and symbols of a nation (Bayard de Volo 2001). First and foremost, they consider themselves as fighters, just like every other militant in the movement. There are clear routines of how mothers use this identity in the everyday; surviving, organising, resisting, ritualising death and struggling for freedom. Militarism is a daily reality, which treats self-defence and the death of loved ones as a necessity, and the remembering of martyrs as a duty.

There is only one academic study on Maxmûr and its history, which traces the people's journey from Bakur to Atruş camp in Iraqi Kurdistan, and eventually to Maxmûr, all the while negotiating with the PKK, the KDP/PUK, the United Nations (UN), and Baghdad (Yılmaz 2016). A handful of studies exist that assess the socio-political relevance of the PKK's martyr cult and how this cosmology gives meaning to those who remain (Bozarslan 2004; Koefoed 2017; Özsoy 2010; Rudi 2018; Weiss 2014), which is why I also draw on militant mothers and the celebration of death in Palestine (Khalili 2007; Peteet 1991, 1997), as well as the Peace Mothers (Göksel 2018) and Saturday Mothers in Turkey (Karaman 2016). This literature acknowledges that for the PKK and its sympathisers both the notion of victimhood as well as the combatants' dead bodies carry a high political value (Weiss 2014), and that martyrs are treated and remembered in culturally specific ways 'as powerful affective and symbolic forces that shape power, identities and struggles' (Özsoy 2010, 30; Rudi 2018). I argue that while Öcalan's liberation ideology gives women a powerful tool to build an alternative life, the burden of losing loved ones does not get lighter because of it but acquires a manageable meaning due to the shared experience of loss for the communal and transnational cause. It is the continuous resistance in the seclusion of the camp that becomes life, and here women are at the forefront.

I collected the data for this chapter through ethnographic research in the camp, which included living with the family of Şehristan and her daughter Şehrivan. This kind of intimate access was only possible due to the fact that all the men in their family had fallen in the armed struggle, which allowed me to stay with the women for extended periods of time. I conducted participant observations by going to many of the events, rituals and wakes with mainly the mother Şehristan and her friends from the women's committee, but also doing interviews with current and retired members of the armed units, as well as PKK cadres currently in organisational roles. Especially in the beginning, Şehristan facilitated access and helped set up most of my semi-structured interviews.[3] Other

---

[3] Foreigners are not allowed to walk freely around the camp but must be accompanied at all times due to security concerns. I managed to loosen this rule somewhat during

than my ethnographic data, this chapter draws on Arzu Yılmaz's research, who wrote a history of the camp in Turkish (2016), as well as the rare journalist/activist books that witnessed the journey to Maxmûr in the 1990s (Laizer 1996; Solina 1997) or that document how the camp is organised now (Herausgeberinnenkollektiv 2012). I also include martyr imagery, the official written camp history (*Rêwîtiya Ber Bi Mexmûrê Ve:* Travelling to Maxmûr 2014) and documents published by the camp's Women's Assembly (*Meclîsa Îştar*).

Militarised Motherhood and Martyrdom

Cynthia Enloe defines militarism as a process that impacts everyday life, stemming from the military. Aspects of the military's disciplining and regulating powers impact social relations, with hierarchy, surveillance, and other forms of authoritarianism becoming a party of everyday life (Enloe 1988, 2000, 2007, 2014). In this process, the institutions of society also become saturated with violence and ideas of combat, martyrdom, victory, heroes and traitors. As violence becomes part of the everyday consciousness, its brutal effects and painful consequences are often neglected (Saigol 2000, 108). This process is deeply gendered, and this chapter will focus on how martyr mothers in particular deal with the processes of militarisation but are at the same time an integral part in the ritualisation and reproduction of militarised bodies as well as the militarised system (Bayard de Volo 2001). Militarisation of the people in Maxmûr did not happen in a vacuum but was a gradual process over the last thirty-five years or so with the people of the camp first being sympathisers, then collaborators and then de facto members of the PKK (Solina 1997). In Maxmûr, this militarisation manifests itself in rituals of the fallen, military marches, the omnipresence of HPG/YJA-STAR fighters and the shared notion that war is good and justified as long as fascism in all its forms exists (interview with Renas, 14 May 2016),[4] and the absolute normalisation of war. '*Şer heye*', 'there is a war' and shrugging of shoulders were common reactions to me questioning fighters or

---

my second visit; thereafter I was allowed to make my own plans and move around unaccompanied.

[4] Renas was a retired guerrilla who was running the guest house in Maxmûr. He had been severely wounded during his time as a sniper in Rojava and could barely use one of his hands. He accepted his new position stoically, even though he would have much preferred to be back at the front line. The last time I met him was in the Qandil mountains during Newroz 2017. He excitedly told me about the new position with the religion committee in Raqqa (Syria), to which he had just been assigned. In January 2018, while working there, he stepped on a land mine and died.

civilians about what was going on in certain places across Kurdistan, mostly while watching the evening news together.

A feminist inquiry into militarised motherhood requires first to theorise 'beyond the now familiar nationalist formulation of women as icons of the nation and recent critiques of that conflation' and to instead 'treat activist motherhood as a paradoxical practice that is simultaneously agential and limiting' (Peteet 1997, 103). This means asking questions about the constructions of femininities and masculinities and tracing what kind of powers are at work, under whose control and with what consequences. Enloe urges the feminist researcher to ask: who causes the militarisation of society? Who is being militarised? What does militarisation mean for daily life? (Enloe 2000). How for example is a mother convinced to let her daughter or son go and fight in the mountains? How is she supposed to cope with her or his death? Using this line of inquiry, I can make assumptions about what it means to be a 'martyr mother', which ideas are attached to it, what spaces for agency open and how they are used. Finally, focusing on motherhood allows me to bring to the fore the workings of power on gender norms and relations in Maxmûr more broadly. When analysing militarism, I am not painting it as a positive aspect of life in Maxmûr, but as normality, as a necessity. The women with whom I spent a lot of time wish for peace, justice and freedom for Kurdistan and Öcalan. But they also know that in the current geopolitical situation the party must continue to fight, even if they do not want their children to join the struggle. In line with party ideology they cannot openly protest against militarisation or the loss of their children; instead they officially only critique and resist Erdoğan's Turkey, Barzani, fascism, Europe, the United States and Capitalist Modernity. I write officially because there are instances of hidden resistances in the camp and especially young people in the camp find new hybrid ways to exist between university life in Erbil and the more conservative or party norms in the camp, as I will further discuss subsequently.

Maxmûr is a place of mixed resistances – between the everyday, the organised, publicly articulated and privately practiced: the mere existence of the camp in this desert village, the refusal of people to give up and return to Turkey before the Kurdish issue is solved and continuing to organise and live according to the party paradigm. To capture this complexity of entangled local- and regional-level forms of violence and resistance, I build on Vinthagen and Johansson's work on everyday resistance. They argue that power and resistance are not the dichotomous phenomenon as is often implied, but mixed and interconnected hybrids.

Agents of resistance often simultaneously promote power-loaded discourses, being the bearers of hierarchies and stereotypes as well as of change. Hence, each actor is both the subject and the object of power – the subject is exposed to the ranking and stereotyping as well as promoting repressive 'truths' – thus being both an agent exercising powers and a subaltern who has been subjugated and reduced to order by disciplinary strategies (Lilja 2008). Resistance is always situated, in a context, a historic tradition, a certain place and/or social space forged by those who rebel. (Vinthagen & Johansson 2013, 13–14)

They further argue that the only approach to grasp the complexities of these entangled power/resistance relations is to acknowledge that power is not singular but decentred and intersectional; therefore resistance is also decentred and intersectional. This means resistance(s) need to be analysed in relations to several powers simultaneously and that power and resistance are interdependent, constituting and affecting each other (ibid., 26). This line of inquiry can highlight which rules, norms and ideals are being challenged, which are maintained and with what discourse, institutions or techniques. Resistance rarely simultaneously undermines all the features of power; instead it mostly undermines some, while reshaping or enforcing others (Richter-Devroe 2011, 36). Furthermore, the PKK that prides itself as the force that resists reactionary forces such as *daesh* has built its own matrix of domination that constrains people, albeit on a very different scale than other parties and movements competing for power in the region.

The all-entrenching force of violence and resistance become more comprehensible when reading it through militant femininities' place in the party's transnational division of labour, and by assessing how women in this particular space of Maxmûr use the discursive and material tools the party offers them. Importantly, research on resistance is not only about direct or indirect action but also about discourse and about those who practice this discourse visibly. 'Resistance runs the risk of being able to marginalize, exclude and silence different articulations of resistance; especially when only some intentions are counted as legitimate' (Vinthagen & Johansson 2013, 38). This chapter does not include those voices in Maxmûr that are not actively organised in the party structures and instead focuses mainly on organised martyr mothers who are involved in the everyday workings of the camp. Even though I had a good rapport with many camp inhabitants and cadres working there, I was an outsider looking in (Al-Ali & El-Kholy 1999; Baser et al. 2019). At the end of my stay, I was still in no position to conclusively say how well the female-led parallel institutions and structures work, how much they can effectively decide for themselves, or what the percentage is of those choosing to stay at the fringes of the organisational structures. For that reason, I posed these questions to the former commanders, who provided some alternative facts about the camp, as I will indicate throughout this chapter.

The PKK and Martyrdom

Only in the last three decades, almost forty thousand people were killed on both sides [of the conflict between the Turkish state and the PKK], while the majority of these were Kurdish guerrillas and civilians. Biological death, however, has not necessarily meant total destruction or exclusion of these dead from Kurdish culture and politics. Rather, the Kurds resurrect their dead through a moral and symbolic economy of martyrdom as highly affective forces that powerfully shape public, political and daily life, promoting Kurdish national identity and struggle as a sacred communion of the dead and the living.

(Özsoy 2010, 1)

Hişyar Özsoy, a scholar who became an HDP MP in 2015, introduces the distinct role martyrs play in Kurdish society and the ongoing struggle for peace and liberation of the PKK. His PhD thesis, which I quote in this chapter, 'explores these multiple struggles over Kurdish dead bodies and the political imaginaries and subjectivities they generate' (ibid., 3). The PKK has a distinct martyr cult that is enshrined in its ideology and everyday practices. Şehîd namirin!, martyrs don't die!, goes the famous slogan that is shouted after every memorial. Members of the party are told that if they lead a meaningful life that serves the party, its leader and the people, and die while doing so, they and their name will live on forever in the hearts of the people. Martyrdom in revolutionary struggles has adapted some of the religious cosmology, such as the idea of sacrifice and eternal life; however, the act itself is performed for the nation that is to be liberated (Khalili 2007, 19). Contrary to religiously connoted martyrdom, there is no clear indication of the hereafter for PKK martyrs; there are no promises given by the leader as to what awaits them in the afterlife. Pious Kurds, including Şehristan, believed that her relatives went to heaven (in Islamic terms); however in the secular discourse of the party, the martyrs have already achieved the greatest goal – to be buried in the soil of the homeland and to become morally pure. 'Martyrs become untouchable after death, no matter their faults in this life, no one can criticise them after they die. You become free, famous and purified all at the same time' (interview with former commander 5, 12 October 2019). The history of the party and its ideology is inscribed in militant bodies and biographies, their reference being an important part of conversation between the party and its social base (Orhan 2016, 134). Everyone who falls in battle becomes a martyr, but heroism is reserved for those who either lived a particularly heroic life or died a particularly spectacular death. I posed the question of who is remembered as a hero and who is remembered less so to a former commander:

This always troubled us. Who decides who is treated like a hero and who is barely mentioned, and according to which criteria? It is decided at the top and it is usually classed in terms of how high and influential and educated people were. One time a few years ago fifteen women died in an operation in Bakur. But only the commander was celebrated as a hero, but fourteen other women died! I knew and liked the commander but that's not the point. (Interview with former commander 4, 11 October 2017)

Those who killed themselves specifically for Öcalan in the earlier years and after his arrest have a particular rank in party history. Zîlan, whom Öcalan heralded as the new *Îştar* after her heroic death, is a good example of being raised into the upper echelon of honour post-mortem. However, these hierarchies in dying put other members of the party under tremendous pressure, to perform, live and die in an equally honourable fashion (ibid.).

In linking the two debates, militarised motherhood and martyrdom, I attempt to grasp the complex lives faced in Maxmûr by those who 'give' to the party. In what follows I will zoom into three key sites of everyday camp life for women in Maxmûr: the martyr house, party work and the private sphere, before making broader assumptions about how the women of Maxmûr challenge prevailing gender norms and relations, and what role 'militant motherhood' plays in the bigger national liberation struggle of the Kurdish Freedom Movement. A key component in my analysis is the management and ritualisation of death. In Maxmûr martyr ceremonies and death wakes are central to everyday life, a site where women show their resistance, enacting the 'linkage between mother, death or sacrifice, and the nation in a way that publicly states and validated mothers moral and political standing as other mothers' (Peteet 1997, 115), or what I call militant mothers.

Spaces of Performance and Resistance

The Martyr House (mala şehîdan)

'The PKK is the people – and the people are here!' is a slogan usually shouted during demonstrations in Bakur, when people want to pledge their allegiance to the party. The meaning of this slogan is probably nowhere truer than in Maxmûr. Historically the people who live here have always supported the party, which was the main reason for the Turkish state burning down their villages in Bakur and forcing them into displacement in the early 1990s. The party in turn has always supported the (at that point) around 17,000 refugees by sending cadres to build and organise the six refugee camps before they arrived in Maxmûr according to party structures, to help with logistics, self-defence and teach its ideology. Maxmûr Camp was established in 1998 and is since regarded as the first place where self-administration according to PKK ideology was put into practice. As such is seen as somewhat of a role model. Or as Öcalan puts it:

The people of Maxmûr [...] I know them well, they are resisting through an unbending struggle. Despite their situation and being under many pressures they never give in. Our people in Maxmûr, they must continue their cultural work and mother tongue education. Maxmûr is like a commune of the oppressed, here Democratic Confederalism can best take shape. (Rêwîtiya Berbi Mexmûre Ve 2014, 42–43)

I understand this quote as the leader's attempt to give meaning and hope to the lives of the camp inhabitants, portraying them as relentless vanguards – the first to resist Turkey's state violence, embracing the liberation ideology, and build the democratic confederal non-state nation. However, the camp also fulfils a geopolitical role of being a PKK camp outside the Qandil mountains, a strategic transfer point between Qandil, Kirkuk, Şengal and Rojava. Hence, the party needs people to stay there, no matter how harsh the living conditions (interview with former commander member 2, 20 July 2018).

Today the boundaries between civil and armed, public and domestic, violence and resistance are blurred, while the historical and present struggle are omnipresent. This manifests itself in almost every family in the camp having lost one or more people to the struggle; almost weekly martyr funerals take place in the camp. It also means that the education system is modelled according to party ideology. School is taught in Kurmancî, women are organised in separate organisational structures and members of the PKK mix with civilians, especially since the party defended the camp against an attack by *daesh* in August 2014.

The *mala şehîdan* is situated in the centre of Maxmûr and was one of the first stone structures built after people settled here in 1998. According to Medya, a party cadre who organised the martyr house and its activities, around 700 people from Maxmûr, have fallen in the armed struggle between the 1980s and 2016. This number includes the people who fell on the treacherous way to Maxmûr and was growing by the week as more people fell in Şengal, Bakur or Rojava during fieldwork. The party decides when these martyrs are announced, and when their memorial is to be celebrated, having to consider and manage the camp's 'morale' and the ability to handle more bad news in order for life to continue.

I spent many hours in the martyr house, mesmerised by the amount of labour that goes into celebrating and honouring the memory of the martyrs. Every Wednesday morning a ceremony takes place at the *mala şehîdan* to remember and celebrate the fallen, attended by the older generation, students and a few members of the PKK. The men sit on the right-hand side, the women on the left, and the guerrillas in the back. Depending on the agenda, these events last around one hour and follow a clear script: they are opened by a party cadre who, after a minute's silence to remember all martyrs, gives a passionate speech about the importance of the martyrs, the struggle, the political situation and the freedom of Abdullah Öcalan. Then follows a longer speech by one of the *mala şehîdan* activists, who, depending on the date, honours the anniversary of an important martyr or event. These memorial events were fascinating in the beginning and very repetitive after a while, reciting the same narrative, the same slogans and the same rhetoric. However, I had also learned early on in my fieldwork that this is a culture of composure; when someone talks, no matter for how long and how uncomfortable you are, you sit and listen. Attending hours of these memorial ceremonies, I got used to the official script, but never became immune to feeling the physical burden, the sadness and injustice that resonates from these walls and the hundreds of images of dead people (Figure 4.1).

Apart from the weekly memorial service, each time someone from the camp falls in the armed struggle, the *mala şehîdan* stages the funeral service.[5] This is a big affair, attended by a few hundred people, the camp leaders and PKK cadres. A table and chairs are arranged on a podium outside the martyr house so that speakers stand behind photos of the fallen and Abdullah Öcalan, while the family members and important camp and PKK members sit in the row behind the table. In front of them the 'organised' people of Maxmûr assemble; the mothers and older men arrive first, then the students march in neat rows and take position in front of the stage. The last ones to arrive are the banner bearers – young people in guerrilla uniforms, carrying party flags. While everyone is walking in and taking their positions, bombastic martyr songs are played loudly, creating an even graver atmosphere. Countless songs have been written to honour the heroic lives of martyrs; one of the most famous ones

---

[5] If the person died elsewhere in Kurdistan (Bakur, Rojava) and the body cannot be brought back to Maxmûr, the camp still holds a martyr commemoration but without a coffin.

Figure 4.1 Maxmûr residents lingering at the martyr house (*mala şehîdan*) after the weekly ceremony. Photo: Peter Käser

is by Xelîl Xemgîn and called '*Ey Şehîd*',[6] an eerie song about how those who fight and fall for Kurdistan will never die.

This ceremony is always performed according to a set script: it begins with a minute of silence in memory of all martyrs. Then a party member opens the ceremony, greeting the family and attendees, and talks about the importance of the struggle, the current political situation in the region, and why they must continue to make the struggle against 'fascism' even bigger, to free Abdullah Öcalan and free Kurdistan. This is followed by two people from the family saying a few sentences about the person who fell, what their motivations for fighting were, and how they are not sad but proud and honoured that their child, brother or sister has 'given their blood, which is now soaking the earth of Kurdistan'. Then everyone claps and shouts '*Şehîd namirin!*' (martyrs don't die), '*Bijî serok Apo!*' (long live the leader Apo), and '*Bê serok jiyan nabe!*' (there is no life without the leader). After

---

[6] This song was composed in the early 1990s when guerrillas fell in the thousands and the music groups close to the party could no longer compose a song for each one of them (Özsoy 2010, 70). These songs have tremendous affective power; many people I interviewed mentioned martyr songs as a reason for becoming aware of injustice committed against the Kurds before joining themselves. For *Ey Şehîd* and other martyr songs see bibliography (multimedia).

this part of the ceremony is over, the decorations and loudspeakers are quickly taken down, while the crowd reassembles outside. Most people then walk in groups of women and men over to the martyr family's house. For the days of the wake (*taziye*, approx. ten days) many families put up a big tent where they welcome their guests.

During these ceremonies nobody cries; instead the family members are composed and proud. As Minoo Koefoed noted, this can be seen as a form of emotional resistance, a way not to let the enemy see weakness, but also as a sign of respect for those who have sacrificed themselves for the nation (Koefoed 2017). I would further add that is due to the fact that Öcalan himself disapproved of weeping:

> The tears of the living for the dead are tears for themselves. They see themselves in the dead. They see the fact that they are living dead ... They are so weak and so much like the dead that they create a mess when one is dead. It did not seem to be as a meaningful thing to face a natural life cycle in this way. In fact, now there is not much weeping for the martyrs. What we have done was to turn the martyrs into a force of life and courage ... [...] A right approach to death, rightly evaluating the link between life and death, defeated fear ... We have created a situation in which physical death would not mean death. This has met a great need for Kurdistan. The fear of death is eliminated and the need to create the feeling of immortality in life has been met. (Öcalan 2000, 268–69, cited in Özsoy 2010, 65–66, *language unchanged*)

This practice of not crying, and the ideological trope of finding strength in the sacrifice made by the martyrs, to honour their death by marching on, is something I observed throughout different parts of Kurdistan. Martyrdom is deemed a necessity by those who resist the oppression of the nation; it is seen as the only route to a meaningful life. Khalili shows that this link of loving life, wanting to live a worthy life and thus being prepared to sacrifice one's life, has been evoked by many post-colonial liberation movements such as the Palestinians, Hizbollah in Lebanon, the Cuban Revolution and the Black Panthers in the United States (Khalili 2007, 19–20). The PKK's martyr culture needs to be situated in that era and political climate, as Öcalan was not only greatly influenced by charismatic Turkish communist and leftist leaders (e.g. Mahir Çayan) but also other revolutionary liberation movements, such as the DFLP, who agreed to train a first generation of militants in Lebanon in the 1980s. They instructed them in guerrilla warfare, the art of propaganda, and civil mobilisation, including how to celebrate martyrs (Marcus 2007, 54–58). The martyr funerals have since become a site where Kurdish Muslim funeral traditions merge with PKK 'party aesthetics' and behavioural codes. Particularly in Maxmûr, a highly politicised and militarised context, martyr funerals include a mix of civil and military elements. For example, in 'the mountains' the bodies of martyrs are not washed and there are no religious rituals, such as praying or death wakes, that accompany the ceremony. In Maxmûr, however, alongside elements of a martyr funeral such as speeches, flags, songs and photos, the martyr body is washed and laid to rest by the Imam, according to Muslim tradition (fieldwork notes, May–August 2016). This hybrid form of the old and the new, the traditional and the revolutionary runs through all aspects of life in this camp.

Both Özsoy and Khalili write about 'hyper-masculine heroism' that is celebrated at martyr memorials, valuing virtues considered masculine: courage, violence and self-sacrifice. From what I have observed men and women receive equal celebratory rituals and because women have such a long history of contributing to and dying for the party, these characteristics have become gender-neutral. Yet every time a woman falls it is emphasised that she was also fighting for the liberation of women in Kurdistan, the women of the Middle East, and potentially the whole world. Thus, the gender politics of the party and its vision for a future Kurdistan become visible and audible at these events.

These dramatically staged martyr funerals, with the heroic songs, colourful flags, fiery rhetoric and the symbols that make up the 'martyr aesthetic', serve multiple purposes. First, they symbolise the martyr's passage into the hereafter and allows people to pay their respect to the dead. Second, it is a ritual to connect the martyr to the land that she or he died for, to mark and claim territory, which is linked to the third aspect: the political and symbolic power of dead bodies. Political ideas and representations of both victimhood and agency can be materialised through dead bodies (Weiss 2014, 163). Martyrs are appropriated and politicised into national symbolism, a part of imagining the struggling nation (Khalili 2007). Moreover, martyrs become the effective figures that create renewed 'feelings of militancy' (Peteet 1991, 151) or *îrade* for the people of Maxmûr. Through martyrdom, a symbolic of 'superior death' is constructed, the relocation of the biologically dead into the symbolic realms of immortality (Özsoy, 2010, 40–44).[7] Lastly, the repetitive act of celebrating and mourning the dead is also a display of power, reinforced by the deliberate use of symbols that retell the story of a collective struggle, an ongoing resistance and a strive towards a future utopia (Wedeen 1999).

---

[7] The large martyr funerals began with the Kurdish uprisings (*Serhildan*) in the early 1990s, during which the state reasserted its power by not only killing fighters and protesters, but also by making it difficult for the families to reclaim the bodies. The massive funerals were a form of resistance and appropriation of death into the struggle and often drew thousands of people into the streets (Özsoy 2010, 45; Weiss 2014).

The Death Wakes (Taziye)

Each time I arrived in Maxmûr, the first thing Şehristan and I did was to go to one of the many death wakes (*taziye*). Entirely gender segregated (apart from young children), the women would sit together in a circle in the garden or the living room, again following a clear script: first the mother, grandmother and other female relatives of the fallen are greeted to express condolences and wish that their 'martyr may rest in peace'. Everyone sits down in silence, usually during a minute of silence or a prayer. Here the women cry. Often the mother starts; overwhelmed by sadness, and perhaps exhaustion, she wipes her tears with her headscarf. The other women, most of whom have previously lost someone, start crying too, feeling the new martyr mother's pain just as much (Karaman 2016). Soon the other women start to console her with encouraging words about how martyrdom is an honour, how she is the mother of all children in Kurdistan, how it will get better; 'One is ok, I have lost three, imagine how hard that is,' I heard one woman say. In these moments a particular form of 'Maxmûr motherhood' is evoked, a combination of Kurdish motherhood and militant motherhood, between victimhood and agency, between suffering and struggling. Yet I always wondered, what does it mean for women, for mothers, to have to be 'OK' with giving so many of their loved ones to the struggle? How do women cope with this cycle of suffering? I found a beginning of an answer in their routine of work and commemoration to keep the dead visually and ritually alive (Wedeen 1999). At the above wake for example, after an exchange of consolation and stories how difficult others had it, the conversation slowly turned to everyday politics and camp chat. By this time tea and water had been served, and sometimes in summer fruit followed. These rounds often turned into lively and loud discussions, only the martyr mother continued to stare blankly into the distance. The meaning and purpose of these extended and repetitive sittings as I understand it are to reassure those grieving that life goes on, that death is part of life, that this is a price for freedom they are expected to pay, but also to demonstrate that those around will help and come back to visit. Each week after the Wednesday martyr ceremony for instance, the women's committee of each neighbourhood would go on a tour through their area, visiting all those women who are sick or have recently lost someone. The same ritual follows in quicker succession – water, well-wishes, lamenting, crying, tea, sharing of stories, political chat and personal banter, before moving on to the next house.

Families and mothers who have lost someone are supposed to cope and be proud – certainly not to blame the party for their loss but find strength in the party ideology and community. This works partly because the PKK itself holds its martyrs in such high esteem. Official party doctrine says:

Understanding the truth of the PKK, which is a 'Martyrs Party' is possible to understand through its truth of martyrs. [...] If today the people of Kurdistan has confirmed its existence in a way without doubt and is walking towards freedom, what lies in the basis of this is the truth of the martyrs of this difficult struggle. In every word said for the Kurd and Kurdistan, in the basis of organizing, institutionalizing, awareness and action; lies the effort, sacrifice and blood of the martyrs. [...] It is not possible for a people to gain their freedom if they do not stand up for its children which puts their lives to the forefront for themselves. [...] The best response we can give to the memories of our great martyrs who have a historic role in the creation of this noble case and in the acquisition of the spirit of resistance, as a struggle and a life stance of superior sacrifice and participation, will be to march steadfastly in the victory line and achieve a high level of success in the direction of our people's expectations. [...] All Kurdistan liberation guerrillas today walk through the footsteps of these heroic martyrs, the Apoist devoted spirit lives at its peak, and as a sacrificial guerrilla army, it lives on the memory of martyrs in its resistance and march. On this basis, we once again remember our martyrs with respect and gratitude, once more with the determination to make the period of struggle we are in a victory period, and once again on this day we repeat the promise that we will definitely defend a life, which is worthy of their memories. (HPG 2017, shortened, *language unchanged*)

This quote is an excerpt from a press statement that was released in May 2017, the PKK's official month of martyrs, and highlights how deeply rooted this struggle is in 'sacred death'. It also gives some key justifications for violence, sacrifice and continuous resistance. An important aspect is the promise to always keep on fighting, to make the struggle even bigger, in honour and memory of those who have fallen. In the first sentence the PKK calls itself a 'Martyrs Party', implying that much of their efforts is for them and that martyrs are right up there with Abdullah Öcalan as the incorruptible bearers of 'truth' (Bozarslan 2004). This is one of the important factors that enables people to make sense of their losses: knowing that their loved ones did not die in vain, but that their struggle will live on as they become a symbol of resistance for those who live.

However, just because this ideology of continuity is spoken and lived, believed and helping with the everyday, it does not mean that the sadness felt by mothers for many years after their loved ones have fallen becomes any less of a burden. As Emine Rezzan Karaman discusses in her work on the construction of motherhood in reference to the Saturday Mothers and Peace Mothers in Turkey, I also observed that the loss of a relative is not an episode but becomes a continued sadness and longing: 'It becomes a way of life in which they [the mothers] embody suffering and mourning.

It turns into something that remains. It permeates their everyday practices, shapes their days and nights' (Karaman 2016, 394). The sorrow of Kurdish mothers has become part of the socio-political fabric across different parts of Kurdistan, their suffering and strength also being the subject of many beautiful and sad songs.[8] Yet the mothers I worked with always evoked *îrade*, their will to continue resisting, until hopefully one day both Öcalan and Kurdistan will be free. *Îrade* can be compared to the Palestinian *sumūd*, which translates as steadfastness and can be defined as an everyday insistence on carrying on with life, economically and culturally, and to seize the opportunities to enjoy life, against all odds. Similar to *îrade*, *sumūd* is an integral but mostly individual and non-organised form of resistance, a form of ideational resistance to maintain hope and continue living and organising with a sense of normality (Richter-Devroe 2011, 33). In the case of the PKK, having *îrade* also means knowing how to repeat the party ideology. So much so that if some of my respondents talked in what I call 'official speech', one could hear Öcalan speaking through them. What differed from woman to woman in Maxmûr is her own personal history, what her life was like before leaving her village in the early 1990, how she met her husband, what her parents were like, how her family members died. As soon as they were uprooted and marched south across the Iraqi border, the stories become as one: that of hardship, starvation and death but also of resistance. Also, their political opinions are seemingly all the same. A friend and interlocutor who comes from a village in Şirnak and also grew up on the front line of the war between the Turkish state and the PKK in the 1990s told me after my first visit to Maxmûr:

They have a will [*îrade*]. They don't need to think. It is bad! They say they are free but in reality, they are just creating a new prison [. . .]. They are my people, I love them but I can't discuss their opinions with them. They only repeat party slogans because that is save and they are afraid to say anything else. In Kurdish we are saying 'the door of their mind closed'. (Fieldwork notes, April 2016)

How closed the minds of my respondents were is not for me to decide, but due to the relentless repetition of party ideology during formal interviews, I eventually stopped doing them and instead resorted to participant observation. This method allowed me to get an intimate impression of what camp life is mainly made of: work.

---

[8] Listen for example to Hozan Serhat, a famous guerrilla musician. Before he starts singing the song *Dayê Dayê* he says, 'The Kurd loves his mother very much. This is a nation of mothers, an earth of mothers.' Or Koma Azad, a guerrilla music group (*Êdî bese lê Dayê*), set to music a letter a guerrilla wrote to his mother, explaining why he joined the revolution and that she shouldn't cry for him. One of the first and most famous Kurdish female singers to sing about mothers was Ayşe Şan (*Lêlê Dayê*), and for a contemporary song see Aynur Doğan (*Dayê Dayê*). See bibliography (multimedia).

The Work

Women in the camp know from lived experiences that only by being organised can they survive, be strong and build the new democratic confederal system. Ever since they fled Bakur in 1994, they have been under attack by the Turkish army and different Kurdish forces in Başûr. Every time the Turkish army undertook another operation against the PKK in the mountains, the people who were fleeing were also targeted, mainly through prolonged embargos, air raids and direct attacks of the camps (Rêwîtiya Berbi Mexmûre Ve 2014).[9] According to camp history writing, fearing their alliance with the PKK and their high degree of organisation, the goal of the Turkish state was to make the conditions of the refugees so unbearable that they would leave the camps and return to Turkey, where they would have been forced to migrate West and assimilate, their villages having been destroyed in the meantime (ibid., 24). Women's independent organisational structures started in Atruş camp as early as 1995. Here they formed their own Free Women's Union of Kurdistan (YAJK), just like the guerrilla women in the mountains. Other institutions such as the foundation for martyr families, education in Kurmancî and self-defence forces to secure the travelling camps were also founded *en route*.[10]

Despite their high degree of organisation and their successes in protesting against unbearable conditions in the camps, or forcing the UNHCR to grant them refugee status after staging a hunger strike in 1995, it took four years before a deal was finally reached between Erbil, Baghdad and the PKK to give these refugees the dusty patch of desolate land close to Maxmûr city. All my respondents recounted the hardship of their journey to Maxmûr but emphasised that nothing compared to the horrors of the first months there: no drinking water, no food, no shelter, just dust, heat and scorpions that killed the children. They all agreed they were sent there to die (ibid., 39; interview with Şehristan Durmaz 22 April 2016; Rahima Bozan 13 May 2016). This struggle for sheer survival lasted from 1998 to 2003, as the camp residents continued to be punished for their support of the PKK. In this period, people were forced to build their own administrative system. It was only after the invasion of Iraq in 2003 that

---

[9] Not just the camps predating Maxmûr but also Maxmûr itself has been attacked numerous times, in 2014 and 2016 by *daesh* and on 6 December 2017 Turkish airstrikes destroyed the headquarters of the self-defence forces (HPG) in the camp (ANF 2017). Since then, the camp has been attacked multiple times by Turkish airstrikes, most recently on 15 April 2020 (Rudaw 2020).

[10] To this day, women attend regular weapons training sessions with the guerrillas in Maxmûr, so that if attacked again, they know how to defend themselves.

the political and economic sanctions against the camp were lifted (Yilmaz 2016, 275–76).

I am making this historical excursion to demonstrate that self-organising has a long history in Maxmûr, processes that have enshrined women's centrality beyond ideology. My data, and the literature used in this chapter, suggest that it is the interplay between existential threats both in their native Bakur, while travelling to Maxmûr, and their life in Maxmûr that enabled the liberation ideology of Öcalan to find such a strong footing. The camp residents were sympathisers and collaborators with the party before they were displaced, but it was the ideology and its focus on specific organisational forms that enabled them to survive as a group. The camp organisational structures have grown over the last twenty years and have been adapted according to party ideology, including the KCK system of co-leadership and the women's quota of 40 per cent in all mixed structures, such as the People's Assembly (*Meclîsa Gel*) since 2003. The quota system is now well established but, as everywhere else, was difficult to implement. 'If the quota did not exist, women would not have stood a chance in the beginning. Because societies in the Middle East are still patriarchal and sexist societies' (Reyhan, quoted in Herausgeberinnenkollektiv 2012, 465). This assessment is understandable from Reyhan's point of view (and in fact many of my respondents' point of view), but I find it more constructive to think of the domestic and local gendered violences as 'masculinist restoration' as introduced in Chapter 1 (Kandiyoti 2013), and the lack of a consistent rule of law that implements legal accountability (Jabiri 2016; Kandiyoti 2007a, 2007b). Moreover, feminist scholars have shown that what Reyhan described as 'patriarchal and sexist' and is experienced by many of my respondents as such is also a result of competing religious and secular ideas of personal and family laws that trump national and international ideas of legality and equality (Mir-Hosseini 1996, 2009; Wudud 2009; Al-Ali 2007; Moallem 2005; Abu-Lughod 2010; Ahmed 1982, 1992; Joseph 2000).

Throughout the 2000s, alongside the quota, women's autonomous system expanded into the women's assembly (*Meclîsa Îştar*), the women's academy (*Akademiya Şehîd Jiyan*), and the women's foundation (*Waqfa Jin*) – each responsible for a certain area of work on different levels of operation in the communes, neighbourhoods and districts, or the camp (Rêwîtiya Ber Bi Mexmûrê Ve, 46–55). For instance, the camp is divided into five districts, each has four neighbourhoods and ten committees, which deal with the everyday work of education, health, organisation, economy, culture, tailoring, arts, craft, foreign relations, diplomacy and media. Within these structures, women plan projects or discuss issues and problems, trying to solve them at the local level during their weekly meetings. Each neighbourhood committee sends a representative to the *Meclîsa Îştar*, which meets bimonthly. The women's assembly is divided into six working areas: ideology, society, organisation, youth, self-defence and politics. Female activists, mothers mainly, since the youth have their own structures, do hold organisational and some decision-making powers but they are also expected to do most of the grassroots work since they themselves have to uphold the functioning of this system that has their liberation as its goal. There is an important interplay between the camp and 'the mountains': some questions are debated on the commune and assembly level, whereas other decisions, mainly regarding security, economy and diplomacy, are taken in the mountains. The camp is in direct contact with the mountains through cadres and the monthly reports written by every assembly about the work undertaken.

Under the leadership of PKK cadres, women are at the forefront of all organisational and ideological projects in the camp. Female party cadres are present on all organisational levels, educating, coordinating and implementing. The female cadres are divided into military (YJA-STAR), ideological (PAJK) and organisational work (*Meclîsa Îştar*), the latter being shared with the 'civilian' camp inhabitants. For example, the weekly women's neighbourhood committee meeting was often led by Zeynep, an older commander who at the start gave passionate speeches, summing up the current political situation, before the civilian spokesperson talked about the everyday issues and future plans. Every single time I witnessed one of these events (committee meeting, *mala şehîdan*, youth meetings and school lessons), I was struck by how long-winded and repetitive these speeches were. Have they not heard everything countless times before? Are they not bored? Could they not make this shorter and snappier? Looking around different rooms I tried to understand people's reactions to these monologues: some women were picking their toes, others were playing on their phone, or whispering silently in the corner, and some keeping a stern face, seemingly listening. I mentioned to one of the students after a particularly long memorial speech, which all students are required to attend, 'Wow he likes to speak a lot!'. 'It's good for us,' she replied, 'the longer he speaks, the later we have to go back to school'.

Another time, during a long speech of a guerrilla at the academy which the students attend to improve their ideological knowledge, I asked Şehrivan whether it always happened like this. 'Yes,' she replied, 'and I don't mind. How could we know [what is happening in regional politics] otherwise?' This acceptance of long hours of sitting and listening I observed across different parts of Kurdistan, from Bakur to Rojava and Başûr, from the cities to the mountains. The trainee guerrillas had to sit through long and hot midday sessions, having numerous statements read to them, and many being clearly bored, but they continued to take part in the performance. This culture of patience goes further than showing loyalty to the party; it is a learned routine and an integral part of organised life. A former cadre told me that this wordiness is due to the culture that Öcalan established; he used to lecture for hours, sometimes days, when he was giving his 'Analyses', and everyone else had to listen. Today, when cadres speak publicly, some of them imitate him, demonstrating how knowledgeable and eloquent they are.

Despite this military discipline, not everything runs quite as smoothly as the neat organisational structures and the party's permanent influence might suggest. When I spent a few weeks in the camp, a new cadre had arrived from the mountains. She took on the role of co-leadership of the camp, responsible for diplomacy, public relations but as a woman, also for women's work. Whenever I met her it was clear that she was not too enthused about her new position, did not really want to engage with the people and was annoyed about the dirt in the streets. Since I was a foreign female guest, she was also responsible for me, a duty that she only fulfilled a couple of times, often not picking up the phone when I called. Apparently, she should have done much more for me, one of the martyr mothers told me: 'I don't like people like her, she is arrogant, and she doesn't do her camp work well, she is never around and never picks up the phone.' I ask about what mechanisms women have if they get sent a cadre they do not like or who does not do the work properly. 'We can write reports and send them to Qandil,' she said, 'if she doesn't improve, she has to go to education'. Later I learned that the situation with that particular cadre only got worse, it even came to a dramatic standoff between the women's committee and her, each shunning the other and not speaking for a few days. The next time I visited and saw them all together, the atmosphere was cold and tense and it became clear to me that the relationship between different strands of 'free women' is not without its challenges. Some cadres look down on civilians or are at least irritated by their slow progress towards a 'free and democratic life'. A female cadre I met in the mountains had previously attended the biennial women's conference in Maxmûr was clearly frustrated with the people there: 'People in Maxmûr are dirty, they don't organise, they don't understand the importance of self-defence, even after *daesh* attacked the youngsters just walk around the camp and want to go to Erbil. They are so capitalist.' I found this quite harsh and tried to defend Maxmûr by drawing the commander's attention to the difficulties of the camp's geographical and geopolitical location. But she wouldn't have any of it:

'No, if they would organise and love their earth more, they would learn how to live off it. You don't need much more than water, bread and olives to survive. Also, they don't need to clean their houses three times a day!' (fieldwork notes, 3 August 2016).

This cadre's assessment resonates with what I have observed in terms of the mountain/city divide, the challenges to make the liberation ideology make sense beyond the mountains, and to reconcile the top down (cadres) with the bottom-up (commune-assembly structure) approaches. How much control is needed to free people? I cannot resolve these tensions conclusively or answer that question, but I am convinced that it is much more feasible to put Öcalan's writings into practice in the seclusion of the mountain life, far away from the challenges of everyday lives of present-day Iraq. The camp exists under very difficult political and economic circumstances, and in many aspects is dependent on the Kurdish Regional Government, which pays for water, electricity, schools and the salaries of the camp municipality employees, while the Iraqi government is responsible for renewing the residents' refugee ID cards. Maxmûr residents are free to go to university in Erbil and work outside of the camp; however, as a result of the ongoing economic crisis in Iraqi Kurdistan, many university graduates remain unemployed and many young people chose to not work in areas controlled by the Kurdish regional government, due to the conflicts between the KRG and the PKK, and by extension the people of Maxmûr, who often bear the brunt of this long-standing feud. In summer 2019, the KRG put the camp under an embargo, after the PKK killed a Turkish secret service agent in Erbil. Since then, Maxmûr residents are banned from leaving the camp, which puts the camp under extra duress (Figure 4.2).

The House

'You never sit still, do you?' I remark, after Şehristan got up again, to do yet another chore around the house or the garden. *'Mecbûr im'*, she simply replied, 'I have to.' Laziness is shameful and there is always something to do – this I had understood by now. And that the never-ending routine of cleaning, cooking, women's committee or assembly work, praying, gardening and visiting friends gives this mother structure and the means to continue. It distracts her from her sorrow and reassures her that she is part of a community that continues to march towards liberation. Everything they do has a purpose – visiting another person who is ill or suffering, organising a conference, a march or attending a training session. Women only go home to do the housework, after the camp and organisational work is finished. Someone could walk into our house at any time to pick

Figure 4.2 View of Maxmûr. Photo: Peter Käser

Şehristan up because some more work needed to be done. When they say 'work', it usually means the core of grassroots democracy – meetings and discussions within the women's or mixed structures. One day Şehristan and I went through her whole weekly routine of house and party work. As we discussed her itinerary I could see her getting anxious, 'Is this [inter-view] going to take much longer? I have work!' she stressed. We laughed, and she told me:

> My life is just work. But I wouldn't want to live without work. Even though I am not well; I only have one kidney, I have high blood pressure, and my legs hurt. The Hevals say go and relax. But I cannot. Because today Serokatî [Öcalan] is still in prison, a million Kurds are refugees, every day there is a new şehîd. If I work I can say I did something for the organisation today. (Şehristan 18 May 2016)

Şehristan often sang while doing the house chores, especially in the kitchen. Sad songs of loved ones who are far away, of revolutionaries who will never come back, of the much-missed homeland, or the revolu-tion in Rojava. I complimented her voice but she shrugged it off. 'I used to love singing. But I stopped after my sons fell,' she sighed deeply. 'My heart is black now.' At one point we looked through her picture albums, which are full of photos of her visiting PKK camps in the mountains, posing with Cemîl Bayık (one of the main leaders of the PKK) and other

Figure 4.3 Maxmûr residents in front of an Öcalan collage. Photo: Şehristan's private album

members of the party. She pointed at different photos: 'He is *şehîd*, she is *şehîd*, he is also *şehîd.*' Seventy per cent of the people in photos were dead. One of my favourite pictures that I came across in her album is an image of her, proudly standing in front of Öcalan as the sun, which illustrates one of the key aspects of militant femininity in the camp and to a certain extent 'civilian' life: being able to endure hardship because women are walking in the line of the leadership (Figure 4.3). Eventually both the leader and Kurdistan will be free and, in the meantime, there is much work to be done. I observed this powerful ideology and the way it is sustained to create much hope and meaning for those living in the camp. Next to the photo album she stored a box with the few belongings she received after her second son fell in the mountains; it contained only a wristwatch, and a small mobile phone. Unpacking the box, she told me his heart-breaking story: he joined the party after both his father and his older brother had died in the struggle. He was only a few months into his training, when he slipped and fell into a river during a thunderstorm and drowned. After a few minutes of her going through the box with me, her daughter grabbed the objects out of her hand and put it back into storage;

'Enough mother', she murmured, knowing when to stop her from remin-
iscing in painful memories for too long.

Finally, after a day's work, we would relax together in the living room.
In those moments the TV would either be showing a Turkish soap opera
(Ottoman drama or wedding competition) or one of the party-affiliated
TV stations such as MED MUZÎK or STERK TV, broadcasting the news
from different wars across the four parts of Kurdistan. 'Are there any
şehîd?' Şehristan always asked when she walked in the room, followed by
the z-z-z clicking sounds if the answer was yes. The violent acts perpet-
rated by the Turkish army or *daesh* were intimately linked to the ordinary
everyday of my interlocutors, and many gestures, facial expressions
and sounds indicated that someone was lost for words in the face of
incomprehensible injustice or unpronounceable sadness (Das 2006, 7).
Watching TV with my 'host family' demonstrated again their deep
connection to the party and its members. For instance, when guerrillas
were shown marching up a mountain, Şehristan would exclaim, 'Oh
how I love them all. They are all my children and the mothers of
Kurdistan are all their mothers!' This is part of the official party script,
but I am convinced she truly feels that way. Whenever fighters stopped
by her house, she fed and hosted them, sometimes they showered and
washed their clothes, as the house was open at any time for those
belonging to this way of life.

Later at night, after the last guests were gone and surely no more cadres
would be walking in, we exercised. Partly on my initiative, because in the
excruciating heat we could barely move during the day, but also because
Şehrivan was soon to be married and wanted to lose a few kilos. I taught
them some home exercises, which made for some of the funniest but also
most intimate and interesting discussions about body (image), health and
eventually sexuality. Both mother and daughter are used to intense physical work in and around the house such as baking bread, but both would
collapse in fits of giggles after a couple of minutes into the exercise. The
mother, otherwise rather strict about what was shameful and what was
not, was throwing her legs in the air. When she could not keep up with us
she started hitting her body where it hurt: 'I have become old, I am only
forty-three but my teeth hurt, I only have one kidney, my knees hurt,
I have high blood pressure and look at my toe,' showing me her infected
toenail. While we laughed a lot during our clumsy attempts to move our
bodies, it became clear that neither of them was happy with the way their
bodies looked and had aged, blaming their hard lives, and the harsh living
conditions in the camp.

After the mother went to sleep, sometimes the daughter and I would
put our heads together and talk quietly about boys and hopes for the

future. Joining the armed struggle was never an option for Şehrivan, she wanted love and a family and to make children for the future of Kurdistan. 'What are all the thousands of guerrillas for if they don't have anyone to liberate?' she asked. When I met her, she was engaged to a man in Bakur, who she was looking forward to marrying. Was her husband a true democratic man, had he managed to 'kill his inner male', as foreseen by the leader? She swayed her head, indicating a half-half; he likes and has understood Apo but he is a bit religious she told me. 'He doesn't like it if I dress revealingly, or if I go to Erbil by myself.' I asked her how she envisioned her life as a married woman, how she will use the paradigm of gender equality then? 'Women and men still have clear roles in a democratic family, but women can also work, and men have to help with the housework,' she explained. She assured me that while the party is doing much for women, certain rules like premarital sex or having children outside marriage will not change for a long time; 'Our culture is like that,' she said before we slept.

Shifting Gender Norms in Exile

The 'free woman' or the 'militant mothers' are both lived and discursive products, constructs in the making within the grander goal of working towards Democratic Confederalism. Despite his incarceration, Abdullah Öcalan still holds a huge amount of power, not necessarily direct power anymore but meaning-giving power, especially for women; his liberation ideology has changed the way women see themselves, and has given them tools to talk about and organise against different forms of oppression. It was Öcalan's ideology that brought them back from patriarchy to matriarchy, which has its origins in Mesopotamia, or so the narrative goes. Women must and will shake off their shackles of enslavement because matriarchy has a 20,000-year-old history in the region, whereas patriarchy is only 4,000 years old, Nilüfer Koç, the Co-Chair of the Kurdistan National Congress (KNK, *Kongreya Neteweyî ya Kurdistanê*) explained to me during our meeting in Erbil.[11] 'When European politicians ask me questions about female fighters I tell them you won't like the answer because you don't like him, but it is all about Abdullah Öcalan' (Nilüfer Koç, 15 April 2016). This is a conviction that I observed over and over again, and I have come to understand that it is rooted in the coherence of the liberation ideology and depending on the place, also in the success of

---

[11] The KNK is a transnational organisation with its main office in Brussels, invested in pan-Kurdish dialogue, to ensure that parties in all four parts of Kurdistan communicate and collaborate.

its implementation. 'Who needs a God when you have Apo! We don't have to pray for him, but he makes people bigger,' Şehrivan half-jokingly told me after I asked her if she was practising religion like her mother. 'For me he is like Plato, Nietzsche and Hegel. His power is to open women's eyes.'[12]

It is beyond the scope of this study to conclusively attest to what extent gender norms and relations have changed among the people of Maxmûr, from when they fled Bakur until today. However, displacement and being forced to organise themselves clearly had a big impact. Research into 'traditional' gender norms and relations in Bakur with a focus on urban migration to Van and Diyarbakir shows that which norms are challenged in the course of migration is highly context specific and dependent on power relations such as class, age and education (Çağlayan 2007; Grabolle-Çeliker 2013). Anna Grabolle-Çeliker in her work on Kurdish migration speaks of a 'Kurdish gender paradigm, understood as a dominant, yet malleable, discourse' and how 'migration has given rise to alternative discourse on gender that compete with the dominant one' (ibid., 185; Kandiyoti 1988). Most of my respondents emphasised how oppressed women were in Kurdish feudal culture, how they had to ask their sons or husbands for everything and were often not being treated better than animals. Certainly, the position of women in society depended on class and geographical location. Despite their displacement and poverty, most of my respondents emphasised that their situation as women was much better in the camp than when they were growing up in Bakur. Everything changed with Serokatî (Öcalan), Rahima, an older martyr mother told me: 'He was the one who showed us that women have a right to liberation, that women are equals.' So, then what is equality between men and women for her? I followed up. 'I have not seen equality', she replied promptly. While this discourse and performance of liberation is both audible and visible in Maxmûr, the reality in the houses often looks different. Those women who want to leave the house and get to work in the camp need someone to fight their corner, if their man is not 'democratic' enough. In Rahima's case it was her son who convinced her husband to let her go. Others tell of the guerrillas doing the rounds through the tents, and later houses to mobilise women, and if necessary to argue for their activism in the public sphere (Solina 1997, 208ff). Other women I spoke to were not allowed to go to school, were married off very young or became second wives. These are all practices that the party has banned and today can lead to the expulsion from the camp (Herausgeberinnenkollektiv 2012, 466).

---

[12] These are some of the philosophers that are being quoted in Abdullah Öcalan's own work. Many members of the movement would argue that Öcalan should be as renowned as they are for his contribution to political philosophy and revolutionary knowledge production.

In Maxmûr interesting hybrid forms exist between the 'traditional' and 'modern', 'communal' and 'capitalist'. Take Şehristan's second teenage daughter Nuroj, who was living and working in Erbil as a waitress and only came home on certain weekends. When at home she was always more interested in sleeping, snap-chatting and taking selfies than helping her mother in the household, talking to anyone or participating in camp activities. Even high male party cadres who had known her since she was a baby and wanted to talk to her about her life could barely draw her attention away from her phone for more than half an hour. This behaviour was pointed out as shameful, so were her ripped jeans. 'Do you know how poor we used to be? People are still poor and you are walking around like this!,' her mother would complain. 'Not in the camp, only in the taxi service back to Erbil!,' her daughter defended herself. At the same time, this moody teenager had 'Öcalan' tattooed on her wrist and the initials of her martyr father and two brothers inked on her knuckles. People are as much affected by the neoliberal system so rapidly advanced by Barzani's government as everyone else in Başûr and are subject to the enduring economic and political crisis. However, they also go through years of party education, and many youngsters spend much of their free time organising for the party. So they oscillate between two worlds, wanting good mascara or a new car, but knowing of the detrimental effects of Capitalist Modernity. In other words: when looking at which gender norms and relations are challenged or remain in place, age matters, and so does the family's socio-political and economic context.

One aspect that has certainly survived from the dominant gender paradigm is domesticity. The family I was staying with had no more males in the household; direct male dominance was gone; no patriarchal bargain needed to be kept. Yet the women of the house cooked, cleaned, gardened and washed just as the 'good wives' that Kandiyoti characterises, living up to the ideal of the clean, hardworking woman (Kandiyoti 1988, 280). 'Iraq is dirty, Maxmûr is dirty!', Şehristan would murmur to herself while cleaning the whole house every day, confirming what Anna Grabolle-Çeliker observed in Van (Bakur): a woman's honour is often judged by their cleanliness of her house and her ability to create a home (Grabolle-Çeliker 2013, 197–198). In Maxmûr the extreme cleanliness and domesticity endure, the house gets vigorously cleaned every day, and as ever I was made fun of as I tried to help. 'Don't you clean your house in Europe?' they laughed. 'Of course I do, but maybe once a week and certainly not like this,' referring to the intensity of their bodily efforts, the rolling up of carpets, the washing of curtains, throwing water mixed with petrol everywhere and scrubbing it out.

At the same time the older daughter of the house, who was very well educated in party ideology, got angry at women who only stay at home

and do housework. One night we were walking through the camp after
having visited her brother's grave, passing a courtyard where a woman of
considerable physical size was sitting on her doorstep. Şehrivan pulled
a disgusted face and said, 'All this woman does is eat and get fat. All some
women do here is stay at home, make children, take care of the children,
make food, eat food.' This example illustrates that by no means all camp
residents are as active as the family I was staying with and that while the
party broke the stigma of working outside of the house, many women
were still subjects of 'housewifisation'.

At the core of militant femininities lies the pledge to give everything to
the struggle, to resist unconditionally, if need be until death. Among the
organised community in Maxmûr, I observed many collective forms of
resistance, such as conferences, rallies and ceremonies, but also private and
personal stories of endurance and hope. However, on a regular basis,
festivities or ceremonies such as *Eid* and also official party holidays were
subdued in 2016 because so many people had died in and beyond the four
parts of Kurdistan (e.g. more than 250 people were killed in a suicide attack
in Baghdad just before *Eid* 2016). In such instances the party would decide
to make this year's event solemn and not festive. This ties into what Jean-
Klein in the context of the first Palestinian Intifada has described as
'suspension of life', postponing joyful events such as weddings until after
set mourning periods and not celebrating cultural or party holidays. She
calls this practice of suspending everyday life a 'form of domestic self-
nationalization as well as a form of resistance, as having hegemonic as
well as liberatory overtones' (Jean-Klein 2001, 91). She argues that suspending everyday routines combines subaltern and oppositional strategies
of resistance with new hegemonic and potentially constraining nation-
building impulses. Or, in other words, the practices are a duplex political
initiative, both nationalist and resistant (ibid., 114–115). Her analysis of
Palestinian's practice to 'self-nationalize', the act of demonstrating commitment and political awareness, I also found to be a dominant feature in
the everyday lives of Maxmûr. This was a practice dictated by the party and
always combined with high expectations for those nationalised bodies to be
present at the formal party events such as conferences and marches. One
key point of criticism during one of the 'criticism and self-criticism' sessions
I attended at the academy was a cadre criticising that not more students had
attended all the women's events in March. 'Friends, I know March is
a busy month for us, but it is important that you attend these events,' she
told them. Thereafter each student who felt personally criticised by this had
a chance to get up and defend herself.

That day, a young woman was sitting in front of me who struck me as
very different from the other students; the way she dressed, composed

herself, the way her leg was constantly shaking reminded me of people who 'have seen war'. We started talking across the bench, and it turned out that she was a twenty-one-year-old former fighter from Cizre who had escaped the urban war in 2016. She told me that she was studying law in Istanbul, planning her Erasmus semester in Spain when the arbitrary arrests, including that of her father, started in Cizre. It was clear that she would go home to fight as a member of the urban youth resistance YPS. Just before the fighting was over, she managed to escape and crossed the border to Iraq illegally, eventually ending up in Maxmûr, where she was waiting until she could go home, spending some of her time in the academy.[13] The flow of young fighters goes both ways. Not all youngsters seeking to liberate Kurdistan join the ranks of the PKK anymore. There is an alternative movement of young people wanting to fight in hotspots such as Rojava, Şengal, or the urban wars that started in Bakur in mid-2015. Some of them no longer want to formally join the PKK, not least because then the party decides where you go and for how long. However, they still received weapons and training from the party. That particular student from Cizre put her motivations as follows: 'I think it's easy to join the PKK. The work in the city is harder, you are very close to the enemy every day, you can get killed every day. To help preserve our culture and work with the people, I want to take that risk, to make that sacrifice' (Geerdink 2016).

I am noting this story in order to demonstrate the co-existence of bodies that live by the party principles, bodies who deviate, bodies who are allies, and bodies who have no choice but to collaborate due to regional necro-politics and border regimes. In this matrix of domination, militant femininities is a concept that includes everyone who sees themselves as members of sympathisers of the party. However, it does not aim to simplify the complex geopolitical context these women move in. In Maxmûr, many different gender norms, forms of activism and resistance exist. Importantly, women's activism is always linked to Abdullah Öcalan, each organisational effort is also taken with the goal of his liberation in mind. For some this might be mere lip service but in ideology-laden contexts such as Maxmûr, he means everything to the organised women. His liberation is also a reoccurring theme in all official spoken and written communication (party goals, internal party reports). During an interview in Maxmûr a fighter told me, when I asked her about what she finds difficult about her life and work: 'I sometimes feel like I was born in the PKK, so there is nothing that is difficult. [...] But it hurts me that

---

[13] I later recognised her in an article by journalist Frederike Geerdink, to whom she had told the same story a few months earlier. For her whole story see Geerdink (2016).

Reber Apo is still in prison. That makes me angry' (interview with Berfin Deniz, 15 May 2016).

As indicated, I did not have access to the part of the Maxmûr residents who were not organised behind party lines. The party does not allow all-out protests but there is recurring resistance against PKK control and policies in the camp. 'I often was called to the camp when there was a problem with the residents,' a former commander recounted. 'Sometimes they put bombs in party buildings, sometimes there was discontent among certain groups. I had to figure out what the problem was and try to find a way to appease them' (interview with former commander 4, 20 October 2017). The party managed to re-legitimise its presence and control after success-fully evacuating and defending the camp against *daesh*. In the following days and weeks, PKK cadres worked tirelessly to ensure that the people who were dispersed to other cities of Iraqi Kurdistan would return to Maxmûr, as they could not afford to lose any of its inhabitants, given the camp's strategical importance (ibid.). Since 2015, the camp has seen an increase of residents migrating to Europe. This is due to a breakdown of the Turkish-Kurdish peace process, which crushed people's hope of returning to Turkey, the continuous attacks on the camp by Turkish airstrikes and *daesh*, blockades by the KDP, and a lack of opportunities for the young people who grew up in the camp, finished university in Erbil but struggle to find opportunities in an ailing Iraqi Kurdish economy.

Conclusion

Women in the Global South have organised around the roles of mother-hood to protest unresolved killings and disappearances and demand justice from the respective authoritarian regimes in places like Argentina, Palestine and Turkey for many years (Karaman 2016, 382). Mothers, who in most nation state constructs have been assigned a domestic and non-political role, within which their primary task along with housework is to give birth to offspring and do childrearing, challenge traditional ideologies about motherhood with their presence and protest in the public sphere, sharing their painful past and wounds inflicted by the state (Peteet 1997). Karaman argues that the transformation into subversive subjects takes place as mothers 'destabilize the assumed separation between private and public sphere by sharing their personal experiences in the public domain as an expression of collective trauma and silenced pasts' (Karaman 2016, 383). Here, I have zoomed into a socio-political and economic context where women lead a whole existence of subversion. Maxmûr mothers share much with their sisters, mothers, aunts and cousins who protest in Turkey as Saturday Mothers (Istanbul) or Peace Mothers (Bakur) and also have their own Peace Mothers in the camp. Yet while their relatives in Turkey turn state violence into maternal suffering, which is also a tool of resistance and political agency, the Maxmûr mothers' reality in the Iraqi desert required more from them: staying in an organised manner in a place where they are not welcome (Iraqi Kurdistan); openly supporting a party that is considered a terrorist organisation by many (PKK); not just protesting once a week but showing one's colours and strong blocks of unity at every martyr funeral and official party celebration. Far from being idle and honourable icons (Peteet 1997, 123), the women in Maxmûr are a crucial piece in the bigger KCK puzzle; their contribution to the organisational work is both important to the KCK but also to the women themselves, who see it as their duty to play a role in the struggle of the Freedom Movement. Their struggle for space and functioning autonomous organisational structures is at the same time one for survival, as the camp comes under repeated attacks, and each and every family 'gives' children to join the fight and has to deal with the devastating effects of their loss.

Militarisation is treated as something entirely normal; fighters walking in and out of your house, driving by on trucks when their front-line shift starts or high commanders stopping by for tea when they have a meeting next door. Militarism, violence and suffering infuse every aspect of life, have become part of the ordinary (Das 2006), and have done so since people pledged allegiance to the party in the early 1980s and were forced to flee in the mid 1990s. The war between the Turkish state and the PKK, and the often hostile conditions in Iraqi Kurdistan, has caused much hardship and loss. Every photo album, every song, every ritual evokes memories of victimhood, loss, longing and struggle. For the people who came to Maxmûr to escape that violence but also to refuse to give into Turkish resettlement tactics, the organisational structures and the ideology of the PKK helps them cope with old and new trauma and create hope for a future democratic confederal nation. This ideology is first and foremost centred on to the person of Abdullah Öcalan. '*Bê Serok jiyan nabe*': Without the leader there would be no life, goes the popular slogan. And for the Mothers in Maxmûr I am sure that this holds true.

The commemoration of the dead is an important part of daily life in the camp, a performance for the residents, demanding physical presence, time and emotional or political reactions (Khalili 2007). This reaction might just be remembering but can also be uplifting by creating a sense of community, and thus strengthening *îrade*. Özsoy's work shows that the body of the martyr becomes a site where the boundaries between the imagined nation and the family are renegotiated; '[t]he nation is thus imagined and practiced in metaphorical terms of an extended family, a militant community comprised of martyrs and those who follow the ideals they have died for; a communion of the dead and the living' (Öszoy 2010, 39).

Militant femininities are thus intimately linked with martyrdom both for fighters as well as female relatives, such as the mothers discussed here. The clearly scripted celebration of martyrs is a part of everyday life, which can be seen as a militant form of community-making and surviving, amidst the horrors of ongoing wars and conflicts. At these celebrations and ensuing wakes, sadness is turned into celebration, loss into hope, death into resurrection (ibid., 53) and, I would add, oppression into resistance and *irade*. Furthermore, the culture of remembering the dead is an important aspect of how the nation (that has no state) is created and performed. In the case of Palestine, Khalili argues that 'commemorative practices [...] all represent, reinterpret, and remember the national past in an ongoing and dynamic way and in so doing, set the stage for crafting future strategies' (Khalili 2007, 214). Suffering, commemoration and continuing life are all gendered insofar as the militant women who featured in this book find meaning through the enactment and implementation of the liberation ideology that puts women at the centre. Ongoing wars and militarism have created more suffering, but have also given women tools to resist and, especially with the backing of the women cadres, have enabled them to challenge certain traditional practices. In other words, militarisation goes hand in hand with a new form of knowledge production. The teaching and living of the liberation ideology drive the transnational division of labour and keep the resistance movement active and functioning. Yet at the same time, the high degree of militarisation and subsequent control, not least over femininities and masculinities, also limits how far these developments go. The importance of controlling individual bodies and their sexuality in this revolutionary project will be the subject of Chapter 5.

5 Unmaking and Remaking Sexuality: Body Politics and the PKK

Introduction

> We are revolutionaries, and as such we want to change society. What is important for us is to free society and free women. In this process, we challenge everything, also sexual identities and what it means to be homosexual or lesbian [...] We don't reject sexuality but in our opinion sexuality is not everything.
>
> (Interview with Leyla Agirî, 25 August 2016)

After my last interview in the mountain base camp of KJAR with commander Leyla Agirî[1] I finally understood. It had taken me long enough. Almost all the way through my fieldwork I struggled with the question 'What happens to sexuality, where does it go?' This is a progressive revolutionary movement, which not only fights for communal economy, and sustainable ecology but centres around the quest for gender-based equality and justice. The women I met in Diyarbakir, Istanbul, Maxmûr, Rojava, Sulaymaniyah, and the guerrilla camps stressed that in their radical approach to women's issues they go further than 'Western Feminism', which allegedly operates at the fringes of a patriarchal system, whereas the Kurdish Women's Freedom Movement has managed to establish parallel organisational structures in which men have no say, and women have to ask no one, not religious, tribal nor political leaders, for permission or legitimisation of any kind (Asya Abdullah, 20 July 2016).[2] In the new society these revolutionaries are trying to build, both in the political and military sphere, other things are more important than sexuality, which in this analysis broadly comprises the sex act, physical pleasure or openly lived sexual identities.[3] And, that in order to

---

[1] In June 2020, Leyla Agirî, one of the key figures in the Kurdish women's movement, was killed in a Turkish airstrike in Rojava.

[2] Asya Abdullah made these remarks at a conference I attended in Sulaymaniyah ('Peace and Stability in the Middle East with Abdullah Öcalan's Thought', 19–21 July 2016), which brought together members of the Kurdish Freedom Movement and sympathisers from all four parts of Kurdistan.

[3] Sexuality has been conceptualized much broader than I have here, as power and knowledge (Butler 1988, 1999; Foucault 1990), as a biopolitical act of resistance (Hamdan 2019), as erotic power and creative source (Lorde 1993), pleasure and desire (Rubin

dismantle the old, and always be at the ready to fight and potentially sacrifice yourself in this struggle, female and male guerrillas have to be strictly disciplined fighters and must not be distracted by sex, love, relationships, pregnancies or broken hearts. The Kurdish women's movement has developed a different understanding of who the 'free woman' is and what her duties on the path to freedom are. As such, this movement and its liberation ideology are deeply gendered, while aiming to desexualise social relations 'at work' for members of the party in order to ensure focus on sustaining the construction of a transnational network, within which Democratic Confederalism shall replace the modern nation state. In this project, women are demarcating the boundaries between 'us' versus 'them'; the democratic confederal project of the Kurdish Freedom Movement versus the barbaric rule of *daesh* or the authoritarian Turkish state. In order to inhabit these roles, women have to subscribe to what I have called militant femininities throughout this book.

In this chapter, I problematise and discuss militant femininities reproductive and productive human labour: the fighter, the politician and the mother, and how the realisation of a division of labour sustains resistance and fosters the making of a non-state nation. Hereby, I consider the often-neglected aspect of the fighters' desexualisation and the general sidelining of issues concerning sexuality in the movement as a whole. What kind of militant femininities are created and lived and how is this part of the subjectivity maintained and policed? What are the tensions that emerge from creating a sexless guerrilla army that comes down from the mountains to liberate society? Second, the chapter discusses what I call 'party bargains' in reference to Deniz Kandiyoti's work 'Bargaining with Patriarchy' (1988, 1998) and Frances Hasso's further development of it in 'Bargaining with the Devil' (2014). Hasso argues 'that patriarchies are malleable and plural and show that women and rights activists unintentionally produce and reinforce them in a variety of bargains' (ibid., 110). This chapter demonstrates that women break out of certain societal constellations by entering the party and subject themselves to new bargains, this time with the party. I argue that in this process of entering the matrix of domination of the Kurdish Freedom Movement, sexuality is perhaps not everything, as Leyla Agirî said, but it is at the heart of how the party controls its militant subjects.

This chapter is by no account written to denounce a lack of freedom due to this 'abstinence contract'; instead, I intend to unpack the liberation ideology once again, using a sexuality lens, focusing on body politics,

---

1992), biology (Fausto-Sterling 2012) and queer identities (Halberstam 1998; 2005), to name only a few.

rules of love and friendship, and the envisioned 'free and equal relationships'. The chapter treats sex and sexuality as a site of violence and resistance. In the wider Middle Eastern region, we have seen instances of how sexuality or nudity can be used in protest (e.g. in Egypt with Aliaa Magda Elmahdy and her nude photo, El Said 2015), but withholding sex and negating sexuality as the Kurdish Freedom Movement is doing, is just as radical an act (Fahs 2010), that arguably strengthens its ranks through control and punishment. I investigate this argument and based on my ethnographic data demonstrate that productive subjectification has to be in accordance with what is perceived as local culture and identity (El Said 2015, 129). Here, the 'abstinence contract' is a key element in the 'party bargain', because it makes female fighters both acceptable to 'traditional society' and traces back their power and beauty to their goddess pasts. I demonstrate that the party is not all about military discipline, but that in the civilian sphere in the cities, under very specific conditions, also advocates for pleasure, love and relationships. As such the party constructs pragmatic structures that produce obedient bodies through disciplinary power as subjects of warfare, as well as spaces for civilian body politics, where difference and intimate relations can be problematised to some extent. This chapter draws on the discussions in previous chapters, which highlighted the fluid boundaries between civil and military, between the cities and the mountains, and shows how militarised gender norms and relations effect the political realm and vice versa (Pugliese 2016).

Talking about sex, sexuality, intimacy and love during my research was challenging. Particularly with members of armed branch of the movement it was not an easy feat, because the official position is that guerrillas do not need physical intimacy, and that there is no sex within the PKK, except for love for your friends, the land, the struggle and the leader. If you break these rules you are seen as a weak revolutionary, someone who has not understood the party ideology correctly and has 'fallen' (*düşkün*). He or she then has to stand trial and usually has to complete another round of education or in more serious cases has to spend time in party prison, until the superiors believe that the person has changed. Questions about sexuality and the control thereof were central in my interviews with the former commanders, as they could speak more frankly about this 'taboo' topic (El-Feki 2013). By calling it 'taboo' I do not mean to reiterate Orientalist tropes relating to sexuality in the Middle East, but instead speak to the growing body of feminist scholarship that looks at the question of intimacy across the region, challenging the private-public binary and complicating tropes around Muslim subjectivities, selves and collectives (Najmabadi 2005; Sehikoglu 2016; Zengin & Sehlikoglu 2016; Sayyegh 2017).

Following a conceptual discussion on how to talk about sexuality during ongoing wars, this chapter zooms into three different contracts of 'party bargains': the fighter, the civil activist or politician, and the mother. These three categories are co-dependent and their boundaries are often fluid: mothers join the armed resistance, and former fighter who spent time in prison become activists in the political sphere (Weiss 2010). I take the body as a departure point in each instance and argue that while conservative gender norms and relations are being challenged in all three realms in which militant femininities work, new and relatively static body policies are institutionalised by the Freedom Movement. In each of these three spheres the new norms regulating gender and sexual relations hold discipline but also emancipatory potential for each woman, just like the rest of the liberation ideology and its implementation does.

Methodological Reflections on Sexuality in Permanent War

I am editing this chapter as the Turkish army invades Rojava in order to establish a 'buffer zone' that would force the SDF to retreat from its shared border with Turkey and cause thousands of civilian and military casualties. In autumn 2019, under the pretence of 'Operation Peace Spring' the Turkish army and its Jihadi affiliates are expected to not only slaughter thousands of people but also use women's bodies to demarcate their power in the region. I have previously worked on this chapter while the Turkish army invaded the Afrin region in February 2018 and took control of Afrin's city centre a month later. Heart-wrenching stories of killings, destruction, lootings, and news reports of the direct targeting of women were coming out of the formerly YPG/YPJ-controlled region (Kizilirmak 2018). It is exactly due to this 'daesh mentality' and what it does to women that so many young women join the party and take up weapons to defend themselves, their families and their land. Feminist scholars have shown that the systematic targeting of women in war operates on a continuum through women's bodies and entrenches women's lives at home and in the public sphere, a fact that is not novel but has become most visible with the emergence of daesh and its abhorrent crimes against Yezidi women and women's bodies in general (Al-Ali 2018). This is also true for the Turkish army, which has a long history of mutilating the bodies of PKK fighters, particularly women (Berger, Friedrich & Schneider 1998; Walton 2016), and thus demarcating the boundary between 'us' versus 'them'; the legitimate Turkish state versus the separatist terrorists, male power versus dishonoured women's bodies.

In such a climate of abhorrent violence and injustice, should or should I not write about sexuality (the practice and identity) or its absence when it comes to the Kurdish women's movement? Should I brush it off as not important in times of war and conflict, and go by their explanation of marginality in the bigger struggle for liberation? For a long time, I was conflicted about this but had a hunch that sexuality and the controlling of people's bodies and desires were really at the core of creating the soldiers needed for this fight or the civilians they are educating. Lara Deeb writes about her decision not to write about the Shia practice of temporal marriage in Lebanon:

[H]ow can we produce honestly critical work about gender and sexuality without fuelling racist stereotypes? One hopes that shedding light on an issue will dispel stereotypes, as they thrive on ambiguity and categorical judgments, but fears that audiences will hear only what they are listening for. This is an old problem, one that has graced myriad conversations at conferences and workshops, the kind of simultaneously ethical, contextual, and methodological problem that refuses to expire. It's also a multi-faceted problem, where orientalist exoticism, Islamophobia, colonial feminism, and the limits of political alliance combine into a repulsive and sometimes paralyzing mix. (Deeb 2010)

Following this argument, I am conscious of how the female fighters have already been orientalised, sensationalised and sexualised in Western (media) depiction and how problematic and essentialising these representations have been. Dilar Dirik (2014) and Adrianne Shahvisi have challenged these representations, the latter noting that

the tone of astonishment in newspaper articles when reporting on women soldiers in Rojava derives not merely from the difficulty in accepting the idea of women as soldiers, or soldiers as women, it also reflects astonishment at West Asian women acting autonomously i.e. brown women saving themselves from brown men, thereby flouting Spivak's (1994) famous dictum, and disrupting the stereotype. (Shahvisi 2018, 3–4)

Aside of the hegemony of Western media's depiction of Kurdish fighters, I am also conscious of my position as a white, Swiss female ethnographer who, writing in London, has the luxury of positionality and resources to engage in conversations about sexuality, while the brutal wars in the region rage on, and many activists, civilians and fighters are losing their lives (Mikdashi & Puar 2016). Why then is it still important to think and write about this issue? Why not, like Deeb, decide not to write about such a contentious issue, in order not to give more fuel to the 'civilizational dichotomy [that] has been put in service of new wars and not political-economic projects in the region'. Deeb leaves the reader with the questions 'How do we responsibly counter stereotypes without giving them importance, quell liberal desires to save the world without denying social problems where they exist, and produce writing that is critical of the politics of neoimperialism without being dismissed as merely polemical?' (ibid.).

I may not find answers to these myriad questions and pitfalls for the feminist ethnographer; I can merely trace my personal and intellectual journey of trying to make sense of the loaded field of sexuality in war (Sjoberg 2015). I first became sceptical when I realised how much the women and men of the movement themselves emphasise how unimportant sexuality is, how romantic and sexual relations do not happen in the party, and how critical questions sometimes resulted in condescending othering of the 'Western feminist', perhaps also because they have heard the question so many times. Why it is so important to peddle this policy, idea and brand of desexualisation? Of course, it is not just branding, there is actual material reality and emancipatory potential in this claim and its lived realities, as I have shown throughout this book. However, the reality is far more complex and laden with intersecting power relations than it is presented to the eager researcher. At the heart of my writing about sexuality, however, lies the conviction that sexuality is not a mere side aspect that can be negated but a key location where subjectivities are formed and controlled.

'To be a critical military analyst is to be a sceptically curious military analyst' (Enloe 2015, 3). In order to do that Enloe urges the sceptical and curious researcher to take 'seriously feminist investigatory questions' (ibid., 4). This means to question the creation and maintenance of femininities and masculinities that are needed to sustain an army; look behind the veil of heroism and martyrdom; spend time with military mothers; and 'develop a higher tolerance for contradiction, confusion, and messiness' (ibid., 8). I take this as a departure point to question the conventional assumptions that the guerrillas are desexualised simply because Abdullah Öcalan once said so and because it is more practical, given the protracted war. I hope that this will help cultivate a more in-depth understanding of the femininities and masculinities that ensure the longevity of this movement, and how the women in different locations negotiate this specific aspect of the 'party bargains' on their path to liberation.

Abandoning sexuality and subscribing to the body politics of the PKK is a bargain that is a necessity if women want to live, fight and die for this party. Hasso calls this navigating of co-existing patriarchies 'Bargaining with the Devil'. In her work this term conceptualises the way feminists navigate the terrain between neoliberal governments and feminist aspirations across the Middle East (Hasso 2014, 110). She argues that male-dominated institutions do not always work against women per se, and that intimate, sexual and family life cannot be analysed in a binary with states, economies or public spheres. Instead, '[f]eminist scholars have shown how nationalist, ethnic, and religious projects – all of which are concerned with their collective reproduction in biological, legal, and cultural terms – work through sex, gender, and marriage' (ibid., 121). In this web of power relations, people are also embedded in a web of relationships, there is no autonomous self, nor autonomous agency, instead we are constituted through political, material, social or military conditions (Mittermaier 2012, 251). In the following analysis, I will first provide a comparative perspective of how previous national liberation movements have handled what was often referred to as the 'woman's question', before sketching out a short history of PKK party body politics and analysing the discourses surrounding the bodies and the (a)sexuality of fighters, politicians and mothers. I argue that body politics is an important transfer point where militancy and belonging are negotiated (Hasso 2016, 107).

Body Politics in National Liberation Wars: A Comparative Perspective

Legal and state institutions have tried to set the boundaries on how people engage in sexual activities and have developed a range of controls and punishments against disobedient bodies to enforce them (Rubin 1992). Today, every country and every state army have a set of norms that enshrine what are acceptable forms of sexual conduct and which sexual identities and practices are deemed lawful (Snitow et al. 1983). Similarly, every national liberation movement in the twentieth century included women in certain capacities and had to negotiate the place and role of sexuality. The Huk Rebellion for example, a peasant revolution in Philippines (1940/50s) that attracted thousands of women into its ranks even had a written document called the 'Revolutionary Solution of the Sex Problem' to regulate sexual activities in the party, essentially allowing male cadres to take a second 'forest wife' (Lanzona 2009, 13–14). Not just the Huk rebellion, but every communist movement after the 1920s had to address the 'women's question' to clarify the social, economic and political place and mobility of women within the communal and national division of labour. Alexandra Kollontai, a Bolshevik revolutionary and minister in the first Soviet government, challenged prevailing notions of family, love and sex. She imagined a society that is capable of 'social love' and multiple bonds beyond the ideas of property and possession (Kollontai 1980, 231). She was also an advocate of the 'glass of water theory', which classified sex as a bodily urge just like thirst and should therefore be stilled as easily (and non-politically) as drinking a glass of water. This was regarded as utopic and controversial: 'My theses, my sexual and moral views, were bitterly fought by many Party comrades of both sexes'

(Kollontai 1971, 43; quoted in Hardt 2017, 786). In 1923, Kollontai was removed from the inner circle of power and sent to Norway as the first female ambassador in diplomatic history (Kollontai 2011).

Most national liberation movements, even though they recruited women into their military and political ranks, only paid lip service to women's equality, which led to contradicting policies concerning gender and sexuality and to tensions within the movements, as the example mentioned earlier illustrates. In the Maoist Movement in India, and the Chinese and Vietnamese revolutions the goal of gender equality was subordinated to the class struggle (Parashar & Shah 2017, 449), and no clear policy on sexual and personal relationships were formulated in the revolutionary agenda. In Vietnam sexual relations were not strictly forbidden but many women postponed sexual relations until after the revolution, when they were treated as scarred and infertile bodies (Lanzona 2009, 245–248). In the Chinese Communist Party, the requirement for the advancement of women was marriage with an important party leader, their authority being hinged on their sexual relations and the political rank of their men (Gilmartin 1995, 108–109). Similar to the PKK, sex between comrades was banned and punished in the LTTE in Sri Lanka. The movement's founder and leader Vellupillai Prabhakaran was an almost divine figure who simultaneously served as the sovereign, the government and the representative of his people. Under the banner of collectivity and discipline, women were tasked to 'through their intensive military training "defeminize" themselves to become "armed virgins" or "birds of freedom" to uphold male honour and valor' (Parashar 2009, 242). The Eritrean People's Liberation Front (EPLF), a Marxist organisation that fought for the independence of Eritrea from Ethiopia from 1970 onwards, initially tried to suppress sexual relations. However, after more women joined the EPLF, they introduced their own marriage law in 1977, treating both men and women as free individuals who could form partnerships based on love and equality. The couples continued to live a communal life with their units while their prime attachment was to the EPLF (Bernal 2001). Although there was a clear recognition of the importance of issues of sexuality as long as the struggle lasted, these ideas were dropped from the national agenda after independence and women struggled to hold on to this equality post-conflict (Hale 2001).

Moreover, thousands of women participated as spies, couriers, nurses, combatants and cooks in the Algerian War of Independence (1954–1962). This war set a precedence for women in liberation movements globally, partly because of women's everyday actions and partly because Franz Fanon suggested to a global audience that revolutionary violence had transformative power for women as well. Through revolutionary actions they could challenge patriarchal and feudal traditions and liberate themselves from their colonised feminine identities and defend their right to exist as autonomous human beings (White 2007). Feminist scholars have problematized Fanon's claim, by showing that women's participation in military operations does not automatically liberate them from exploitative relationships, that the psychological costs of war might be much more damaging than Fanon suggest, and that in Algeria, as in many other contexts, women's participation in national wars of liberation did not lead to long-term inclusion of women in the post-independence nation (Lazreg 1994; Salhi 2010; White 2007). Feminist scholars have further shown that sexuality is not only controlled during times of revolutionary struggle, but also during invasions and occupations (Al-Ali 2007), in state armies (Enloe 1993), nation-building processes (Najmabadi 2017) and reproductive politics (Puar 2017).

This short comparative perspective serves to illustrate that the PKK is not unique in negotiating women's roles within their movement, or policing the intimate relationships of its militants, neither in comparison to other Marxist-Leninist movements, nor state armies or state-building processes. However, apart from the LTTE, it is the only movement that forbids sexual relations in their totality for those who become armed militants. The way the that sexuality is regulated in the PKK, reminds us that the social contract always goes hand in hand with the 'sexual contract' (Pateman 1988), but also that this needs to be situated within the party's specific cultural and religious context. As a movement that emerged in a predominantly Muslim geography, values attached to the family, mothers and women's honour influenced the party, as discussed in the previous chapters. Moreover, the first generations of PKK cadres, among them Öcalan himself were married and some joined the party with their partners. It was only after the third party congress in 1986, where the characteristics of the militant were fixed that marriage, romantic and sexual relations were banned (interview with former commander 5, 12 October 2019).[4] In his defence writing in the mid-2000s, Öcalan finally made the 'abstinence contract' official by tying the liberation of women (and women cadres) to the liberation of the land and men. According to his argument, women cannot fulfil their revolutionary duties if they are kept in the slavery of marriage. He, however, strongly

---

[4] With the expansion of PKK rule into Northeastern Syria (Rojava) the rules concerning relationships and marriage have changed somewhat. While YPG/YPJ cadres are still not allowed to have relationships, married men can join the YPG. Married women are discouraged albeit not banned from joining. Much rather, the YPJ focuses on educating women early on and encourages them to obtain the identity of a 'free woman' and refrain from getting married in the first place.

advocates for love, as long as it transcends the sexual dimensions, the enslavement of women, and patriarchal culture as a whole (Öcalan 2010, 476–482). Contrary to many other national liberation movements, this means that militant women, at least in the armed sphere, do not have to carry the burden or pregnancies, gender-based violence, sexuality transmitted diseases, childrearing and housework. Instead women and men live sometimes in separate and often in mixed camps as comrades. What this means for the women I worked with and how they negotiated their femininity and sexuality within this new power matrix will be subject for the remainder of this chapter.

PKK's Body Politics: A Short History

Ideas of femininity and beauty for guerrillas and cadres working in the city have shifted over time. Zîn, a female cadre working in Sulaymaniyah, with whom I talked at length about body and sexuality in the diaspora, the different parts of Kurdistan, and in the mountains recounted how in 1999, when she joined the party in Europe, the dress code was very strict:

We dressed very unfeminine. [...] Standard was a loose pair of jeans, a big checkered shirt, which covered your hips and had long sleeves, and sometimes even a turtleneck sweater underneath that. The hair was tied in a ponytail, then sneakers and a backpack. That was standard cadre dress. We made sure we don't accentuate our female body parts. A lot changed after 2000, I assume that this was due to the developments in the fight. (Interview with Zîn, 27 August 2016)

After Abdullah Öcalan's arrest, the PKK went through an ideological and military crisis, with saw thousands of fighters and many cadres leaving the party. After 2004, when Öcalan released his new paradigm from prison in the form of his defence writings (abolishment of fighting for a Kurdish state, and a struggle for Democratic Confederalism instead), and the official announcement of Democratic Confederalism in 2005, did the party start to reorganise and regain momentum. Zîn linked the paradigm shift to slowly changing self-conceptions of what it meant to be revolutionary, a militant. In the 1980s, some women in the guerrilla were veiled, many had short hair and did not pluck their eyebrows or other facial hair. The idea was that the less attention you paid to your looks, the freer you were; the more you rejected common beauty standards, the more you had shed 'system life'. On the other hand, if a woman accentuated her feminine attributes too much, it was seen as a sign of wanting to get men's attention.

What is femininity? I think back then there weren't many discussions about it. Or what is womanhood? How do we have to understand it, what does it mean? I think for a long time there wasn't much engagement with this topic. But I do remember that after 2000 our sleeves got shorter, our things became a bit tighter, a bit more feminine. We sometimes wore sandals after that, a bracelet or a necklace. These things were for a long time frowned upon, because they were seen as jewellery and a free woman does not adorn herself. That was the prevailing understanding. (Ibid.)

The influence the guerrilla struggle had on the activists working in the politic sphere meant that similar beauty standards applied for women in the cities. 'Female guerrillas had embraced this kind of femininity [masculine femininity] as a way to legitimize themselves as fighters, and the style soon spread to nonguerrilla militant and activist women [...] in the cities.' (Düzel 2020, 183). Throughout the 1900s and 2000s, as the women's movement grew in size and power, questions of femininity were discussed at length; what does it mean to be a woman, to liberate women, and how does this affect the body? For example, Zîn elaborated, do women only take care of their outer appearance and wear jewellery because they want to please and attract the opposite sex? Goddesses in matriarchal societies such as in the Neolithic times were also depicted wearing jewellery, and they seem to have been independently powerful. Today many of the female party members wear bracelets and necklaces, which are often handmade with yarn and stones during the long winter months, when the snow prevents them from doing much else, apart from reading and education. This shift described by Zîn resonates with changing beauty practices in wider Kurdish society. Esin Düzel found that beauty plays an integral part in the way that women in Diyarbakir cultivate their political position, a shift that happened in the early 2000s, when the movement's focus on gender-equality mean that women became more visible in politics, at protests, and in the growing NGO sphere:

In this socially and politically fraught context, Kurdish women's beauty practices were charged with an extra layer of meaning. In the 2000s, gender equity became particularly important in the movement's efforts to distinguish itself from the ruling Islamist AKP party and from what the movement considered to be a gender-backward Middle East. Kurdish women were thus positioned as the catalyzers of a bottom-up, thorough transformation toward a democratic and autonomous society. (Düzel 2020, 183)

The new empowered Kurdish woman portrayed in Düzel's work on beauty salons in Diyarbakir, needed to navigate the fine line between embracing her 'natural beauty' and falling into the trap of Capitalist Modernity, which seeks to objectify and commodify bodies for capitalist consumption (ibid., 184). Düzel terms this a balancing act between 'moral autonomy' and 'moral unity', which speaks to my concept of 'party bargains', a process of taking on board the ideological canon and the political manoeuvring space it enables, and in certain instances, like in beautification practices, making it their own. Or as Düzel found, '[w]hile the ideal of naturalness can be a means of moral disciplining, it can also be made into a space for individuality, creativity, and self-care' (ibid., 189).

According to numerous accounts from my respondents, being 'unfeminine' was never the understanding of a 'free woman' for Öcalan. The early PKK cadres acted out of their own sense of contemporary revolutionary aesthetics, surely also influenced by the Turkish and other leftist movements. This dress code, however, was strictly enforced. An ex-guerrilla interviewed in Switzerland, recounted a story of a female guerrilla was allegedly killed for having rolled up her sleeves during a march on a hot summer day. The commander repeatedly told her to dress 'properly'. When she refused to roll her sleeves down, he took her behind a rock and shot her on the spot (former commander 4, 11 December 2017).[5] This apparently happened in the 1990s in the mountains, far away from Öcalan, who created his ideology and politics in Damascus, where the party headquarter was based until 1999. There, he had his own understanding of beauty; apparently, he was the one who eventually asked women to start taking care of themselves, let their hair grow long and pluck their facial hair (fieldwork notes, August 2016).

At the Academy in Damascus there was a swimming pool. Öcalan encouraged women to go swimming as part of their education, with the goal of overcoming body shame and strengthen their bodily awareness. This was a big deal, not only because women's bodies were more visible in a swimsuit, but also because many women (and men) depending where they were from in Kurdistan, did not know how to swim (interview with Newroz, 25 August 2016). Zîn recounted: 'One friend told me that she couldn't get herself to go into the water, after which Öcalan grabbed her, threw her in and held her under water. Just to test how she would resist against it. For him, this pool was very important pedagogically, for the women. [...] With the men he just played.' This may sound cultish, even abusive and depending which accounts of the party's training camp you weigh more it might just have been (Çürükkaya 1997). My data from that period are insufficient and inconclusive but I did confront one male commander with the more cultish elements of the party (e.g. its leadership cult)

---

[5] These kinds of stories are passed on by word of mouth and have not been independently verified. However, during the 1980s and 1990s there are many accounts of party commanders (and Öcalan) ordering to kill their own people for transgressions or suspicion of treason (Çürükkaya 1997; Marcus 2007).

and he simply brushed it off as 'every strong movement has cultish elements'. Cult notwithstanding, Öcalan seemed to be very concerned with women's beauty. 'Those who fight become free; those who are free become beautiful; those who become beautiful are loved', is one of his sayings that link his understanding of beauty to that of the liberation of the land (Öcalan 1994, quoted in Düzel 2020, 183). Commander Eyrehan told me that Öcalan was the one who taught them to stand straight, look confidently ahead, and speak loudly and clearly. That he pushed them to challenge the burden of shame and honour being attached to women's bodies, and to not see menstruation as a sickness (nexweşî), as was usually the case in rural Bakur in the early 1990s. 'He would tell us that it is not shameful or dirty, but that it can be a source of strength and power'. This was perhaps true in Syria, where Öcalan produced this knowledge. The reality of being a fighter with a female body in the mountains looked different, as one former commander told me:

All Kurds say slogans about women, or Bijî Gerîlla! (long live the guerrilla), but they don't know what happens in the mountains. They don't understand or can't understand. Menstruation is a big problem. We had [in the 1990s] no pads in the mountains. You couldn't talk about it. If the commander told you to go and do something you had to do it. But you are on your period and can't carry so much weight. It was still something shameful for women then. (Interview with former commander 3, 11 May 2018)

She also told me that women get colder, need more sleep and food, and can carry less weight during their period. If you are on an operation you cannot wash, and it starts to smell. Often when the guerrillas did not have pads they had to cut up their clothes and use the rags as pads. Another former commander shared the following story:

I have one memory: one [male] comrade went to a spot where we had previously hidden supplies; some flour, salt and bread and two packs of pads. It was winter and very very cold. When this comrade went to the hiding place and saw the pads he didn't understand what they were but saw that they were soft and warm and stuck them to his ears. He grew up in the village and couldn't read or write. When he came back and I saw what he had on his ears I didn't know if I should laugh or cry. I just said 'give me these, these are for women'. And he replied in protest, 'but heval, these are so nice and warm!' [laughs] (Interview with former commander 1, 14 May 2018)

These two interview excerpts illustrate that while men and women become the same in fighting and dying in the PKK, the women have to transgress not only more societal norms and expectations, but also overcome a different physical reality. This was used against them in the 1980s and 1990s when men tried to keep them from fighting as equals. Today, female guerrillas have better access to sanitary products, and they have more say in how they want to look. If they chose to pluck their eyebrows and wax body hair, they can do so. Many women have hormonal problems that can result in facial hair or acne. In that case they can write a report to the women's health committee and be sent to the doctor in the nearest town. This is a big shift; a few years ago, the women would have been criticised for not being revolutionary enough when caring about their looks. But according to Zîn, this is still not enough:

> [...] I do think that the body discourse is not being held sufficiently, this might also be due to the fact that we are currently in a time where everything is very political. I think many ideological projects and discussions of the women's movement were held in peaceful times, when there was a ceasefire or something. [...] At the moment there is a war and many things need to be organised, so little time remains to tackle new ideological projects or open new chapters. This is a problem in my opinion. It's not that the movement is dogmatic and closes itself off to certain topics. That's not it. But right now, there is so much war and death. And if you come now and say I would like to discuss this and that, they would say 'hello', we are currently in a different phase, this is not our most important problem. (Interview with Zîn, 27 August 2016)

According to the Kurdish Freedom Movement the Kurdish nation can only be free if its women are free, the national question is thus intimately linked to the 'women's question'. This quote illustrates that the same simultaneity does not apply to issues around sexuality, which are bracketed off as non-essential and postponed until more peaceful times when the revolution is not under constant duress.

The Desexualised Cadre Party

Today it is mainly women who discuss questions of gender norms and relations in the party. Every time I asked a male informant about issues related to women, they would either repeat the forever same liberation slogans, or say 'ask the women comrades'. The idea that party members would refrain from romantic or physical relationships, however, was suggested by the male leader Öcalan when the party took shape, with the argument that they would be operating under conditions of war and that relationships would be dangerous and a hindrance to the cause. Some founding members were married (such as Öcalan himself) and continued their relationships for a while. Others agreed to continue living as comrades. Sakine Cansız, the female co-founder of the PKK, fell in love with one of her comrades during her time in prison (1979–1990) and describes in her memoirs the difficulties she faced after her release, when she found out that he had allegedly betrayed the movement. Her conviction, however, never wavered:

I would have never given up the struggle for a man and a romantic relationship. Even during the early years of the movement, I refused to have relationships, which were incompatible with the struggle. If Şener [her partner] committed treason, the relationship has finished. All there was left to do for me was to continue struggling. (Cansız 2018, 69–70, *my translation*)

Öcalan later ordered the killing of Şener, which Sakine had to accept. There is no open criticism of the leadership in her memoirs, but it becomes evident that she struggled with the way the party had developed during her absence. The only serious challenge to the 'abstinence contract' came after Öcalan's arrest in 1999 and was pushed by his brother Osman. During the eighth congress at the end of 2003, Osman suggested party internal 'social reforms', including the right to relationships. 'He was an idiot, a feudal *gundi* (villager). He wanted to live like a tribal leader, where women served him. He said this reform is for everyone, but we understood that it is just for him', a woman who was in the guerrilla from 1993–2004 told me. The reform was rejected by women and men alike and Osman left the party in 2004. 'He was not a good man. He married a former guerrilla who he left soon after. Then he went to one of the big tribes in Başûr and got himself a very young girl' (interview with former commander 3, 31 March 2018).

Going back to *Women of a Non-State Nation: The Kurds (2001)*, the first, and for a long time, the only book on 'Kurdish women' I re-read sentences like: 'Women have been denied the right to control their own bodies, sexuality, and sexual desire. The right to control women's sexuality is conferred on the male members of the family, tribe, community, nation and the modern state' (Hassanpour 2001, 227). I am tempted to say that once a woman joins the PKK, her sexuality is no longer in the hands of a male or state power, but in the hands of the party, and so women only switch their bargaining partner. While this is perhaps true, the practice thereof is not quite so simple, because by becoming a party subject, women gain a whole new set of tools and a different form of bodily autonomy. Once a party member for example, no men can make unwanted advances, and if someone does, there are strict protocols of prosecution in place. Furthermore, as I have argued in Chapter 3, through education and internalising the ideology, women gain a history, self-confidence and find their voice, which has allegedly been buried since the Neolithic times. Over the years, I have heard many arguments about why the party institutionalised the sex ban. Explanations range from needing to abide by conservative societal norms, so families would let their daughters go to the mountains, to the need to focus on the struggle against a male-dominated system and nothing else, to the danger of becoming pregnant or dependent on a partner, or the argument that romantic love could lead to preferences amongst comrades, when everyone should be equal. These are the more practical arguments, the ideological argument stresses that the conditions have to be created first for women and men to be truly equal, before relationships should be formed and lived. This refers to Öcalan's concept of the 'free and shared life' (*jiyana azad û hevpar*), the leadership's vision of the relationships of the future, where free men and women in the revolutionised society will have truly equal relationships.[6] In the meantime it would be non-sensical to have relationships with men, when they are fighting against a male dominated system. However, this always and only concerns civilians; guerrillas will remain sexless forever. Moreover, I often encountered the argument that guerrillas are somehow above romantic human relationships, that their task holds something sacred, and that there is no space for earthly urges such as the pleasures of the flesh (Solina 1997; Herausgeberinnenkollektiv 2012; Wolf 2004).

Power and control play an important part in this process of becoming a militant, not just the party's control over its members, but members in relation to each other, and each member's *oto-kontrol* (self-control) over her or his body. I asked Sipan, a male commander, how *oto-kontrol* works precisely:

First, you have to believe. If you believe you can resolve things in your body. Sexuality, hunger and other things. After you believe you can control yourself with *perwerde* [education]. Because in *perwerde* you learn how you can control yourself. And then in practice, often you cannot find free time. So you cannot think about sex.

IK: What exactly do you have to believe?
Your ideology. Apoism. I believe in Apoism! The ideology says you can control yourself, you can educate your body, teach your body. Women or men, there is no difference.

IK: What are the techniques for that?
First, you have to delete some things in your mind. And you have to believe. You have to trust yourself. When you say I cannot do something, you can't do it. But when you say I can do this, I can control myself for example, everything is possible. That's why I said you have to believe first, in the ideology and yourself. You can lie about everything to everybody. But you cannot lie to yourself. (Interview with Sipan, 5 September 2016)

The belief Sipan describes here is central in the process of subjectivation and education is a key site where this belief is strengthened and refined. Party education not only gives people an intellectual education, and an identity, but also regulates their life with each other. The night Zemyan and I walked down the mountain from one camp to the other, she told me that if

---

[6] The Kurmancî word *hevpar* can also be translated as collective, the idea being that both partners are equally free and responsible.

someone acts out (e.g. falls in love, has sex or disobeys the rules in another way), he or she has to go back to education where most people find their way back to the right path. I later asked Sipan to clarify this for me:

Perwerde cannot give you everything. *Perwerde* is for you to have free time to think [...]. About yourself, your work, your practice. Because in practice you are always with your friends, maybe 20–30 people, but in *perwerde* you are with yourself. You have free time just for thinking. You don't have work, you don't have anything; no phone, no internet. You only have books, you can read. Because when you read you can think. So you can understand your problems and how to improve. So after a problem you have to go to *perwerde*. It means, you have to be relaxed, but in work you cannot be relaxed. Only when you are relaxed you can think. (Interview with Sipan, 5 September 2016)

What sounds like a comfortable retreat is in fact a highly disciplinary and punitive process, where disgraced party members have to relearn to perform their allegiance. After education, they have to face criticism and self-criticism and renew their oath (*soz*) in front of comrades and commanders. With one hand on Öcalan's book and the other as a fist at your heart, gaze upward, they pledge allegiance to the flag, weapon and honour, and to the martyrs, comrades, the party and leader Apo.[7]

According to this narrative, in education you learn to control your mind and bodily urges, which in turn should give you the power to persevere and 'make the struggle bigger'. A commander who spent twenty-four years in the party and did not have an intimate relationship for twenty-two of those years explained the process of desexualisation differently:

You become cold. The sexual energy that people have goes after a while. You always see death, you are always close to death. Life there is so difficult. That is the first thing. And second, you always have to control yourself, also with regards to sex [...]. As a result, your psychology, your body, and your hormones change. For example, when I didn't get my period for two years the doctor in Iraq said it is early menopause. I was 38. Now I am 42, and the doctor here said no this is not menopause. Why did I not get my period? Because of the life we lived. We were always cold, hungry or tired, this all has an impact on your psychology and your body. But again, you are supposed to use *oto-kontrol*. (Interview with former commander 2, 20 July 2018)

What she powerfully described as 'becoming cold', and Sipan termed 'deleting certain things in your mind', shows that *oto-kontrol* is a powerful tool for continuing the struggle and surviving life in the party, though with unpredictable and painful physical side effects. Meanwhile, in the women's

---

[7] The full oath in Kurdish: *Ez li ser al, çek û namûsa xwe soz didim. Soz didim şehîdan, soz didim hevalan, soz didim gel, soz didim partiyê, soz didim serok Apo. Soz didim. Soz didim. Soz didim.*

academies, every imaginable discussion about philosophy, ideology, liberation and also sexuality has been and continues to be held:

> I think this is the biggest difference between the Kurdish women's movement and other women's movements. Two things. Firstly ideological: I assume that no other movement has fought the ideological fight as hard as the Kurdish movement. And then the state of being organised. I think there isn't any other women's movement in the world that is as well organised. But these two things depend on each other again, the ideological struggle and being organised, it as a dialectic process. So we are well organised because we are so ideological, and we are so ideological because we are so organised. (Interview with Zîn, 27 August 2016)

What Zîn describes as a dialectic process here reflects the claim of exceptionalism and sustainability: because the women's movement is organised in the armed, political and ideological sphere, it can safeguard its achievements and advance more rapidly than other women's movements. Within this expanding set of ideas, crucial discussions have been held around the concepts of relationships, marriage and family. Since the mid-1990s Öcalan has pushed his party members to think about what it would mean to revolutionise personal and family relations. At first, it was part of the intellectual exercise trainees had to do during their time at the Academy in the Beqaa Valley or in Damascus. The questions and outcomes (his 'Analyses') were recorded, transcribed and sent to the camps in the mountains. He was not only concerned with dismantling the existing order but in revolutionising society by addressing these questions. Since then, the theoretical and ideological discussions around sexuality have been held during times of cease fires or relative peace (e.g. 2000–2005, 2013–2015), and were considered secondary when the wars resumed. Importantly, ideas around a female guerrilla's purity, an almost mystical untouchable hero status, extend beyond her years as an active fighter. Nerina Weiss traces the story of Zehra, a former guerrilla, who after many years in a Turkish prison takes up political cadre work. When she decides to get married and therewith transgress the norms attached to her status, she is accused of betrayal and removed from her position. Zehra turns into a *persona non grata* because she chose to be desired, rather than merely being loved for fighting, as envisioned by the party and illustrated in the Öcalan quote mentioned earlier (Weiss 2010).

Friendship and Love

Concepts such as friendship and platonic love are key to holding the party together. Especially the concept of friendship (*hevaltî*) carries a great deal of meaning and weight. Upon joining the guerrilla ranks, recruits cut the ties with their family and civilian life. They become a *Heval*, which means friend in its literal translation but also carries the meaning of comrade. *Hevals* are trained and expected to give everything to the struggle and if need be to die for their friends. They also become equal insofar as that it does not matter where they are from (rural, urban, class, education) everyone is treated the same way, and it is not people's intellectualism or the lack of it that counts, but their practice. Practice means accumulation of life and battle experience and becoming proficient at a certain discipline (sabotage, sniper etc.). Education and ideology play a crucial role in getting people to become good comrades. In class and daily life in the education camps, recruits learn to look out for each other and treat each other with generosity and kindness, but also criticise each other if needed (fieldwork notes, August 2016). Friendship is also based on communal life: everyone pulls his or her weight in the camp, from the high commander to the new recruit, and washing, cooking, and cleaning are not only left up to the subaltern. Friendship also means taking care of the lesser abled. In each camp I went to, there was at least one person who was in some way handicapped. These women and men receive some education and training but cannot participate in the armed operations. However, their peers are expected to treat them with dignity and respect. One young girl I met in one of the guerrilla camps was found abandoned in a city of Rojhelat, so the cadres decided to take her to the mountains. There she would not speak for months, having been traumatised by her violent past. When I met her, her speaking had improved and she constantly ran around making tea, cooking, and trying to please her comrades. 'Sit down, relax', the commanders told her. 'No I cannot, I am a guerrilla now,' she replied and hurried up the hill towards another chore. 'We'd rather have her here where she is treated well, than back in society where the system treats people like her terribly,' the commander told me (ibid.).

As I have argued throughout this book, education is a core component of the PKK and almost every party member expressed pride in the intellectual achievements of the movement. However, that does not mean that if a new recruit joins, he or she gets to influence theory or knowledge production. It means memorising and internalising the ideology. If new fighters have a background in political philosophy and have been to university they are still treated like everyone else. Because living the communal life also requires cultivating a discourse that everyone understands. 'There is no point in me speaking in big words or theoretical concepts because I came from a university, if my friend from the village doesn't understand', another commander assured me. 'In the beginning I showed off my theoretical knowledge, I wanted to have these big discussions in education. Until one teacher got angry, telling me we will speak again once I had been to the frontline a few times'. This shows that the fighters only get to speak about the philosophies of liberation, when they have proven themselves on the battlefield. Even then they not able to challenge the ideology. A former commander told me about her frustration with these set ways:

When I joined the party, I thought everyone can talk and criticise freely. Before the PKK was like that; all Hevals could discuss and there wasn't one boss. It was a really good group and the [intellectual] quality was high with Mazlum Doğan, Hayri Durmuş and Kemal Pir. There was Haki Karer as well, they were intelligent and smart people. Many of the first generation were arrested [before and during the 1980s coup] and died, and Öcalan went to Syria. He built an academy in the Baqaa valley. There his whole behaviour changed, from then on, everyone said 'yes leader'. People couldn't speak their minds. And then many people came back from prison and were shocked. Before they could just say Heval Ali – Öcalan's other name is Ali – and they could speak in a friendly manner. But now it was different, there was a distance and you had to say yes to everything. (Interview with former commander 3, 11 May 2018)

She later told me that is was exactly this lack of being able to criticise that eventually pushed her to leave the party, combined with the fact that she disagreed with the political direction the party was taking after the arrest of Öcalan.

One night in the mountains, I asked commander Nurhak about love, 'You have been a commander for many years, you must have seen people falling in love, even though it is not allowed?'. She replied:

Yes I did, it happens. But when you realise it, you talk to them and they understand. One time I had these two fighters in my group who fell in love, everyone saw it and knew it, they were cute. They didn't act on it, but he would save his sugar cube to secretly give to her later when they were shaking hands, because he knew she loved sugar. Or she would give him an apple, but he would cut it in seven pieces to give one to everyone in the group. They could never be a couple, always saying that their struggle for Kurdistan is more important and that they will use that love for each other to make their struggle bigger. He later became şehîd. (Fieldwork notes, 24 August 2016)

This romantic story of shared and communal love is also deeply tragic. Not every commander is as lenient and understanding as Nurhak. Loving couples are usually separated, have to write a self-critical report, are sent to different parts of Kurdistan, and most likely never see each other again. Because officially, love is platonic in the party. Yet people still have sex and some women get pregnant. Especially former commanders shared many harrowing stories about the killing of pregnant women, of forced abortions or expulsion from the party, especially during the 1980s and 1990s. Today, if a woman fighter gets pregnant she has three choices:

abortion, give birth and give the child to a sympathiser family (e.g. in Maxmûr) or leave. Whatever her decision, if she decides to stay in the party after, she would still have to go through the same criticism/self-criticism and education procedure as anyone else who transgresses and would only be welcomed back after about one year of punishment (interview with former commander 2, 20 July 2018). Officially, party members are allowed to love but cannot act on it in terms of favouring that person or having physical intimacy. *Hevals* are equal in life and death, during a battle you are obliged so save everyone equally. Romantic love is seen as a civilian desire. As a revolutionary you learn to redirect that love elsewhere: towards your friends, your leader, your land and its struggle. Love itself becomes communal. According to Zîn:

In our movement a lot is about sociality: how to you strengthen that part of an individual. It is not about killing the individual and sacrificing yourself for society. But our movement has shown that you can live this feeling (of sociality) not only with one person. Because we carry so many people in our hearts, countless people really. There are different forms of love. [...] I think that for true love between two people, social love is necessary. To really experience love on the individual level you have to also be social. And I think this is the main problem in society. That this social component is missing. (Interview with Zîn, 27 August 2016)

Zîn's assessment of the different forms of love can also be found in the official party ideology, in which Öcalan, particularly from the 1990s onwards, envisaged the revolution to be a 'revolution of love' (Öcalan 1999, quoted in Çağlayan 2020, 73). In his interpretation of love, it is no longer possible to experience love in the old family structure, with its oppressive structures for both men and women. 'Instead, real love could only be realized by replacing sexual love with love for the *patrie*' (ibid.). As a result, love was desexualised and became a communal love for the people, the comrades and the leadership. This resonates with Marxist literature on love, which suggests that a love, which is free of appropriation and possession has the power 'to generate social bonds and organise social relationships' in a radically new way (Hardt 2011, quoted in Salih 2017, 744, Berlant 2011).

The Tireless Politician

Bringing these partly revolutionised gender norms and relations down from the mountains and into the civilian spheres is a daily challenge. No doubt, policing sexuality makes sense for the army, which has to be always at the ready and disciplined, but also a safe and equal space for women.

But what is the position of sexuality within a free and democratic relationship, outside mountain life? One cadre put it as follows:

Sexuality can be a tool for reproduction and a part of life, but it is not life itself. People are degraded to sex slaves in daily life. The dominant ideology is responsible for that, it makes people insignificant and reduces them to their desires. In contrast, human relationships should be built on mutual understanding. That is also true for the relationship between men and women. Sexual relationships can be an expression of that, but they are not essential and not permanent. A society that is reduced to its desires is burdened by too many aggressions. Women become a tool to satisfy these desires and are used as birth machines. (Şafak, quoted in Herausgeberinnenkollektiv 2012, 107, *my translation*)

One of the core goals of the Kurdish women's movement is illustrated in this quote: to take women out of the house, and out of the familial control, where she has been reduced to a labourer. This resonates with Marxist and queer feminist critiques of the nuclear family as a site for women's oppression and exploitation or as a space that reproduces and enforces heteronormative values (Butler 2002; Fraser & Nicolson 1988; Peterson 1985). Usually the party disseminates its liberation ideology through cadres who organise the women's activities in the cities through education, media campaigns and conferences. In Diyarbakir, like in other cities in Turkey's southeast, where the movement has a long history and strong social backing, the women's movement used to run numerous institutions, cooperatives and academies. These structures were organised under the umbrella of KJA, the Congress of the Free Women. Not all KJA members were also members of the PKK; they were politicians, lawyers, activists, but they all followed the party line in terms of language and organisational structures. Networks of parallel power structures were built to counter the state, to build an alternative way of governing. Before the state-backlash from 2015 to today, each civilian woman close to the movement or working in its structures as an activist, would sooner or later go through a party education course. KJA offered educational courses in Jineolojî and a one-month KJA course was mandatory for every woman who wanted to work in a municipality in Bakur.

Contrary to 'the mountains', relationships are not forbidden in the civilian sphere; women can work for KJA and be married and have children; however, home life comes after party life. The women of the movement often assured me that relationships sooner or later become unequal, that the man will show his true patriarchal face, even if this is not visible from the start, and will try to control women, restrict their freedom of movement, or have family expectations. Ideally, the civilian woman would thus control and restrict her bodily desires and focus solely on the struggle, which means putting all her energy into organising work. Ayşe Gökkan told me of the importance of *oto-kontrol* for women:

Women should decide for herself, what women want is important for us. But *oto-kontrol* is important for us too, because men use women and we are against that. Men use women and they kill them because of honour. When we discussed this, we realised that we are nothing for men, only a sex tool. In capitalism, women's bodies are for sale, they use women's bodies everywhere. [...] When two people love each other, they can have sex freely. But after sex men use women. That's why we say you should be aware of this. Generally, we think if men's mentality is like this, you can't have free [equal] relationships with men. (Interview with Ayşe Gökkan, 14 November 2015)

This illustrates that the 'abstinence bargain' is also applicable in the civilian sphere, albeit in an adapted form that tries to prevent women from entering unhealthy and unequal relationships. Some party members have similar views on having children; do not have them, or do not have too many because you will become a slave to the family. Sakine Cansız, murdered in Paris in 2013, one of the founders and most important female figures of the PKK, is quoted to have said:

This [patriarchal family] is a system that we reject. That's why we are against the classical family. This is the core of our critique for the family and the patriarchal structures, that women are seen as birth-mothers *[Gebär-Mütter]*. Instead we say that if children don't have the possibility to grow up in a free society and speak their own language, it is better they are never born. Instead of living in slavery, we prefer to not exist. This is our philosophical departure point. (Herausgeberinnenkollektiv 2012, 68, *my translation*)

She goes on to argue that due to politics of oppression and marginalisation, Kurdish men have no other domain available for domination than the family, thus they think that a big family is a sign of power, but that this is all burdened onto the shoulders of women. In this case, sexuality has nothing to do with love anymore. 'That's why it is important for us that women create their own sphere of influence, their own self-confidence. Sexuality cannot be used as a tool for domination, but there needs to be (bodily) autonomy of women' (ibid.). She refers to a sentiment that I encountered many times: as long as relationships cannot be 'democratic and free', meaning equal and free of power hierarchies, women should better stay far away from men. This raises the question of same-sex intimacy; if men dominate everything and women are free, why not shift to sex, love and intimacy with women? (Najmabadi 2005, 2013). It certainly happens in the cities, like everywhere, but it also happens in the mountains, albeit rarely. Again, this is a taboo subject that was difficult to broach during fieldwork and could only be addressed during interviews with former cadres: 'I only saw it [homosexual relations] a few times. It is not acceptable and usually the party would send them back to their families' (interview with former commander 5, 12 October 2019). The same harsh policing is not practiced in the cities but in both places the old and new notions of honour need to be preserved, and physical and emotional intimacy need to be controlled in order to have an army of militant subjects, who do not find freedom and fulfilment in pairs but in the larger communal movement.

The women of KJA in Diyarbakir were bearing the double burden of being a politician or activist while also doing housework, and being a mother, sister, wife or friend. If women wanted to be respected by the movement, they had to continuously perform and demonstrate their allegiance; working tirelessly in the public sphere, organising people, events and demonstrations. Working included many communal teas, smoking cigarettes, pacing up and down the garden, endless meetings and discussions. In the evenings they would continue their work by visiting the homes of martyr families to pay their respects and discuss politics. Earthly things like sleep, intimacy or privacy seemed negligible. This does not mean that they did not come together around a table and share deliciously prepared food, but it was usually a hasty affair given the context of permanent war; within a few minutes the first women would push their plates away and light a cigarette.

Aside from theory and practice, considering how the war has intensified since mid-2015, and how horrendous Turkey's state violence against Kurds has been, sexuality and intimacy simply became marginal. 'The war permeates your whole life; it comes right into your bedroom. How can you have a good relationship under these circumstances?' I often heard during my time in Diyarbakir.

The Steadfast Mother

One way to assess how gender norms and relations are being challenged when it comes to body and sexuality is to assess the changing understanding of what shame and honour mean to women of different ages and in different contexts I conducted fieldwork in between the cities and the mountains.[8] This was not my primary research focus but as a woman

---

[8] As a side activity, I made a list of *şerm-s* during my time in Maxmûr, incomplete as it is: crossing your legs while sitting and speaking with people formally, sitting in a relaxed manner in front of guerrillas or men, laziness, being idle, riding a bike, exposing your body during sports, ripped jeans (fashion), talking back to your parents, being a single parent, chewing gum (especially during the wakes), revoking invitations, arrogance, unreliability, and celebrating festivities when there are too many martyrs.

living in the region I became very receptive to the exclamation of '*şerm e!*' (it is shameful!). It would be said just flippantly and teasingly in conversations, but even then, it says a lot about a continuing set of societal norms that determine what is deemed right and wrong. An interesting hybrid place to observe the party's quest to change ideas of womanly shame, other than the mountains is Maxmûr. One evening in the summer of 2016, Şehristan, her two daughters and I were walking home after an event, when a few kids were cycling past. The daughters told them to stop, wanting to borrow the bikes for the ride up the hill. The mother, otherwise supportive of women's liberation according to the party script, shouted out in horror, 'You are not getting on these bikes, how shameful!' The daughters just ignored her and rode off. The mother stomped up the hill, murmuring to herself in anger. As I do so often, I laughed in order to diffuse the situation and asked: 'Why is this shameful?' 'It is not proper for girls to ride bikes', was her curt answer. 'Why not?' I inquired, 'It is cultural,' she replied. I could not get much more out of her before the girls returned, laughing and making fun of their mother's conservatism. The mother, while active in so many of the party's and town's organisational bodies and an avid admirer or Abdullah Öcalan himself, was clearly holding on to a set of more conservative norms of shame and honour.

Another evening, during my third stay with the family, relaxing after a big dinner Şehristan told me: 'Isabel you are like a daughter to me, you will always be my daughter'. Before this stay I had been very sick with a painful stomach infection, the bloating side effect of which made me look about four months pregnant. We started joking about my big belly and about how I might be pregnant, which led to me saying that I do not want to get married and that in Europe you can have children without being married. There the fun ended; with a stern face the mother said: 'If you ever have a child without getting married, you will no longer be my daughter'. Again, my half-naïve/half-researcher question – why? 'In our culture it is not possible, and it would be shameful for everyone'. End of discussion. In the late hours, after the mother was asleep, the daughter and I kept discussing these societal limits or 'borders' (*sinor*) as she called them. After I told her a bit about my experiences she told me that things concerning women's sexuality cannot be changed by the Kurdish Freedom Movement alone but will only change over generations.

The Kurdish women's movement has a large ideological canon that explains the toxic interplay between state, capitalism, patriarchy (Hennessy 2000) and religion and its results for women and the construction of woman's 'honour'. In August 2016, I was in a car with Newroz, a commander of KJAR, the women's branch working in Rojhelat. We were both being driven back to the mountains, where I was to spend another week in party education. During the two-hour drive we started talking about shame and honour and I told her how I was getting tired of everything being shameful and that I thought it was one of the problems of Kurdish society as I had come to understand it, to attach so much potential shame to women's bodies. Newroz was pleased with my comments and later repeated them to the highest commander of the camp, Leyla Agirî. She confirmed that this is one of their key, but most difficult, battles; to remove notions of shame and honour from women's bodies and to remove these bodies out of male, familial, conservative and religious control. As the party mobilises more women into its ranks, it moves them from one matrix of domination into the other. Once a member, the recruits gain a new understanding of what it means to be a woman. Here, the civil/mountain divide is huge. Female guerrillas are very much aware of the problems and construction of the concepts of shame and honour, often having been victims of it themselves, before joining the party. They know how the female body has always been and continues to be a battleground for different political narratives and claims of power (Gill & Brah 2014; Gill 2014; Ortner 1978; Schneider 1971; Welchman & Hossain 2005; Wikan 2008). When mirrored with the grim reality of Rojhelat or Iraqi Kurdistan, where women are killed on a regular basis because they dare to overstep or are believed to have overstepped certain lines of their bodily and family honour, the two spheres seem worlds apart (Alinia 2013; Begikhani, Gill & Hague 2015; Fischer-Tahir 2009). However, feminist scholarship on gender and sex-based violence in the Middle East, and on Kurdish women in Iraqi Kurdistan in particular, have complicated the binary between shame and honour and have argued that while ideas around shame and honour persist in society, any analysis thereof needs to consider the family, society and the state's role in failing to institutionalise and implement the rule of law, and contributing to and maintaining structures of physical, emotional, mental and financial violence against women (Abu-Lughod 2011; Jabiri 2016; Joseph 1999; Keli 2018).

The education course I participated in was also attended by seven female refugees from Rojhelat, who were living in and around Ranyia, a city in Northern Iraq. PJAK, the Iranian branch of the PKK, is not only investing in education in the villages and cities of Rojhelat, but they also mobilise the Rojhelati refugees. The course covered the basics of Abdullah Öcalan's liberation ideology: the importance of education; the history of the PKK; the history of PKK women; Jineolojî; and the Iranian regime and women. To end the week the women all went through the criticism and self-criticism (*platform*) exercise.

Also in this camp, the day was structured around a disciplined routine: breakfast at 6.00 a.m., the morning lesson from 7.30–11.00 a.m., followed by a lunch break and lessons again from 1.00–4.00 p.m. The education tent was a few hundred metres from the communal area, a simple construction that provided shade in the 45-degree heat in those August weeks. Almost all the women had brought their babies or young children to the camp. The youngest ones crawled around the tent during our lessons, whereas the older ones were being entertained with crafts and other activities by the guerrillas in the communal area. Each day a different cadre was our teacher and it became clear that they all followed the main education books but, depending on the teacher, this was more or less engaging and critical. The first day, for example, Şervin only read from a book for hours on end, with short intermissions, when we watched educational videos about a famous female martyr. Şervin also repeatedly used the opportunity of having a European in her course, to make her points about the weak, victimised, sexualised European women, who even as a feminist, remains marginal and an object of capitalism. 'Isn't it like this Isabel?', she would say to seek my approval of her arguments. When I said, 'Well, yes and no, there are different capitalist and state systems and many women's movements that understand how it is all linked', she nodded impatiently, wanting to bring her argument to a close, back to what Abdullah Öcalan said about the matter. Şervin was also one of the defenders of the argument that homosexuality is a side product of capitalism and that lesbianism is a reaction to feminists hating men, as will be further discussed subsequently.

The PKK is by no means a monolithic organisation and its ranks are made up of women with different experiences and levels of education prior to joining the party, or interest in furthering their knowledge beyond Öcalan's books. Nurhak for example, our teacher on the second day, had been in the party for more than twenty years, eight of which she had spent in a Turkish prison. There, she read constantly and still gets her friends in Turkey to send her books to the mountains. When I met her, she had retired from active combat and was working in 'diplomacy', a broad term that encompasses everything from knowledge production, to teaching, organising in the cities, to actual foreign relations. She was a fantastic storyteller; her lessons were engaging and full of hope. We all hung on her every word when she told us about how women discovered wheat cultivation in Neolithic times, or when she told us the story of Şahmaran, the mythical snake women and guarding of female wisdom. Her fiery and heartfelt slogans of resistance were optimistic that the party truly is the alternative: 'Women are deliberately kept like imprisoned falcons, believing that they are not capable of things, not able to fly. But you can overcome these borders if you strengthen yourself, if you love yourself and open your eyes to the condition you are kept in' (fieldwork notes, 24 August 2016).

Özgür, our teacher on the third day told us that her name (meaning freedom in Turkish) was given to her because she had always been a rebel in the party, constantly running into trouble because she liked to do things her way and not the party way. She was working as a KCK activist in the civilian sphere for many years, before the heavy state crackdown on the KCK in the late 2000s made her work too dangerous. That is when she joined the guerrilla. She was also clearly bored in her role as head of this academy and anxious to get back to the front line. I later saw her in a music video about the defence of Afrin, joyous and wide-eyed. During her lesson, she made complex connections between state and domestic violence, demonstrating the continuum of violence using women's bodies. She also talked freely about what kind of sexuality the party believes in:

Friends, now I am going to say something a bit embarrassing but we are amongst women so I can be relaxed. Why does the man always want to be on top during sex? [. . .] Why do they instantly turn away and falls asleep when they are done? It's because of the male mentality, we say every family is a small state and the man wants to oppress women. (Fieldwork notes, 25 August 2016)

She went on to talk about the importance of consensual sex, also in marriage, about foreplay and how important it is that women get aroused before sex in order to experience pleasure. She told the women that Apo is against women getting married younger than twenty-five, and that they should not have more than two children, but instead raise those well in order to build a better society. She gave them tips of how to take care of their bodies and live a healthy and active life. She talked at length about the importance of mothers, to break old stereotypes of shame (nakedness, breastfeeding, marrying at an older age), and raise more conscious patriots who know their history and culture and refuse to be assimilated into the Persian culture. 'Don't just give your children tablets and computers, tell them stories, teach them about mythology and sociology, and spend time with them'. In her lesson she made mothers the key force behind building a stronger community, saying that they are crucial to building an awareness that can resist the imperial powers and regimes who want to keep Kurds ignorant and poor. I doubt that Şervin could have given us this lesson and that the ease with which Özgür talked came largely from her experiences pre-party, as well as the many discussions she seemed to have been part of within the party, which revolved around female liberation and its links to body politics.

A lot of the education also consisted of the women sharing their experiences, often heart-breaking stories of poverty and suffering, at the hands of their families or the Iranian state. This course was about spreading Öcalan's ideas and gaining more civilian support, but for the women themselves it was also a space to be heard and listened to, by the ever-understanding and supportive guerrillas. I was left conflicted, as always: amazed by the thoroughness and identity-creating strength of this ideology and movement and overwhelmed by its density and claim to truth. Nevertheless, it also became clear that while there is one unifying 'truth', given by Abdullah Öcalan, there are many women in the party who find their own words to speak about, teach and live it.

Body Politics within the PKK: The Question of LGBT

So far, I have read my data from a heteronormative position, because the movement upholds a strict gender binary and persons of diverse sexual orientation, gender identity or gender expression are a topic that is sparsely talked about in daily conversation or formal interviews. The movement has an uncomfortable relationship with LGBT issues, due to a mix of conservatism, and sexual identities generally being a marginal subject in the larger struggle for Kurdish liberation. Additionally, they say life in the mountains is not well suited for queer folks, due to the camps often being gender-segregated, which means men live and work mostly with men and women with women.[9] Towards the end of my fieldwork I started asking the members I had a good rapport with about their views on LGBT issues. The answers varied. One male commander told me: 'This is an army, if you join you become a soldier and have to control your sexuality. It doesn't matter if you are hetero or homosexual. If you can do that, it is no problem for me, but if your sexual orientation causes problems within the army, you have to leave' (interview with Agir, 5 July 2016). A female commander told me that homosexuality is an illness invented by the Greeks and accentuated by Capitalist Modernity. According to her homosexuals had problems due to bad experiences in their life, which can be solved through party education (interview with Newroz Cizre, 25 August 2016). Other respondents emphasised that the

---

[9] Women and men are never alone for more than two hours. Two hours are considered enough to discuss work-related issues; everything that exceeds this time frame is considered dangerous, potentially leading to romantic or sexual temptations.

PKK hesitates to embrace LGBT issues because of the need to appeal to a conservative constituency. A cadre who worked in the civilian sphere reiterated that while she had always supported the struggle of queer folks, to her sexuality is something private and not a social or political category and should not be treated as such (fieldwork notes, August 2016).

Some of the opinions noted here reflect the personal experiences of party members who do not categorically reject homosexuality, while others who do are indicative of the party line: Öcalan was always clear in his view of same-sex love and intimacy, describing it as 'unnatural', a 'cancer of society' and a result of Capitalist Modernity, a system that seeks to dominate all of society, and men who as a result dominate women and other men, turning them into homosexuals (Öcalan 2013b, 124). In 2013, Öcalan, in his conversation with Pervin Buldan and Selahattin Demirtaş, who visited him on Imralı Island as part of the peace process talks between 2013 and 2015, is quoted to have said: 'The concept of gender liberation (*cinsiyet özgürlükçü*) that you always use is not correct. Do not use this concept again because everyone understands its differently. It is more important to say women's liberation. Use this in all institutions' (Öcalan 2015, 104–105). Here, Öcalan orders his party to focus its struggle on women, and not use terminology that could give grounds to call for the equality of queer folks. Despite this, the HDP, an alliance of Kurdish and Turkish leftists, anti-capitalist, anti-racist, anti-homophobic, anti-nationalist, anti-sexist and pro-peace ethnic religious minority organisation, in 2015, ran with an inclusive party programme (Burç 2018). The top PKK commanders such as Cemîl Bayık subsequently criticised them, saying that the HDP should stay away from 'marginal groups' in Beyoğlu, arguing that the Kurdish people are not ready for this alliance (interview with former commander 2, 20 July 2018; interview with former commander 5, 12 October 2019; Haberler 2014).

Women from the movement have also written about this topic, for example in the Jineolojî book, which is a collection of essays by female prisoners (Özgür Kadın Akademisi 2016). I asked an LGBT activist and party sympathiser from Diyarbakir to tell me about its content during our interview.[10] He emphasised that this book was very important for women's struggles but in terms of sexuality and LGBT issues it was not satisfying for him. He picked one of the articles that addresses the issue specifically and paraphrased the author who says same-sex couples reproduce problematic and oppressive gender norms, for example one woman is fem and the other is butch. And that same-sex couples cannot reproduce, hinting that homosexual relations are abnormal. According to my interlocutor:

[10] It was only later that I had certain parts of the book translated.

There isn't any politics on LGBTI, there is only a part of an article. But we know [...] that the Kurdish political movement doesn't want to talk about these issues. And I also mean the youth organisations, KJA, and other women cooperatives. Also [...] they have written this book in prison, where they discuss all these issues. But they are not involved in LGBTI issues. And also in the mountains, they haven't got any idea. Maybe they don't want [to be involved] because the PKK is a social movement, Islam is social, women's problems are social, capitalism critique is social, but sexuality maybe not social, it may be personal. [...] They talk about sexuality but not free sex, free sex should not be the issue. But you must have a politics on sexuality, and partnership, relationship, marriage. (Interview with anonymous, 2 December 2015)

He stressed that the PKK is not homogenous and that of course you cannot say it is homophobic. But that it is very difficult as a homosexual guerrilla in the mountains, or for a LGBT group who wants to march visibly alongside the movement during protests for example. According to him, the LBGT movement needs the endorsement of the leadership:

If he [Öcalan] says homosexuality is not an illness, it is not forbidden, it is not a sin, it is not a part of immorality or part of assimilation, decadence of capitalism, if he said something like that and argued his opinions with many many references, if he did something like that it would be OK. But I think he won't be so clear because of the society. Because PKK is a social movement. (Ibid.)

This assessment speaks to the movement's difficult navigation between conservatism, discomfort and necessity, and supports Maha El Said's argument that effective resistance has to be in accordance with what is perceived as local culture and identity (El Said 2015, 129). LGBT issues are an area that challenges the party's essentialist binary between femininity and masculinity and its strict control thereof. The HDP made a promising start when it endorsed all LGBT groups ahead of the 2015 elections, but evidently, the question of sexuality remains, and understandably so. Zîn explains:

Our revolution is based on simultaneity, but many things we cannot do simultaneously. On such topics [sexuality, femininity, love], the ideological process continues, these things are being discussed and have an influence on life. And our lives have an influence on the theoretical production process. But it is not one line, but fluctuates. [...] This is the dialectic of our struggle. [...] There is no dogmatism or absolutism. (Interview Zîn, 27 August 2016)

More research is needed to trace this dialectic relationship between struggle and theory, mountains and cities, between Öcalan and his followers. How do discussions in the mountains influence the civilian spheres and vice versa? Where are the spaces where critical ideological questions can be discussed, since Öcalan is cut off from communication and cannot send any more decrees? Members of the party often stressed that their ideology is not dogmatic, that there are spaces for criticism and development. However, I argue that this is only true for those who are high up in the structures, and have given a lot to the struggle; only then can people contribute to the intellectual or policy discussions, within the limits set by the leadership. If people in the lower ranks raise critical questions, either through their sexual identity or political and intellectual concerns, they are told that with enough party education they would learn and understand. Or they would be met with a stern face or a pitiful smile, which says, 'Oh look at the poor liberal/feminist/bourgeois/reactionary, she didn't get it'. Or they would be completely sidelined. Only if you have done the soldier march for long enough, can you be an ideologue. Perhaps the current socio-political developments in Rojava, as well as the work that is being done by the Jineolojî committees in Europe, where members of the women's movement are in ongoing discussion with LGBT groups, will push the party and its strict ideology to soften and expand, in order to incorporate different political views and non-binary sexual identities and practices (Al-Ali & Käser 2020).

Conclusion

People – journalists, activists, politicians and academics, myself included – were deeply affected by the Kurdish women's movement, its female fighters and their quest for liberation that became so visible with the Rojava Revolution. I needed to take five steps back after fieldwork, and continuously so throughout the writing process, because not only had I sometimes fallen for the excellent branding, but had also become militarised throughout the twelve months of fieldwork and the numerous visits in the following years. I never lost my criticality, but I also needed to remind myself of Cynthia Enloe's words:

To be sceptical is to be energetically wary of simplistic descriptions and facile explanations. To be sceptical is to have a hunch – a hunch that, of course, will need to be explored and tested – that things are more complicated than they are being portrayed. To be sceptical calls for a deepened curiosity. Militarization – which commonly involves the unquestioning admiration of a masculinized military institution – is a process that minimizes analytical curiosity, especially a feminist-informed sceptical curiosity. (Enloe 2015, 7)

Yes, I was an admirer, mainly of the feminine institutions created by the formidable women of this movement, both in the armed and civil spheres.

But throughout I had a hunch that surely more coercive power goes into creating these subjects, and probably sexuality plays a big part in that. The goal of this chapter was to put this hunch and the ensuing explorations into words. Clearly, the conundrum persists: desexualisation can be read as a radical act of resistance, a disruption of key intersections between sexuality and 'institutions that control reproduction, pleasure and women's bodies' (Fahs 2010, 445). In that line of argumentation, removing sex is an important aspect in the 'party bargain' that opens the doors to a new subjectivity and allows for a communal fight for independence in a region where Kurds fight for their sheer existence. On the other hand, it can be read as one of the control mechanisms of a masculinized military institution, purposefully limiting the subversive power that lies in sexuality by negating sexual relationships and intimacy (Lorde 1993). This conundrum speaks to a central dilemma in feminist movements and scholarship in the past forty years, which addresses the various intersections between sexuality and politics; 'between the struggle to claim the body as a site of political and social power, while also valuing its role as a source of pleasure' and intimacy (Fahs 2010, 446). Here, I recognised that many women I worked with did not have another choice than to abide by the party's rules; it is a war, and women need to find a way to bargain at every intersection with different matrices of domination. For some, entering these bargains can be truly emancipatory. Others find it hard to 'become free', to shed 'system life', 'become the goddess' or 'kill the dominant male' (Duzel 2018; Grojean 2014). Some parts of the militant femininities and masculinities remain a necessary performance that members are prepared to undertake in order to be part of the movement and be able to fight the enemy in its different guises. Many internalise the performance, and really try to implement what is expected from them, and others again truly embody it. Most former commanders I spoke to confirmed that they often fell in love but stuck to the 'abstinence contract' for most of their time in the party, and particularly the women felt it would negatively impact their work if they did not.

Öcalan's writings and the Kurdish women's movement's praxis have clearly challenged the construct of shame and honour and reconfigured it according to their liberation ideology. They have developed their own ideology of freedom and liberation and removed some aspects of patriarchal control from the female body. Friendship, love, marriage and family have been given a new meaning in that process. In this ideology sexuality as a key feature in capitalist society is being dismantled. 'Sex is not everything', Leyla Agirî told me, and finally I understood. While I understood and agreed, I now know that the reality is far more complex than what the clear-cut ideology makes us believe. Many people within the party still have sex but in the dark of the night or in the shade of a bush. The punishment when caught in the act is harsh. Furthermore, I continue to be sceptical about the new essentialism of femininity and the strict binary between women and men; women are the centrepiece of the new society, men remain the enemy. What happens if you do not fit, because of your sexual orientation or other parts of your identity? 'If you don't agree with the party you just don't join', one cadre responded when confronted with my concerns. People join the party voluntarily and subscribe to a certain set of rules. But what if the ideology is brought down from the mountains to the cities and made into laws, what then? The party will continue to hold discussions on the (for them not so) pressing issues of sexuality. Places like Rojava and the discussions in the Jineolojî camps in Europe will perhaps challenge the party to rethink their strict body politics and might challenge their binary concepts. It is possible that these discussions might not consider sexuality to be an important and intimate source of selfhood and subversive power (Lorde 1993), and it might take a while. 'Come back in thirty years', I was often told when I asked the uncomfortable questions.

Conclusion

I met Mizgîn on a warm spring afternoon in a refugee camp in Switzerland. Mizgîn had been a member of the PKK for twenty-four years, spending her last years in the party as a top KCK commander. In spring 2017, she left the party and fled to Europe. A mutual friend and fellow former commander had arranged our meeting, and over many cigarettes and cups of tea, we told each other our stories, discussed the state of the world, and the women's questions that not only plague the four parts of Kurdistan. With great sadness in her eyes and many deep sighs, Mizgîn told me about how she joined the party as a teenager, her time spent in Syria with Öcalan, her many years of struggle, her increasing doubts, and that seeing how things were run at the very top, particularly in relation to the urban wars in 2015–2016, finally gave her the impetus to leave. At a different table on the terrace another asylum seeker was playing sad PKK revolutionary songs on his *baglama*.[1] Mizgîn nodded in his direction and indicated that we should keep our voices down. She assumed that the musician was also from the PKK and did not want anyone to know who or where she was. 'If they would have found me in Iraq after I left, they would have killed me. Here they can't.'[2] We managed not to cry over the immense injustices she witnessed as a Kurd, as a woman, and as a party member and now a refugee, and instead laughed about the absurdity of us meeting on these lush Swiss hills. 'You know, Öcalan really understood the condition of women in the Middle East well. And as long as women are part of the struggle, the PKK will persevere,' she assured me.

With her remarks Mizgîn once again confirmed that despite all the complexities and contradictions, women are the backbone of the Kurdish

---

[1] *Baǧlama* or *saz* is a stringed musical instrument used in Kurdish, Persian, Turkish, Armenian, Azeri and Assyrian music.

[2] Joining the armed branch of the party is a commitment for life, leaving is considered treason (Gürbüz 2012). Normal rank and file guerrillas can leave without risking their lives, unless they steal money or kill someone from the party. However, high cadres, such as Mizgîn, cannot leave and will be killed or imprisoned, depending on their position and the status of their families, if caught (interview with former commander 5, 12 December 2019; interview with Mizgîn, 20 July 2018).

Freedom Movement. It is due to them that the movement is pushing well beyond the armed struggle, continuously creating more spaces, using the liberation ideology to their advantage. These political and military spaces previously claimed are under constant attack and need vigilant defence at all times. The very necropolitical conditions that structure the geographic locations of this movement consistently drive the politicisation and militarisation of bodies, keeping them engaged in resistance against reactionary and antagonistic state and non-state actors. Moreover, the conviction that this struggle is just, and that all sacrifices are made for the purpose of liberating women, Kurds, the land and the leadership drive the struggle forward.

This book has set out to understand the trajectories of the women in this movement: who and where they are, how they got there and what powers keep them engaged at the many front lines between the cities and the mountains of Kurdistan. The boundaries between the armed and the political struggle are fluid at best; some of my interlocutors were mothers, before finding refuge in the mountains; others continued to work as civilian activist after having been imprisoned for their armed resistance. Throughout the chapters, I focused on how the production of ideology as knowledge about the 'right' way to live and die and the distinct organisational tools give the women of the movement the means to continue their life and work in spite of extreme hardship. I have asked whether new imaginaries and practices emerged that challenged gender norms and relations beyond the battlefield, because women's liberation has been endorsed by the leadership, is enshrined in the written ideology and is being put into practice by women themselves. Moreover, I was interested in how the PKK has assigned new meanings and practices to gender, sexuality, comradery and liberation, arguing that this has opened new spaces for women to participate in the struggle on equal footing with men but has also led to new mechanisms of coercion and control over the militant body.

The PKK began its struggle as a classic guerrilla organisation, which formulated its ideology along the axis of Marxism-Leninism, Fanonian ideas of violence and self-sacrifice, and a vision of an independent Kurdistan carved out of Turkey by a 'people's war'. Particularly in the early 1990s, gender inequality started to become a key ideological theme in Öcalan's work. Öcalan presents the history of civilisation, among other things, as a history of the enslavement of women and of the 'dominant male', and both were regarded as the foundation of state formation and economic exploitation. Therefore, the party's struggle for equality, freedom and democracy required an analysis of the ways in which gender hierarchies have been created and intersect with other power relations. The liberation of women was tied to the liberation of the nation as a whole, and women pushed for their own organisational and decision-making structures from 1993 onwards in order to expedite women's separation from men, ideologically and practically (Jongerden 2017, 240–241). Over the next decade, as the party's ideology developed into Democratic Confederalism, women's liberation became a cornerstone of the new paradigm. This transformation was achieved due to women's tireless struggle for autonomous organisational structures in the political and armed spheres, not under the banner of feminism, but of women's liberation and after 2008 Jineolojî.

In writing a partial history of the Kurdish women's movement, my goal was to highlight areas and periods of contention, in which women fought, politicised and resisted against internal adversaries and external enemies. Following the women's own narrative, I demonstrated that the main factors that shaped them, their struggle and their liberation ideology were severe state repression; the symbolic power of early martyrs; the women's liberation ideology of 1998; Öcalan's arrest in 1999; the formation of the first women's party in the same year; the ensuing power struggles within the legal and illegal party; the women's quota and the co-presidency system; their success in Turkish electoral politics after 2005; the Rojava Revolution since 2012; and the ongoing repression of the political movement in Turkey, including the imprisonment of key political figures such as Sebahat Tuncel and Gültan Kışanak. Cockburn writes: 'If violence is a continuum, our movements have to be alliances capable of acting in many places, at many levels, and on many problems simultaneously' (Cockburn 2004, 44). Kurdish women know from embodied experience the extent to which patriarchal power violently infuses every institution and all aspects of life. They speak of a trinity of oppression; the state, capitalism and patriarchy, and the need to struggle against all three simultaneously, long beyond direct armed confrontation. Overall, the history I narrated suggests that the party is only as strong as its women and that it is the women who change it from the inside and push it forward with all their might – until they burn out, leave wounded or disillusioned, or get killed – because it is women who have the most to gain or indeed lose from the party's success and longevity.

Women join the party for many reasons: from needing to escape a violent context, to seeking a place to struggle for freedom and justice for Kurds, or because they adhere to the principles set out by the movement and its charismatic leader Abdullah Öcalan, to name only a few. Once a member they go through education and learn that their purpose is to become 'free' by fighting, to become militants who are able to resist and commit violence, and to become revolutionaries who will stop at nothing to build a utopic future. Part of the process of subjectivation (Butler 2004;

Mahmood 2001, 2005) entails the learning of *oto-kontrol* and *îrade*, the will to fashion mind and body according to the framework set out by what I call militant femininities and to fight and sacrifice themselves for a vision of a more just future. The parameters of militant femininities help those who join the party to obtain an identity, a vocation and a communal network of love and compassion for the dead, which constructs meaningful relations and rituals among the living. This identity and practice are learned in party education and strictly policed within its ranks, particularly in the military branches. In the political realm, activists have more leeway to decide which part of the identity assemblage is played up or down, silenced or foregrounded (Puar 2007).

At first, many of my interviewees would repeat the same liberation jargon back to me, a pattern that was difficult to break through as an academic who is not part of the Kurdish (diaspora) community. Most active members are bound to stick to certain official narratives, particularly during recorded interviews with international visitors. I do not mean to imply that these narratives were not representing parts of my respondents' everyday reality, but they were intended to relay a unified story that clearly brushed over more complex and messier personal and political dynamics of being in this movement. However, I also understood that the question of 'official' and 'unofficial' narratives creates a false dichotomy between what is visible and invisible to the outsider's eye (Al-Ali & El-Kholy 1999; Davis 2008; Enloe 2015). Instead, I found that this liberation ideology is one of the main tools of resistance, which women wield in the activist, political and armed spheres, as they translate it into everyday practices and labour for women to work towards a future utopia. This labour includes performing as a unified block, building political alliances, and staging visible and audible actions such as conferences, demonstrations and cultural events. Most importantly though, the historically rooted women's structures enabled them to slowly but steadily push their members into important political positions, where they have decision-making powers, access to state funds and international networks (Kışanak 2018; Watts 2010). Some women might simply repeat the catchy party slogans about freedom and equality, while others have organised as part of the wider women's movement since the early 1980s, pushing Öcalan to amend the official ideology according to their achievements and needs. My findings resonate with Al-Ali's and Taş's argument that 'the processes linked to interpreting, translating and circulating Öcalan's writings are constitutive of a dialectical process between ideology and political practice that is influenced not only by the different positionalities of political actors but also by historically varying political conditions' (Al-Ali & Taş 2018c, 19). The idea of 'liberation' in the

Kurdish Freedom Movement creates a competing 'blueprint' for justice, peace and freedom that is implemented by a transnational grassroots movement. This determination and far-reaching vision, together with the strong (semi-)autonomous women's structures, help the movement to survive the ongoing military and state backlashes and the individuals to endure harsh battles, the loss of friends or time in prison.

Feminist scholarship has problematised the emancipatory potential of women's armed participation in national liberation wars, usually coming to a 'yes ... but' conclusion: yes women participated, sometimes in the same ranks as men, but they were pushed back into the private sphere post-conflict, which at best has led to 'ambivalent emancipation' (Rajasingham-Senanayake 2001) and at worst has further entrenched male dominance and male privilege (White 2007). At the same time, scholars have challenged the static tropes of women's roles in highly militarised places of conflict – the victim, mother, fighter, peacemaker – and have instead started to pay attention to how women are engaged in politically motivated violent acts (Gentry & Sjoberg 2015). Feminist IR scholars have argued that both women and men 'do not make choices (to commit political violence or otherwise) independent of either the other people or social structures around them' (Gentry & Sjoberg 2015, 137–38). This line of enquiry was important to the analyses in this book, as it enabled me to show the continuum between violence and resistance, and how the women of the Freedom Movement navigate their particular subjectivation. I have embedded this particular subjectivation in different matrices of domination. This has led to a more robust understanding of the forms of violence affecting the everyday lives of my interlocutors, since patriarchal violence in the family and community, gender-based violence, economic exploitation, and the structural and institutional violence committed by the state and its institutions, or the PKK for that matter are generated by a multiple and interrelated organisation of power (Collins & Bilge 2016). The movement frames its oppression and resistance intersectionally, showing how their particular form of domination is shaped by the interplay of nationalism, ethnicity, gender, class and neoliberalism (Crenshaw 1991; Collins 2000; Collins & Bilge 2016).

Yet still not enough is known about women's agency in nationalist movements, and women fighters in many cases continue to be seen as reproducing behaviour associated with men. The women of the Kurdish Freedom Movement argue that because they are central to all political, armed and ideological efforts taken, their army and their politics are not reproducing masculinist notions of war and violence. While I remain sceptical about the latter, I have highlighted how in the medium term, women in this party are building political and military structures that are capable of combatting not only *daesh* but also '*daesh* mentality' – (gender-based) violence and injustice behind the front lines in communities, families and relationships (Charter of the Social Contract 2014).

My study writes against both the idealisation and the exceptionalism of women with guns and for a better understanding of women's self-perception as revolutionaries who put their own bodies at the front lines. Bodies are both objects and effects of violent practices and are key sites of political subjectivation, resistance and the transformation of power relations (Butler 2004; Hyndman 2004; Wilcox 2015). Violence takes many forms in the four different parts of Kurdistan: neoliberal restructuring, Turkish imperialism, acute wars and armed conflicts, violence against women and minorities, and the destruction of heritage sites, to name a few. While non-violence is not an option for many stateless people like the Kurds, or many women in the movement, their participation is part of an increasing militarisation of Kurdish society and contributes to the continuation of a 'tragic mind' that views revenge, violence and militarisation as the surest provider of hope and justice (Begikhani et al. 2018; Bozarslan 2004). The PKK has built its own matrix of domination and uses violence and modes of coercion, albeit at a very different scale. This matrix spans the mountains and cities and distributes new forms of knowledge about what liberation, freedom and a democratic and confederal future should look like. Women resist violent contexts and practices by joining the party, but not without subjugating themselves to a different set of rules, enabling them to go on and commit violence. I have called this 'party bargains', a means for the recruits to continue life and make sense of a region defined by ongoing wars and insecurities. The revolutionaries interviewed for this book confirmed that structural, political, symbolic and everyday forms of violence were an integral part of their life before the party and that in the party they learned to transform that violence into resistance, to then go on and commit violent acts in the name of self-defence, liberation and Democratic Confederalism.

In these processes, conservative gender norms and relations have certainly been challenged by the Kurdish women's movement, mainly by women pushing into and claiming spaces that used to be seen as male spaces (Puwar 2004). The specific relationship between the resistance in the mountains and the cities, both benefiting from each other's sacrifices and successes, allowed them to expand their hold on these spaces. In order to create the militant revolutionaries that can be mobilised for political action or war, norms around femininity and masculinity had to be rewritten in order to enable communal living, women's ascendance and power-sharing in the movement. Each male member is tasked with 'killing the dominant male', whereas each female member sets out to become like Zîlan, the modern-day goddess Îştar. Throughout the 1980s and 1990s, clear discursive and performative boundaries were put around the 'free woman' and the 'free man'. Heteronormativity is still presumed, however, not by evoking hyper-masculine soldier types but through the creation of militant femininities and masculinities (Peterson 2010, 17–18). Yet most of my respondents assured me that these norms are never dogmatic but subject to constant rethinking and further development, both in the party and the society it depends on. How the party engages with LGTB issues is a telling example of this:

> Officially it is not easy to say 'we don't like gays', because they are people and part of the community. So the official party position right now is that the conditions in the mountains are very difficult for them, because of the separate men and women structures. This is similar to before with the women: in the beginning men didn't want women there so they said the mountains are not suitable for them, then women changed this. (Interview with Sipan, 25 August 2016)

Commander Sipan shared an optimistic forecast with me; however, contrary to LGBT folks, women had Öcalan on their side to fight against 'male mentality' in the party and wider society. Over the last few years, it was mainly the HDP and the women working on Jineolojî in the four parts of Kurdistan and in Europe who were and are engaged in discussions with different LGBT groups and are working towards creating a more inclusive ideology (Al-Ali & Käser 2020), despite the backlash from certain conservative elements in the party. For now, particularly in 'the mountains', there is a clear binary between male and female and little fluidity or acknowledgement that gender and therefore masculinity and femininity are performed. Instead, according to party ideology, genders have an essential and natural core that was lost over the course of modern history and needs to be rediscovered in order to achieve a society based on gender equality and justice.

Nationalism, gender norms and sexuality are socially and culturally constructed, often mutually constitutive and play an important role in helping to create an 'us'/'them' distinction by excluding the 'other' (Mayer 1998, in Giles & Hyndman 2004; Mullholand et al. 2018; Puar 2007). In the Kurdish case, 'us' are those who are following the 'truth' as set out by Abdullah Öcalan and who are fighting for Democratic Confederalism, and 'them' are those enslaved by Capitalist Modernity. Existing post-colonial and transnational feminist literature has also shown that women often become the 'iconic representations' of cultural and/or ethnic-national identity, particularly during national liberation movements and the creation of nation states (Einhorn 1993; Enloe

1993; Yuval-Davis & Anthias 1989, 1999; Yuval-Davis 1997). This case study shows that wherever the party holds power, women become the markers of 'freedom': they demarcate the boundaries between 'us', a gender-equal society based on radical democracy, and 'them', the barbaric other – *daesh*, the Turkish and Syrian regimes and the racist and capitalist world order. Importantly, this is a desexualised non-state nationalism, where the nation needs to be liberated first before 'equal and free' relationships can be had. This is true for the guerrillas, who are to refrain from any sexual activity, and for the activists, who are encouraged to practise self-control in order to not fall victim to being abused by men or distracted from the struggle. I have traced the links between body, sexuality and the liberation ideology and shown that the 'abstinence contract' is an integral part of gaining access to a movement that is able to fight for a particular version of a new society and a key location through which the movement controls its members.

Clearly, with the Kurdish Women's Freedom Movement it is never a neat-cut either/or case, but very much an either/and (Weber 2016), or better a both/and; this movement complicates and confirms, reinvents and reproduces theories and tropes on war, gender, sexuality and nationalism. Despite or perhaps because of these contradictions, the women's movement has made tremendous gains in terms of gender-based equality and justice far beyond the guerrilla ranks. It is too early to say whether these gains will be sustainable, not least because the movement as a whole is under sustained attack from all sides in all four parts of Kurdistan. Yet the historical trajectory of the autonomous women's structures, the mechanisms in place to defend them, the developments in Rojava and the continuous resistance in Bakur give us informed reason to be optimistic that women will continue to be not only the markers but also the makers of the emerging democratic confederations in the region.

All my informants confirmed that the emergence of the PKK and the parallel struggle for women's liberation has played an important role in the emancipation of women, first in Bakur and now in Rojava, and to a lesser extent in Başûr and Rojhelat. This emancipation, however, did not come without its contradictions, having on the one hand raised 'female consciousness' and simultaneously assigned new and relatively fixed roles to women. 'What does the term militant mean to you?' I asked a former guerrilla, who spent ten years in the mountains, when I started fleshing out my concept of militant femininities:

Militant means to be a sheep; you have to be faithful, loyal, and don't ask any sceptical questions. What the shepherd [Öcalan] says counts. It's a bit like between god and humans. Öcalan is not a man, he is a god. If you accept this, you get the identity as a militant. (Interview with former commander 4, 11 October 2017)

Similarly, a former commander who spent twelve years in different parts of Kurdistan said: 'You are a good revolutionary or a good militant if you work like a donkey, don't ask any questions and always say "yes sir"' (interview with former commander 5, 12 October 2019). People's view of the party after they left depends on their experiences during their time 'in the mountains' and on why and under what circumstances they left. Not everyone's assessment is as harsh as those of the two interlocutors quoted here. The accounts I have read (Bingöl 2016) and other interviews I conducted suggest an emotional attachment to the party, particularly to their fallen comrades, that lasts long beyond active membership. The interlocutor who felt like a sheep, however, had spent years questioning how the ideology was produced and implemented and witnessed the discrepancy between theory and practice. It was the latter that eventually pushed her to leave. The interlocutor who evoked the image of a pack animal left the party because he felt unfairly treated and tried after an alleged crime. Both sentiments are also reflected in Oliver Grojean's work, who analyses the 'new man' that each recruit has to become. He argues that Öcalan alone has the monopoly on the interpretation and definition of the 'truth' and he 'alone "is" the key to liberation – as opposed to just possessing it – and able to judge the level of investment required of each person if they are to become a true Man' (Grojean 2014, 10). I have argued that in order to gain access to this new identity of a revolutionary, both men and women unlearn and relearn masculinity and femininity and enter into a bargain with the party: in the armed wing they live in abstinence, give up privacy, and individualism, and in turn gain a whole new existence, a whole new life as revolutionaries.

I concur with Handan Çağlayan who argues that, from a gender perspective, the discursive transformation from women into goddesses and the 'party bargains' that are made in this transition involve a number of contradictions. For example, the process of becoming party subjects is not open to all women, but only to women who fulfil the requirements of militant femininity and its specific configurations in the armed, political and activist sphere. Generally, women are asked to desexualise themselves when entering the public spaces dominated by the party, similarly to other anti-colonial national movements (Aktürk 2016; Najmabadi 1997). Respectable and honourable participation in the public sphere is strictly predicated upon an idea of purity, an unfaltering attachment to the homeland, fighting and very likely dying for it. Substituting sexual love for the love for the homeland is enough reason to be excluded from the 'liberated' women's identity (Çağlayan 2008, 22; Weiss 2010). Civilian activists are asked to curb their sexuality, resist Capitalist Modernity and focus on building a communal life. Mothers in Maxmûr for example are tasked with building and reproducing the revolutionary structures, giving birth to and 'giving' new fighters to the struggle and finding solace and meaning in the ideology of Öcalan when tragedy hits again.

To address this tension between liberation and obedience, and trace the process of 'becoming', I proposed the concept of militant femininities, mapping out how women in different realms of labour, at home, at the front lines and in the city contribute to the making of a new political system in semi-autonomous organisational structures in order to safeguard their central positioning within the movement as a whole. For most of my respondents, omitting sexuality is one of the many tools they use to resist male violence and dominance to strengthen their ranks. In practice they avoid emotional dependency, pregnancy and punishment. The controlled and disciplined body then becomes the political and tactical tool of advancing women's liberation. Paying attention to the coercion that goes into body and identity politics also means gaining a more nuanced understanding of what kind of femininities and masculinities are needed for the political project in the making and to what extent women play a productive and/or reproductive role in that process.

This research is based on a feminist curiosity about what happens to gender and body politics during a struggle for national liberation. How do the norms attached to femininity need to be reconfigured to fit the cultural, political and military conditions of the Kurdish 'state of statelessness' the PKK operates in? I posed the question of what happens to femininity in war to the former commanders I interviewed:

Femininity in war is not possible. I think women's mentality and war do not match, unfortunately. But at the same time, we had to fight, and we still have to fight. There is a slogan by Öcalan: when she fights, she is beautiful and when she is beautiful she is loved, or something like that. Maybe political struggles are ok but life in the mountains is very difficult and femininity is not possible. (Interview with former commander 3, 11 May 2018)

Mizgîn, who had been a warrior for more than two decades, was also very clear about this:

Femininity in war is impossible. War is against women. It is against all of humanity. But the nature of men is closer to war. But women and war ... war destroys women. As much as they say we are fighting for freedom, no! Women can fight with ideas, they are really strong at that. [...] Öcalan says women are very important for him. When women joined the war, it caused huge damage. 90% of women were martyred. Those who survived, like me, realised that the reality of war destroys your body, your psychology and your soul. In war you are abandoning your femininity. (Interview with Mizgîn, 20 July 2018)

These accounts resonate with Aaronette White's critical analysis of the transformative capacity of revolutionary violence. Her comparative work, which looks at the aftermath of political violence during the anti-colonial wars on the African continent, shows that while wars have produced powerful new identities for women, Fanon was overly hopeful about the therapeutic potential of revolutionary violence, because he neglected the gendered aspects of armed conflict:

Contrary to Fanon's optimistic predictions, participation in revolutionary violence does not necessarily contribute to the mutual recognition and equality of women in the aftermath of war. Indeed, many aspects of gendered violence work against it. [...] Even in circumstances where revolutionary violence is justified, the long-term psychological costs of war may be far more damaging for women and men than Fanon suggested. (White 2007, 880)

White is not suggesting that struggles for national liberations should be conducted in a pacifist manner, as this is not an option for many women who face the onslaught of masculinist restorations in different contexts globally (Kandiyoti 2013). Instead she unpacks the interrelationships of gender, war and post-war reconstruction, a period when male dominance and privilege challenges and sidelines women's wartime contributions (White 2007, 880). Similar to White, Philippe Bourgois found that people do not escape unscathed from the oppression they rise up against and an omission thereof diminishes the real human cost wrought by political repression and war and obscures our understanding of the 'greyness of violence'. 'The challenge of ethnography, then, is to check the impulse to sanitize, and instead to clarify the chains of causality that link structural, political and symbolic violence in the production of an everyday violence that buttresses unequal power relations and distorts efforts at resistance' (Bourgois 2004, 433). In present-day Kurdistan, a context shaped by necropolitics, invasions and occupations, it is difficult not to see and portray the Kurdish revolutionaries as anything less than noble resistors, who are building a new system based on gender equality amidst protracted wars and conflicts. I have navigated these challenges by zooming into different matrices of domination and the embodied epistemologies of war, asking questions about the women's everyday practices, some of which do not get told in the official party history. We rarely read about what experiencing or committing violence really does to women and men in the movement. We do not hear about how 'mountain life' or the process of desexualisation marks women's bodies in the long run or what happens to those who transgress the established parameters of the militant. Instead, most of my interlocutors would tell me about how women have gained political, intellectual and physical spaces using a multi-pronged approach of a simultaneous armed, political and ideological struggle. Members of the movement know that lasting peace cannot be achieved through war, that neither the Turkish government nor the PKK can win this forty-year conflict. Wherever possible, the movement builds the grassroots structures for Democratic Confederalism and advocates for gender equality and ethnic and religious pluralism. And as far off as peace might still be, the militants engaged in this ongoing struggle are already living their version of freedom. Or as Commander Eyrehan put it before I left the mountains:

Now in the Middle East, it is very difficult; violence, destruction and massacres are everywhere. But no matter how bad it is, if there are people in this horror who have hope and believe in something, who are fighting against this, that is freedom. (Interview with Eyrehan, 2 August 2016)

Appendix

Table I.1 *Organisational structure – Kurdish Freedom Movement*[1]

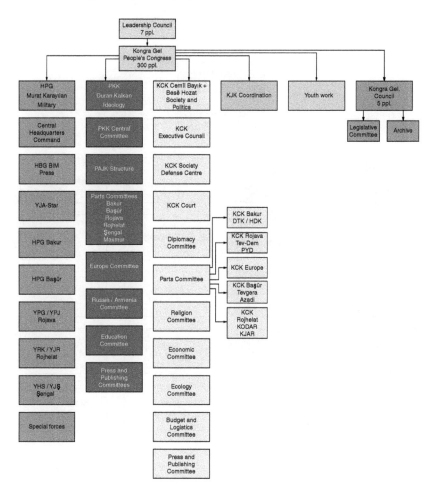

[1] Each member or former member of the movement whom I asked to draw the organisational structure of the Kurdish Freedom Movement and its women's branch drew a different chart, depending on where they were positioned within its branches (rank, armed/civil, women/men), which led to many lengthy discussions, about who has how much power and is subjected to whose rule. What I reproduced here is a distillate of these different sketches that aims to demonstrate (1) the three main areas of work (military, ideology and politics), (2) that despite the restructuring of the party structure, the KCK is in fact on the same organisational level as the HPG and PKK, and (3) the male leadership, particularly in the PKK and HPG, remains firmly intact. The women's movement staffs its own structures and elects its own representatives for the top positions, however, some of them have to be signed off by the main leadership. This is not a complete illustration (the everyday workings are much more complex) but a simplified visualisation of some of the (sub)structures the movement operates through.

Table I.2 *Organisational structure – Kurdish Women's Freedom Movement*

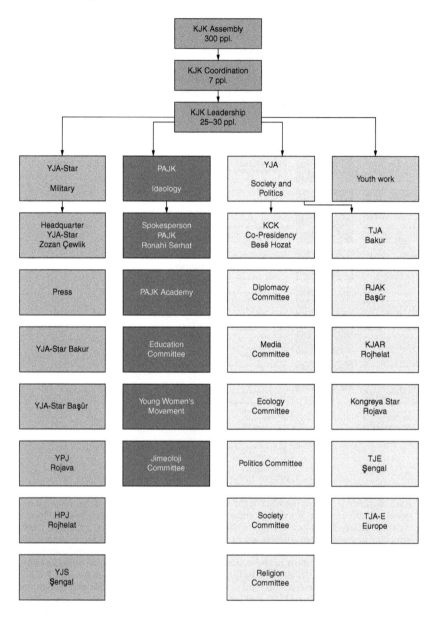

References

Abu-Lughod, Lila. 1993. *Writing Women's Worlds: Bedouin Stories*. Berkeley: University of California Press.

1998. *Remaking Women: Feminism and Modernity in the Middle East*. Princeton Studies in Culture/Power/History. Princeton: Princeton University Press.

2010. 'The Active Social Life of "Muslim Women's Rights": A Plea for Ethnography, Not Polemic, with Cases from Egypt and Palestine'. *Journal of Middle East Women's Studies* 6 (1): 1–45. https://doi.org/10.2979/MEW.2010.6.1.1.

2011. 'Seductions of the "Honor Crime."' *Differences* 22 (1): 17–63. https://doi.org/10.1215/10407391-1218238.

2017. 'Commentary on "Ethnography as Knowledge in the Arab Region" by Lila Abu-Lughod'. *Contemporary Levant* 2 (1): 67–70. https://doi.org/10.1080/20581831.2017.1322230.

Ahmed, Leila. 1982. 'Western Ethnocentrism and Perspectives of the Harem'. *Feminist Studies* 8 (3): 521–34.

Aktürk, Ahmet Serdar. 2016. 'Female Cousins and Wounded Masculinity: Kurdish Nationalist Discourse in the Post-Ottoman Middle East'. *Middle Eastern Studies* 52 (1): 46–59. http://doi.org/10.1080/00263206.2015.1078793.

Al-Ali, Nadje. 2007. *Iraqi Women: Untold Stories from 1948 to the Present*. London: Zed Books.

2009. *What Kind of Liberation? Women and the Occupation of Iraq*. Berkeley: University of California Press.

2018. 'Sexual Violence in Iraq: Challenges for Transnational Feminist Politics'. *European Journal of Women's Studies* 25 (1): 10–27. https://doi.org/10.1177/1350506816633723.

Al-Ali, Nadje and Heba El-Kholy. 1999. 'Inside/Out: The Native and the Halfie Unsettled'. *Cairo Papers in Social Science* 22 (2): 14–40.

Al-Ali, Nadje and Isabel Käser. 2020. 'Beyond Feminism? Jineolojî and the Kurdish Women's Freedom Movement'. *Politics & Gender*: 1–32. https://doi.org/10.1017/S1743923X20000501.

Al-Ali, Nadje and Nicola Pratt. 2011. 'Between Nationalism and Women's Rights: The Kurdish Women's Movement in Iraq'. *Middle East Journal of Culture and Communication* 4 (3): 339–55. https://doi.org/10.1163/187398611X590192.

2016. 'Gender, Protest and Political Transition in the Middle East and North Africa'. In *Handbook on Gender in World Politics*, edited by Jill Steans and Daniela Tepe-Belfrage, 127–36. Cheltenham: Edward Elgar.

Al-Ali, Nadje and Nicola Pratt, eds. 2009. *Women and War in the Middle East: Transnational Perspectives.* London: Zed Books.

Al-Ali, Nadje and Latif Taş. 2017. '"War Is like a Blanket": Feminist Convergences in Kurdish and Turkish Women's Rights Activism for Peace'. *Journal of Middle East Women's Studies* 13 (3): 354–75. https://doi.org/10.1215/15525864-4179001.

2018a. 'Reconsidering Nationalism and Feminism: The Kurdish Political Movement in Turkey'. *Nations and Nationalism* 24 (2):453–73. https://doi.org/10.1111/nana.12383.

2018b. 'Clashes, Collaborations and Convergences: Evolving Relations of Turkish and Kurdish Women's Rights Activists'. *Journal of Balkan and Near Eastern Studies* 21 (3): 1–15. https://doi.org/10.1080/19448953.2018.1497754.

2018c. *Dialectics of Struggle: Challenges to the Kurdish Women's Movement.* Middle East Centre Paper Series 22. London: London School of Economics. www.lse.ac.uk/Middle-East-Centre.

Alexander, M. Jacqui and Chandra Talpade Mohanty. 2010. 'Cartographies of Knowledge and Power: Transnational Feminism as Radical Praxis'. In *Critical Transnational Feminist Praxis,* edited by Amanda Swarr and Richa Nagar, 23–45. SUNY Series. Albany: State University of New York Press.

Alinia, Minoo. 2013. *Honor and Violence against Women in Iraqi Kurdistan.* New York: Palgrave Macmillan.

2015. 'On Black Feminist Thought: Thinking Oppression and Resistance through Intersectional Paradigm'. *Ethnic and Racial Studies* 38 (13): 2334–40. https://doi.org/10.1080/01419870.2015.1058492.

Alison, Miranda. 2003. 'Cogs in the Wheel? Women in the Liberation Tigers of Tamil Eelam'. *Civil Wars* 6 (4): 37–54. https://doi.org/10.1080/13698240308402554.

2009. *Women and Political Violence: Female Combatants in Ethno-National Conflict.* Contemporary Security Studies. London: Routledge.

Allsopp, Harriet. 2014. *The Kurds of Syria: Political Parties and Identity in the Middle East.* London: I. B. Tauris.

Alkan, Hilal. 2018. 'The Sexual Politics of War: Reading the Kurdish Conflict Through Images of Women.' *Les Cahiers Du CEDREF. Centre d'enseignement, d'études et de Recherches Pour Les Études Féministes* 22 (October): 68–92.

Amrane-Minne, Danièle Djamila and Farida Abu-Haidar. 1999. 'Women and Politics in Algeria from the War of Independence to Our Day'. *Research in African Literatures* 30 (3): 62–77.

ANF. 2015. 'Declaration of Political Resolution Regarding Self-Rule'. ANF News. Accessed 5 September 2018a. https://anfenglish.com/kurdistan/dec laration-of-political-resolution-regarding-self-rule-13498.

2017. 'Makhmur Martyrs Laid to Rest in Qandil'. ANF News. Accessed 12 September 2018b. https://anfenglish.com/kurdistan/makhmur-martyrs-laid-to-rest-in-qandil-23558.

2018a. 'KJAR Calls upon Women to Join Protests in Iran'. ANF News. https://anfenglish.com/women/kjar-calls-upon-women-to-join-protests-in-iran-23962.

2018b. 'YJCR's Call for Women in Iran and Rojhilat'. ANF News. https://anfenglish.com/women/yjcr-s-call-for-women-in-iran-and-rojhilat -24098.

2018c. 'The Developments in Iran and the Importance of the PJAK Project'. ANF News.

2018d. 'KJAR Proposal for Women in Iran and Eastern Kurdistan'. ANF News. https://anfenglishmobile.com/women/kjar-proposal-for-women-in-iran-and-eastern-kurdistan-29202.

https://anfenglishmobile.com/features/the-developments-in-iran-and-the-importance-of-the-pjak-project-28766.

Angey, Gabrielle. 2018. 'The Gülen Movement and the Transfer of a Political Conflict from Turkey to Senegal'. *Politics, Religion & Ideology* 19 (1): 53–68. https://doi.org/10.1080/21567689.2018.1453256.

Aras, Ramazan. 2013. *The Formation of Kurdishness in Turkey: Political Violence, Fear and Pain*. Routledge Studies in Middle Eastern Politics. New York: Routledge.

Ayboğa, Ercan. 2018. 'Demokratischer Konföderalismus: Eine Utopie Wird Wahr'. In *Konkrete Utopien: Unsere Alternativen Zum Nationalismus*, edited by Alexander Neupert-Doppler. Stuttgart: Schmetterling Verlag.

Bahng, Aimee. 2018. *Migrant Futures: Decolonizing Speculation in Financial Times*. Durham: Duke University Press Books.

Bayard de Volo, Lorraine. 2001. *Mothers of Heroes and Martyrs: Gender Identity Politics in Nicaragua, 1979-1999 / Lorraine Bayard de Volo*. Baltimore: Johns Hopkins University Press.

2012. 'A Revolution in the Binary? Gender and the Oxymoron of Revolutionary War in Cuba and Nicaragua'. *Signs: Journal of Women in Culture and Society* 37 (2): 413–39. https://doi.org/10.1086/661727.

2018. *Women and the Cuban Insurrection: How Gender Shaped Castro's Victory*. First Edition. New York: Cambridge University Press.

Bayat, Assef. 2013. *Life as Politics: How Ordinary People Change the Middle East*. Stanford: Stanford University Press.

Beauvoir, Simone de. 1997. *The Second Sex*. London: Vintage.

Begikhani, Nazand, Aisha K. Gill, and Gill Hague. 2015. *Honour-Based Violence: Experiences and Counter-Strategies in Iraqi Kurdistan and the UK Kurdish Diaspora*. Burlington: Ashgate.

Begikhani, Nazand, Wendelmoet Hamelink, and Nerina Weiss. 2018. 'Theorising Women and War in Kurdistan: A Feminist and Critical Perspective'. *Kurdish Studies* 6 (1): 5–30.

Behar, Ruth. 1996. *The Vulnerable Observer: Anthropology That Breaks Your Heart*. Boston: Beacon Press.

Berger, Andreas, Rudi Friedrich, and Kathrin Schneider. 1998. *Der Krieg in Türkei-Kurdistan: Über Die Kriegführung Und Die Soldaten Der Türkischen Armee*. Lamuv Taschenbuch. Göttingen: Lamuv Verlag.

Berlant, Lauren. 2011. 'A Properly Political Concept of Love: Three Approaches in Ten Pages'. *Cultural Anthropology* 26 (4): 683–91. https://doi.org/10.1111/j.1548-1360.2011.01120.x.

Bernal, Victoria. 2000. 'Equality to Die For?: Women Guerrilla Fighters and Eritrea's Cultural Revolution'. *PoLAR: Political and Legal Anthropology Review* 23 (2): 61–76. https://doi.org/10.1525/pol.2000.23.2.61.

Bingöl, Berivan. 2016. *Bizim Gizli Bir Hikayemiz Var. Dağdan Anneliğe Kadınlar.* Istanbul: İletişim Yayınları.

Birch, Nicholas. 2006. 'Death Comes Easily to the Young Women of Batman'. *The Irish Times.* 13 May 2006. https://www.irishtimes.com/news/death-comes-easily-to-the-young-women-of-batman-1.1002474.

Bourgois, Philippe. 2004. 'The Continuum of Violence in War and Peace: Post-Cold War Lessons from El Salvador'. In *Violence in War and Peace*, edited by Nancy Scheper-Hughes and Philippe Bourgois, 425–34. Oxford: Blackwell.

Bozarslan, Hamit. 2012. 'Between Integration, Autonomization and Radicalization. Hamit Bozarslan on the Kurdish Movement and the Turkish Left. Interview by Marlies Casier and Olivier Grojean'. *European Journal of Turkish Studies. Social Sciences on Contemporary Turkey*, no. 14. http://journals.openedition.org/ejts/4663.

2000. '"Why the Armed Struggle?" Understanding the Violence in Kurdistan of Turkey'. In *The Kurdish Conflict in Turkey: Obstacles and Changes for Peace and Democracy*, edited by Ferhad Ibrahim and Gülistan Gürbey, 17–30. Münster: LIT Verlag.

2004. *Violence in the Middle East: From Political Struggle to Self-Sacrifice.* Princeton: Markus Wiener Publishers.

2008. 'Kurds and the Turkish State'. In *The Cambridge History of Turkey*, edited by Reşat Kasaba, First Edition, 333–56. Cambridge University Press. https://doi.org/10.1017/CHOL9780521620963.013.

Bozarslan, Mahmut. 2017. 'Iconic Armenian Church Survives War but Not Plunder in Turkey'. Al-Monitor. 2017. https://www.al-monitor.com/pulse/originals/2017/12/armenian-church-plundered.html.

Bruinessen, Martin van. 2001. 'From Adela Khanum to Leyla Zana: Women as Political Leaders in Kurdish History'. In *Women of a Non-State Nation: The Kurds*, edited by Shahrzad Mojab, 95–112. Costa Mesa: Mazda Publishers.

Burç, Rosa. 2018. 'One State, One Nation, One Flag – One Gender? HDP as a Challenger of the Turkish Nation State and Its Gendered Perspectives'. *Journal of Balkan and Near Eastern Studies*, August, 1–16. https://doi.org/10.1080/19448953.2018.1497755.

Butler, Judith. 1988. 'Performative Acts and Gender Constitution: An Essay in Phenomenology and Feminist Theory'. *Theatre Journal* 40 (4): 519–31.

1999. *Gender Trouble: Feminism and the Subversion of Identity.* New York: Routledge.

2002. 'Is Kinship Already Heterosexual'. *Differences: A Journal of Feminist Cultural Studies* 13 (1): 14–44.

2004. *Precarious Life: The Powers of Mourning and Violence.* London: Verso.

1997. *The Psychic Life of Power: Theories in Subjection.* Stanford: Stanford University Press.

Çağlayan, Handan. 2007. *Analar, yoldaşlar, tanrıçalar: Kürt hareketinde kadınlar ve kadın kimliğinin oluşumu.* Istanbul: İletişim Yayınları.

2008. 'Voices from the Periphery of the Periphery: Kurdish Women's Political Participation in Turkey'. Unpublished conference paper. Torino, Italy.

2012. 'From Kawa the Blacksmith to Ishtar the Goddess: Gender Constructions in Ideological-Political Discourses of the Kurdish Movement in Post-1980 Turkey. Possibilities and Limits'. *European Journal of Turkish Studies. Social Sciences on Contemporary Turkey*, no. 14 (June). http://journals.openedition.org /ejts/4657.

2020. *Women in the Kurdish Movement: Mothers, Comrades, Goddesses*. London: Palgrave Macmillan. https://doi.org/10.1007/978-3-030-24744-7.

Çaha, Ömer. 2011. 'The Kurdish Women's Movement: A Third-Wave Feminism within the Turkish Context'. *Turkish Studies* 12 (3): 435–49. https://doi.org/10 .1080/14683849.2011.604211.

Cansiz, Sakine. 2015. *Mein ganzes Leben war ein Kampf. Band 1: Jugendjahre*. Neuss: Mezopotamien Verlag.

2014. *Mein ganzes Leben war ein Kampf. Band 2: Gefängnisjahre*. Neuss: Mezopotamien Verlag.

2018. *Mein ganzes Leben war ein Kampf. Band 3: Guerilla*. Neuss: Mezopotamien Verlag.

Casier, Marlies. 2011. 'Beyond Kurdistan? The Mesopotamia Social Forum and the Appropriation and Re-Imagination of Mesopotamia by the Kurdish Movement'. *Journal of Balkan and Near Eastern Studies* 13 (4): 417–32. https://doi.org/10.1080/19448953.2011.621792.

Çelik, Selahattin. 2002. *'Den Berg Ararat Versetzen' Die Politischen, Militärischen, Ökonomischen Und Gesellschaftlichen Dimensionen Des Aktuellen Kurdischen Aufstands*. 1. Aufl. Frankfurt am Main: Zambon.

Chaliand, Gérard, ed. 1993. *A People without a Country: The Kurds and Kurdistan*. London: Routledge.

'Charter of the Social Contract'. 2014. *Peace in Kurdistan* (blog). 7 March 2014. https://peaceinkurdistancampaign.com/charter-of-the-social-contract/.

Chatterjee, Partha and Pradeep Jeganathan, eds. 2000. *Community, Gender and Violence*. Subaltern Studies 11. New York: Columbia University Press.

Chisholm, Amanda and Joanna Tidy. 2017. 'Beyond the Hegemonic in the Study of Militaries, Masculinities, and War'. *Critical Military Studies* 3 (2): 99–102. https://doi.org/10.1080/23337486.2017.1328182.

Çiçek, Cuma. 2017. *The Kurds of Turkey: National, Religious and Economic Identities*. Library of Modern Middle East Studies. London: I.B. Tauris.

Cixous, Hélène. 1976. 'The Laugh of the Medusa'. *Signs* 1 (4): 875–93.

Clark, Jessie Hanna. 2015. 'Green, Red, Yellow and Purple: Gendering the Kurdish Question in South-East Turkey'. *Gender, Place & Culture* 22 (10): 1463–80. https://doi.org/10.1080/0966369X.2014.991701.

Cockburn, Cynthia. 1998. *The Space between US: Negotiating Gender and National Identities in Conflict*. London: Zed Books.

2004. 'The Continuum of Violence: A Gendered Perspective on War and Peace'. In *Sites of Violence: Gender and Conflict Zones*, edited by Giles, Wenona and Hyndman, Jennifer, 24–45. Berkeley: University of California Press.

2007. *From Where We Stand: War, Women's Activism and Feminist Analysis*. London: Zed Books.

Cohen, Dara Kay. 2013. 'Female Combatants and the Perpetration of Violence: Wartime Rape in the Sierra Leone Civil War'. *World Politics* 65 (3): 383–415. https://doi.org/10.1017/S0043887113000105.

Cohn, Carol, ed. 2013. *Women and Wars: Contested Histories, Uncertain Futures.* Cambridge: Polity Press.

Coleman, Simon and Pauline von Hellermann, eds. 2013. *Multi-Sited Ethnography: Problems and Possibilities in the Translocation of Research Methods.* New York, London: Routledge.

Collette, Carolyn P. 2013. *In the Thick of the Fight: The Writing of Emily Wilding Davison, Militant Suffragette.* Ann Arbor: University of Michigan Press.

Collins, Patricia Hill. 1996. 'What's in a Name? Womanism, Black Feminism, and Beyond'. *The Black Scholar* 26 (1): 9–17.

2000. *Black Feminist Thought: Knowledge, Consciousness, and the Politics of Empowerment.* Rev. 10th anniversary edition. New York: Routledge.

Collins, Patricia Hill and Sirma Bilge. 2016. *Intersectionality.* Cambridge: Polity Press.

Connell, R. W. and James W. Messerschmidt. 2005. 'Hegemonic Masculinity: Rethinking the Concept'. *Gender & Society* 19 (6): 829–59. https://doi.org/10.1177/0891243205278639.

Connell, Raewyn. 1987. *Gender and Power: Society, the Person, and Sexual Politics.* Stanford: Stanford University Press.

2005. *Masculinities.* Second Edition. Cambridge: Polity.

Crenshaw, Kimberlé. 1991. 'Mapping the Margins: Intersectionality, Identity Politics, and Violence against Women of Color'. *Stanford Law Review* 43: 1241–99. https://doi.org/10.2307/1229039.

Cürükkaya, M. Selim. 1997. *PKK: die Diktatur des Abdullah Öcalan.* Frankfurt am Main: Fischer.

Daly, Mary. 1978. *Gyn/Ecology: The Metaethics of Radical Feminism.* Boston: Women's Press.

Darici, Haydar. 2011. 'Politics of Privacy: Forced Migration and the Spatial Struggle of the Kurdish Youth'. *Journal of Balkan and Near Eastern Studies* 13 (4): 457–74. https://doi.org/10.1080/19448953.2011.623869.

2015. 'The Kurdish Self-Governance Movement in Turkey's South East: An Interview with Haydar Darici'. 22 December 2015. http://www.criticatac.ro/lefteast/kurdish-self-governance/.

Das, Veena. 2006. *Life and Words: Violence and the Descent into the Ordinary.* Berkeley: University of California Press.

Davis, Angela. 2008. 'A Vocabulary for Feminist Praxis: On War and Radical Critique'. In *Feminism and War: Confronting U.S. Imperialism*, edited by Robin Riley, 19–26. London: Zed Books.

Deeb, Lara. 2010. 'On Representational Paralysis: Or, Why I Don't Want to Write about Temporary Marriage'. Jadaliyya. 1 December 2010. http://www.middleeastdigest.com/pages/index/364/on-representational-paralysis-or-why-i-dont-want-t.

Demir, Arzu. 2017. *Die Rojava Revolution.* Zambon Verlag.

Derrida, Jacques. 1978. *Spurs: Nietzsche's Styles.* Chicago: Chicago University Press.

Dicle, Amed. 2016. 'Dead Bodies on the Street and the Unforgiving War in Kurdistan'. Kurdish Question.Com. 22 January 2016. http://kurdishquestion.com/oldarticle.php?aid=dead-bodies-on-the-street-and-the-unforgiving-war-in-kurdistan.

Dietrich Ortega and Luisa Maria. 2012. "Looking beyond Violent Militarized Masculinities: Guerrilla Gender Regimes in Latin America." *International Feminist Journal of Politics* 14 (4): 489–507. doi:10.1080/14616742.2012.72 6094.

Dirik, Dilar. 2014. 'Western Fascination with "badass" Kurdish Women'. *Al Jazeera*, 2014. https://www.aljazeera.com/indepth/opinion/2014/10/western-fascination-with-badas-2014102112410527736.html.

2018. 'Overcoming the Nation-State: Women's Autonomy and Radical Democracy in Kurdistan'. In *Gendering Nationalism*, edited by Jon Mulholland, Nicola Montagna, and Erin Sanders-McDonagh, 145–63. Cham: Springer International Publishing.

2021. *The Kurdish Women's Movement: History, Theory, Practice*. London: Pluto Press.

Doğan, Zülfikar. 2015. 'Struggling to Keep Up, Conflict Causes Major Economic Setback in Turkey's Poorest Region'. Al-Monitor. 2015. https://www.al-monitor.com/pulse/en/originals/2015/09/turkey-pkk-clashes-wreaks-economic-havoc-in-poorest-region.html.

Duran, Aram Ekin. 2016. 'Conflict in Diyarbakir Hits the Economy'. Deutsche Welle. 1 March 2016. https://www.dw.com/en/conflict-in-Diyarbakir-hits-the-economy/a-19084398.

Duzel, Esin. 2018. 'Fragile Goddesses: Moral Subjectivity and Militarized Agencies in Female Guerrilla Diaries and Memoirs'. *International Feminist Journal of Politics*, January, 1–16. https://doi.org/10.1080/14616742.2017.1419823.

Düzel, Esin. 2020. 'Beauty for Harmony'. *Comparative Studies of South Asia, Africa and the Middle East* 40 (1): 180–92. https://doi.org/10.1215/1089201X-8186170.

Eccarius-Kelly, Vera. 2012. 'Surreptitious Lifelines: A Structural Analysis of the FARC and the PKK'. *Terrorism and Political Violence* 24 (2): 235–58. https://doi.org/10.1080/09546553.2011.651182.

Einhorn, Barbara. 1993. *Cinderella Goes to Market: Citizenship, Gender, and Women's Movements in East Central Europe*. London: Verso.

El Said, Maha, Lena Meari, and Nicola Pratt, eds. 2015. *Rethinking Gender in Revolutions and Resistance: Lessons from the Arab World*. London: Zed Books.

El-Feki, Shereen. 2013. *Sex and the Citadel: Intimate Life in a Changing Arab World*. London: Chatto & Windus.

Enloe, Cynthia. 1988. *Does Khaki Become You? The Militarization of Women's Lives*. London: Pandora Press.

1990. *Bananas, Beaches and Bases: Making Feminist Sense of International Politics*. Berkeley: University of California Press.

1993. *The Morning After: Sexual Politics at the End of the Cold War*. Berkeley: University of California Press. https://www.ucpress.edu/book/9780520083363/the-morning-after.

2000. *Maneuvers: The International Politics of Militarizing Women's Lives.* Berkeley: University of California Press.

2007. *Globalization and Militarism: Feminists Make the Link.* Lanham: Rowman & Littlefield Publishers.

2014. *Bananas, Beaches and Bases: Making Feminist Sense of International Politics.* Second Edition. Berkeley: University of California Press.

2015. 'The Recruiter and the Sceptic: A Critical Feminist Approach to Military Studies'. *Critical Military Studies* 1 (1): 3–10. https://doi.org/10.1080/23337 486.2014.961746.

2017. *The Big Push: Exposing and Challenging Sustainable Patriarchy.* Oxford: Myriad Editions.

Erren, Lorenz. 2008. *'Selbstkritik' Und Schuldbekenntnis: Kommunikation und Herrschaft unter Stalin (1917-1953).* München: R. Oldenbourg Verlag.

Exo, Mechthild. 2020. 'Making Connections: Jineolojî, Women's Liberation, and Building Peace'. In *Building Free Life: Dialogues with Öcalan,* edited by International Initiative 'Freedom for Abdullah Öcalan – Peace in Kurdistan', 147–66. Oakland, CA: PM Press.

Fahs, Breanne. 2010. 'Radical Refusals: On the Anarchist Politics of Women Choosing Asexuality'. *Sexualities* 13 (4): 445–61. https://doi.org/10.1177/1363 460710370650.

Fanon, Frantz. 1968. *The Wretched of the Earth.* New York: Grove Press.

Fausto-Sterling, Anne. 2012. *Sex/Gender: Biology in a Social World.* Routledge.

Fischer-Tahir, Andrea. 2009. *Brave Men, Pretty Women? Gender and Symbolic Violence in Iraqi Kurdish Urban Society.* Berlin: Europäisches Zentrum für Kurdische Studien.

2012. "Gendered Memories and Masculinities: Kurdish Peshmerga and the Anfal Campaign in Iraq." *Journal of Middle East Women's Studies* 8 (1): 92–114.

Flach, Anja. 2003. *Jiyanekê din – ein anderes Leben: zwei Jahre bei der kurdischen Frauenarmee.* 1. Aufl. Köln: Mezopotamien Verlag.

2007. *Frauen in der kurdischen Guerilla: Motivation, Identität und Geschlechterverhältnis in der Frauenarmee der PKK.* Köln: PapyRossa Verlag.

Flach, Anja, Ercan Ayboğa, and Michael Knapp. 2016. *Revolution in Rojava: Frauenbefreiung und Kommunalismus zwischen Krieg und Embargo.* Hamburg: VSA: Verlag.

Fluri, Jennifer. 2009. '"Foreign Passports Only": Geographies of (Post)Conflict Work in Kabul, Afghanistan'. *Annals of the Association of American Geographers* 99 (5): 986–94. https://doi.org/10.1080/00045600903253353.

Forensic Architecture. 2019. 'The Killing of Tahir Elçi ← Forensic Architecture'. n.d. Accessed 12 October 2019. https://forensic-architecture.org/investiga tion/the-killing-of-tahir-elci.

Foucault, Michel. 1990. *History of Sexuality: The Will to Knowledge.* Harmondsworth: Penguin Books.

1991. *Discipline and Punish: The Birth of the Prison.* Reprint. Penguin Social Sciences. London: Penguin Books.

Fraser, Nancy and Linda Nicholson. 1988. 'Social Criticism without Philosophy:
    An Encounter between Feminism and Postmodernism'. *Theory, Culture &
    Society* 5 (2–3): 373–94. https://doi.org/10.1177/0263276488005002009.
Friedan, Betty. 1965. *The Feminine Mystique*. Harmondsworth: Penguin.
Gambetti, Zeynep. 2005. 'The Conflictual (Trans)Formation of the Public
    Sphere in Urban Space: The Case of Diyarbakir'. *New Perspectives on
    Turkey* 32: 43–71. https://doi.org/10.1017/S0896634600004106.
    2009. 'Politics of Place/Space: The Spatial Dynamics of the Kurdish and
    Zapatista Movements'. *New Perspectives on Turkey* 41: 43–87.
Gambetti, Zeynep and Joost Jongerden. 2011. 'The Spatial (Re)Production of the
    Kurdish Issue: Multiple and Contradicting Trajectories—Introduction'.
    Journal of Balkan and Near Eastern Studies 13 (4): 375–88. https://doi.org/10
    .1080/19448953.2011.621785.
    eds. 2015. *The Kurdish Issue in Turkey: A Spatial Perspective*. First Edition.
    Milton Park, Abingdon, Oxon: Routledge.
Garzan, Hevala Rûken. 2015. *Dîroka Tevgera Jina Azad: Vegotin û Nîqaşên
    Waneya Dîroka Tevgera Jina Azad Dewraya Ş. Reşîd Ya Ocaxa PKK*.
    Matbaya Azadî: Ocaxa PKK ya Sakine Cansiz.
Geerdink, Frederike. 2016. 'Survivors of the City Wars'. Byline. Accessed
    5 September 2018. https://www.byline.com/column/57/article/1331.
Gentry, Caron E. and Laura Sjoberg. 2015. *Beyond Mothers, Monsters, Whores:
    Thinking about Women's Violence in Global Politics*. London: Zed Books.
Giles, Wenona and Jennifer Hyndman, eds. 2004. *Sites of Violence: Gender and
    Conflict Zones*. Berkeley: University of California Press.
Gill, Aisha K. 2014. 'Introduction: "Honour" and "Honour"-Based Violence:
    Challenging Common Assumptions'. In *'Honour' Killing and Violence*, edited
    by Aisha K. Gill, Carolyn Strange, and Karl Roberts. London: Palgrave
    Macmillan.
Gill, Aisha K. and Avtar Brah. 2014. 'Interrogating Cultural Narratives about
    'Honour'-Based Violence'. *European Journal of Women's Studies* 21 (1):
    72–86. https://doi.org/10.1177/1350506813510424.
Gilmartin, Christina K. 1995. *Engendering the Chinese Revolution: Radical Women,
    Communist Politics, and Mass Movements in the 1920s*. Berkeley: University of
    California Press.
Gökalp, Deniz. 2010. 'A Gendered Analysis of Violence, Justice and Citizenship:
    Kurdish Women Facing War and Displacement in Turkey'. *Women's Studies
    International Forum* 33 (6): 561–69. https://doi.org/10.1016/j.wsif.2010.09.005.
Gökarıksel, Banu. 2017. 'Feminist Perspectives on the 2016 Military Coup Attempt
    and Its Aftermath in Turkey'. *Duke University Press News* (blog). 24
    February 2017. https://dukeupress.wordpress.com/2017/02/24/feminist-
    perspectives-on-the-2016-military-coup-attempt-and-its-aftermath-in-turkey/.
Göksel, Nisa. 2018. 'Losing the One, Caring for the All: The Activism of the
    Peace Mothers in Turkey'. *Social Sciences* 7 (10): 174. https://doi.org/10
    .3390/socsci7100174.
Gonzalez-Perez, Margaret. 2006. 'Guerrilleras in Latin America: Domestic and
    International Roles'. *Journal of Peace Research* 43 (3): 313–29.

Grabolle-Çeliker, Anna. 2013. *Kurdish Life in Contemporary Turkey: Migration, Gender and Ethnic Identity*. London: I.B. Tauris.

Graham, Stephen. 2004. 'Introduction'. In *Cities, War, and Terrorism: Towards an Urban Geopolitics*, edited by Stephen Graham, 1–25. Studies in Urban and Social Change. Malden: Blackwell Publishing.

Gregory, Derek. 2004. *The Colonial Present: Afghanistan, Palestine, and Iraq*. Malden, MA: Blackwell Publishers.

Grewal, Inderpal and Caren Kaplan. 1994. *Scattered Hegemonies: Postmodernity and Transnational Feminist Practices*. Minneapolis: University of Minnesota Press.

Grojean, Olivier. 2014. 'The Production of the New Man within the PKK'. *European Journal of Turkish Studies*. http://ejts.revues.org/4925.

2017. *La Révolution Kurde: Le PKK et La Fabrique d'une Utopie*. Cahiers Libres. Paris: La Découverte.

Grosz, Elizabeth A. 1994. *Volatile Bodies: Toward a Corporeal Feminism*. Indiana University Press.

Gunes, Cengiz. 2012. *The Kurdish National Movement in Turkey: From Protest to Resistance*. New York: Routledge.

2019. 'Developments in the Kurdish Issue in Syria and Turkey in 2017'. *European Yearbook of Minority Issues* 16 (1): 211–29. https://doi.org/10.1163/22116117_01601010.

Gunes, Cengiz and Welat Zeydanlioglu, eds. 2014. *The Kurdish Question in Turkey: New Perspectives on Violence, Representation and Reconciliation*. New York: Routledge.

Guneser, Havin. 2018. 'Democratic Confederalism – Democratic Autonomy'. In *Your Freedom and Mine: Abdullah Öcalan and the Kurdish Question in Erdoğan's Turkey*, edited by Thomas Jeffrey Miley and Federico Venturini, 330–36. Montréal: Black Rose Books.

Gürbüz, Mustafa. 2012. '"Sold Out to the Enemy": Emerging Symbolic Boundaries in Kurdish Politics and Strategic Uses of Labelling Treason'. *European Journal of Turkish Studies* 14. http://ejts.revues.org/4629.

Haber Erciş. 2018. 'Yıkılan Newroz Anıtı'nın yerine saat kulesi dikildi'. Haberercis.com. July 7. http://haberercis.com/guncel/yikilan-newroz-anitinin-yerine-saat-kulesi-dikildi-h298538.html.

Haberler. 2014. 'HDP'den PKK'lı Cemil Bayık'a "Marjinal" Tepkisi'. Haberler. com. 2014. https://www.haberler.com/hdp-den-pkk-li-cemil-bayik-a-marjinal-6411012-haberi/.

Halberstam, J. Jack. 2005. *In a Queer Time and Place: Transgender Bodies, Subcultural Lives*. New York: NYU Press.

Halberstam, Judith and Jack Halberstam. 1998. *Female Masculinity*. Durham: Duke University Press.

Hale, Sondra. 2001. 'The State of the Women's Movement in Eritrea'. *Northeast African Studies* 8 (3): 155–77. https://doi.org/10.1353/nas.2006.0006.

Hamdan, Mohammed. 2019. '"Every Sperm Is Sacred": Palestinian Prisoners, Smuggled Semen, and Derrida's Prophecy'. *International Journal of Middle East Studies* 51 (4): 525–45. https://doi.org/10.1017/S0020743819000680.

Harding, Sandra. 1986. *The Science Question in Feminism*. Ithaca: Cornell University Press.

Hardt, Michael. 2017. 'Red Love'. *South Atlantic Quarterly* 116 (4): 781–96. https://doi.org/10.1215/00382876-4235005.

Hassanpour, Amir. 2001. 'The (Re)Production of Patriarchy in the Kurdish Language'. In *Women of a Non-State Nation: The Kurds*, edited by Shahrzad Mojab, 227–63. Costa Mesa: Mazda Publishers.

Hasso, Frances S. 2014. 'Bargaining with the Devil: States and Intimate Life'. *Journal of Middle East Women's Studies* 10 (2): 107–34.

Hasso, Frances Susan. 1998. 'The "Women's Front": Nationalism, Feminism, and Modernity in Palestine'. *Gender and Society* 12 (4): 441–65.

2005. *Resistance, Repression, and Gender Politics in Occupied Palestine and Jordan.* Syracuse: Syracuse University Press.

Hasso, Frances Susan and Zakia Salime, eds. 2016. *Freedom without Permission: Bodies and Space in the Arab Revolutions.* Durham: Duke University Press.

Hennessy, Rosemary. 2000. *Profit and Pleasure: Sexual Identities in Late Capitalism.* First Edition. New York: Routledge.

Henry, Marsha. 2017. 'Problematizing Military Masculinity, Intersectionality and Male Vulnerability in Feminist Critical Military Studies'. *Critical Military Studies* 3 (2): 182–99. https://doi.org/10.1080/23337486.2017.13 25140.

Herausgeberinnenkollektiv, c/o Cenî – Kurdisches Frauenbüro für Frieden e.V., and c/o Cenî – Kurdisches Frauenbüro für Frieden e.V., eds. 2012. *Widerstand und gelebte Utopien: Frauenguerilla, Frauenbefreiung und Demokratischer Konföderalismus in Kurdistan.* Neuss: Mezopotamien Verlag.

Hermez, Sami. 2017. *War Is Coming: Between Past and Future Violence in Lebanon.* Philadelphia: University of Pennsylvania Press.

Herold, Marc. 2004. 'Urban Dimensions of the Punishment of Afghanistan by US Bombs'. In *Cities, War, and Terrorism: Towards an Urban Geopolitics*, edited by Stephen Graham, 312–29. Studies in Urban and Social Change. Malden: Blackwell Publishing.

Hester, Helen. 2018. *Xenofeminism.* Cambridge: Polity Press.

hooks, bell 2001. *Ain't I a Woman: Black Women and Feminism.* London: Pluto Press.

1984. *Feminist Theory from Margin to Center.* Boston, MA: South End Press.

1989. *Talking Back: Thinking Feminist, Thinking Black.* New edition. New York: Routledge.

n.d. *Understanding Patriarchy.* https://imaginenoborders.org/pdf/zines/Underst andingPatriarchy.pdf.

HPG. 2017. 'Understanding the PKK Truth Is Possible by Understanding Its Truth of Martyrs'. Hezen Parastin. 19 May 2017. http://www.hezenparastin.com/eng/index.php?option=com_content&view=article&id=1674:understanding-the-p kk-truth-is-possible-by-understanding-its-truth-of-martyrs&catid=37:anakarar gah-alamalar&Itemid=300.

Hyndman, Jennifer. 2004. 'Mind the Gap: Bridging Feminist and Political Geography through Geopolitics'. *Political Geography* 23 (3): 307–22. https://doi.org/10.1016/j.polgeo.2003.12.014.

2010. 'The Question of "the Political" in Critical Geopolitics: Querying the "Child Soldier" in the "War on Terror"'. *Political Geography* 29 (5): 247–55. https://doi.org/10.1016/j.polgeo.2009.10.010.

İmset, İsmet G. 1992. *The PKK: A Report on Separatist Violence in Turkey (1973-1992)*. Turkish Daily News Publications. Istanbul: Turkish Daily News Publications.

In der Maur, Renée, Jonas Staal, and Dilar Dirik, eds. 2015. *Stateless Democracy*. New World Academy Reader, #5. Utrecht: BAK.

Irigaray, Luce. 2011. 'This Sex Which Is Not One (1977)'. In *Cultural Theory: An Anthology*, edited by Imre Szeman and Timothy Kaposy, 449–53. Oxford: Wiley-Blackwell.

Jabiri, Afaf. 2016. *Gendered Politics and Law in Jordan: Guardianship over Women*. Cham: Palgrave Macmillan. https://doi/10.1007/978-3-319-32643-6.

Jacobs, Susie M., Ruth Jacobson, and Jen Marchbank, eds. 2000. *States of Conflict: Gender, Violence, and Resistance*. London: Zed Books.

Jayawardena, Kumari. 1986. *Feminism and Nationalism in the Third World*. London: Zed Books.

Jean-Klein, Iris. 2001. 'Nationalism and Resistance: The Two Faces of Everyday Activism in Palestine during the Intifada'. *Cultural Anthropology* 16 (1): 83–126.

Jineolojî Committee Europe. 2018. *Jineolojî*. Neuss: Mezopotamien Verlag.

JINHA. 2016. 'Women Marchers: "This Will Spread to Cities"'. Jinha, Jin News Agency. 12 January 2016. http://jinha.com.tr/en/ALL-NEWS/content/view/42018#.

Jongerden, Joost. 2007. *The Settlement Issue in Turkey and the Kurds: An Analysis of Spatial Policies, Modernity and War*. Leiden: Brill Academic Publishers.

2017. 'Gender Equality and Radical Democracy: Contractions and Conflicts in Relation to the "New Paradigm" within the Kurdistan Workers' Party (PKK)'. Edited by Hamit Bozarslan. *Anatoli. De l'Adriatique à La Caspienne. Territoires, Politique, Sociétés*, no. 8 (October): 233–56. https://doi.org/10.4000/anatoli.618.

2018. 'Conquering the State and Subordinating Society under AKP Rule: A Kurdish Perspective on the Development of a New Autocracy in Turkey'. *Journal of Balkan and Near Eastern Studies*, August, 1–14. https://doi.org/10.1080/19448953.2018.1497751.

Jongerden, Joost and Ahmet Hamdi Akkaya. 2011. 'Born from the Left: The Making of the PKK'. In *Nationalism and Politics in Turkey: Political Islam, Kemalism and the Kurdish Issue*, edited by Marlies Casier and Joost Jongerden, 123–42. New York: Routledge.

2012. 'The Kurdistan Workers Party and a New Left in Turkey: Analysis of the Revolutionary Movement in Turkey through the PKK's Memorial Text on Haki Karer'. *European Journal of Turkish Studies. Social Sciences on Contemporary Turkey*, no. 14. http://journals.openedition.org/ejts/4613.

2013. 'Democratic Confederalism as a Kurdish Spring: The PKK and the Quest for Radical Democracy'. In *The Kurdish Spring: Geopolitical Changes and the Kurds*, edited by Mohammed M. A. Ahmed and Michael M. Gunter, 163–85. Costa Mesa: Mazda Publishers.

Joseph, Suad. 1993. 'Connectivity and Patriarchy among Urban Working-Class Arab Families in Lebanon'. *Ethos* 21 (4): 452–84. https://doi.org/10.1525/e th.1993.21.4.02a00040.

ed. 1999. *Intimate Selving in Arab Families: Gender, Self, and Identity.* First Edition. Gender, Culture, and Politics in the Middle East. Syracuse, NY: Syracuse University Press.

ed. 2000. *Gender and Citizenship in the Middle East.* First Edition. Contemporary Issues in the Middle East. Syracuse, NY: Syracuse University Press.

2005. 'Learning Desire: Relational Pedagogies and the Desiring Female Subject in Lebanon'. *Journal of Middle East Women's Studies* 1 (1): 79–109.

Kadioğlu, Ayşe. 1996. 'The Paradox of Turkish Nationalism and the Construction of Official Identity'. *Middle Eastern Studies* 32 (2): 177–93. https://doi.org/10 .1080/00263209608701110.

Kampwirth, Karen. 2002. *Women and Guerrilla Movements: Nicaragua, El Salvador, Chiapas, Cuba.* University Park: Pennsylvania State University Press.

Kanafani, Samar and Zina Sawaf. 2017. 'Being, Doing and Knowing in the Field: Reflections on Ethnographic Practice in the Arab Region'. *Contemporary Levant* 2 (1): 3–11. https://doi.org/10.1080/20581831.2017.1322173.

Kandiyoti, Deniz, ed. 1991. *Women, Islam, and the State.* Basingstoke: Macmillan.

2007a. 'Between the Hammer and the Anvil: Post-Conflict Reconstruction, Islam and Women's Rights'. *Third World Quarterly* 28 (3): 503–17. https:// doi.org/10.1080/01436590701192603.

2007b. 'Old Dilemmas or New Challenges? The Politics of Gender and Reconstruction in Afghanistan'. *Development and Change* 38 (2): 169–99. https://doi.org/10.1111/j.1467-7660.2007.00408.x.

1987. 'Emancipated but Unliberated? Reflections on the Turkish Case'. *Feminist Studies* 13 (2): 317–38.

1988. 'Bargaining with Patriarchy'. *Gender and Society* 2 (3): 274–90.

1998. 'Gender, Power and Contestation: Rethinking Bargaining with Patriarchy'. In *Feminist Visions of Development: Gender Analysis and Policy,* edited by Ruth Pearson and Cecile Jackson, Routledge studies in development economics:135–51. London: Routledge.

2013. 'Fear and Fury: Women and Post-Revolutionary Violence'. Open Democracy, 50.50. 1 October 2013. http://www.opendemocracy.net/5050/ deniz-kandiyoti/fear-and-fury-women-and-post-revolutionary-violence.

Karaman, Emine Rezzan. 2016. 'Remember, S/He Was Here Once: Mothers Call for Justice and Peace in Turkey'. *Journal of Middle East Women's Studies* 12 (3): 382–410. https://doi.org/10.1215/15525864-3637576.

Käser, Isabel. 2021. 'A Struggle within a Struggle: A History of the Kurdistan Women's Freedom Movement 1978-2019'. In *The Cambridge History of the Kurds,* edited by Hamit Bozarslan, Cengiz Gunes, and Veli Yadirgi, 893–919. Cambridge: Cambridge University Press.

Kaufman, Joyce P. and Kristen P. Williams. 2010. *Women and War: Gender Identity and Activism in Times of Conflict.* Sterling: Kumarian Press.

Katz, Cindi. 2007. 'Banal Terrorism. Spatial Fetishism and Everyday Insecurity'. In *Violent Geographies: Fear, Terror, and Political Violence*, edited by Derek Gregory and Allan Pred, 349–61. New York: Routledge.

Keli, Haje. 2018. *The Continuum of Violence against Women: An Ethnographic Study of Female Genital Cutting, Domestic Violence and the State Response in Iraqi Kurdistan*. PhD thesis: SOAS University.

Khalidi, Ari. 2017. 'Turkey Trustee Dismantles Memorial Statue for Massacre Victims'. Kurdistan24. 9 January 2017. http://www.kurdistan24.net/en/news/c f89f77f-208e-4e26-b934-19c80e4023dc/Turkey-trustee-dismantles-memorial -statue-for-massacre-victims.

Khalili, Laleh. 2007. *Heroes and Martyrs of Palestine: The Politics of National Commemoration*. Cambridge: Cambridge University Press.

2010. 'The Location of Palestine in Global Counterinsurgencies'. *International Journal of Middle East Studies* 42 (3): 413–33. https://doi.org/10.1017 /S0020743810000425.

2013. *Time in the Shadows: Confinement in Counterinsurgencies*. Stanford, California: Stanford University Press.

Khalili, Laleh and Jillian Schwedler, eds. 2010. *Policing and Prisons in the Middle East: Formations of Coercion*. Columbia University Press.

Kizilirmak, Zeynep. 2018. 'Dozens of Girls Missing in Afrin'. ANF News. 31 March 2018. https://anfenglish.com/news/dozens-of-girls-missing-in-afrin-25829.

Kışanak, Gültan. 2018. *Kürt Siyasetinin Mor Rengi*. Facsimile edition. Ankara: Dipnot Yayınları.

KJA. n.d. *Free Women Congress*. Diyarbakir.

Koefoed, Minoo. 2017. 'Martyrdom and Emotional Resistance in the Case of Northern Kurdistan: Hidden and Public Emotional Resistance'. *Journal of Political Power* 10 (2): 184–99. https://doi.org/10.1080/2158379X.2017.133 5838.

Kollontai, Alexandra, A. 1980. *Selected Writing of Alexandra Kollontai*. New York: Norton.

Kollontai, Alexandra, A. 2011. *The Autobiography of a Sexually Emancipated Communist Woman*. New York, NY: Prism Key Press.

Küçükkıca, İclal Ayşe. 2018. 'The Relationality between the "Free Women's Movement of Kurdistan" and the "Feminist Movement in Turkey" Building Solidarity or Coalition in Peace and Wartime'. In *Patriarchat Im Wandel: Frauen Und Politik in Der Türkei*, edited by Hürcan Aslı Aksoy, 133–56. Frankfurt: Campus Verlag.

Kurt, Mehmet. 2017. *Kurdish Hizbullah in Turkey: Islamism, Violence and the State*. London: Pluto Press.

Laizer, S. J. 1996. *Martyrs, Traitors, and Patriots: Kurdistan after the Gulf War*. Zed Books Ltd.

Lanzona, Vina A. 2009. *Amazons of the Huk Rebellion: Gender, Sex, and Revolution in the Philippines*. Madison, WI: University of Wisconsin Press.

Lazreg, Marina. 1994. *The Eloquence of Silence: Algerian Women in Question*. New York: Routledge.

Leezenberg, Michiel. 2016. 'The Ambiguities of Democratic Autonomy: The Kurdish Movement in Turkey and Rojava'. *Southeast European and Black Sea Studies* 16 (4): 671–90. https://doi.org/10.1080/14683857.2016.1246529.

Lorde, Audre. 1993. 'The Use of the Erotic: The Erotic as Power'. In *The Lesbian and Gay Studies Reader*, edited by Henry Abelove, Michèle Aina Barale, and David M. Halperin, 339–43. London: Routledge.

Lorentzen, Lois Ann and Jennifer E. Turpin, eds. 1998. *The Women and War Reader*. New York: New York University Press.

2007. *Sister Outsider: Essays and Speeches*. Berkeley: Crossing Press.

Lower Class Magazine and Unrast e. V, eds. 2017. *Konkrete Utopie: Die Berge Kurdistans und die Revolution in Rojava – Ein Reisetagebuch*. Münster: Unrast.

MacKenzie, Megan H. 2012. *Female Soldiers in Sierra Leone: Sex, Security, and Post-Conflict Development*. New York: New York University Press.

Mahmood, Saba. 2001. 'Feminist Theory, Embodiment, and the Docile Agent: Some Reflections on the Egyptian Islamic Revival'. *Cultural Anthropology* 16 (2): 202–36.

2005. *Politics of Piety: The Islamic Revival and the Feminist Subject*. Princeton: Princeton University Press.

Mandıracı, Berkay. 2016. 'Turkey's PKK Conflict: The Death Toll'. International Crisis Group. 20 July 2016. http://blog.crisisgroup.org/europe-central-asia/2016/07/20/turkey-s-pkk-conflict-the-rising-toll/.

Marcus, Aliza. 2007. *Blood and Belief: The PKK and the Kurdish Fight for Independence*. New York: New York University Press.

Massey, Doreen. 1994. *Space, Place and Gender*. Cambridge: Polity.

2004. 'Geographies of Responsibility'. *Geografiska Annaler. Series B, Human Geography* 86 (1): 5–18.

Mazurana, Dyan. 2013. 'Women, Girls, and Non-State Armed Opposition Groups'. In *Women and Wars*, edited by Cohn, Carol, 146–68. Cambridge: Polity Press.

Mazurana, Dyan E., Karen Jacobsen, and Lacey Andrews Gale. 2013. *Research Methods in Conflict Settings: A View from Below*. Cambridge: University Press.

Mbembé, Achille. 2003. 'Necropolitics'. *Public Culture* 15 (1): 11–40.

McClintock, Anne. 1991. '"No Longer in a Future Heaven": Women and Nationalism in South Africa'. *Transition*, no. 51: 104–23.

McDowall, David. 2001. *A Modern History of the Kurds*. London: I.B. Tauris.

McNay, Lois. 2000. *Gender and Agency: Reconfiguring the Subject in Feminist and Social Theory*. Cambridge: Polity Press.

Mies, Maria. 1986. *Patriarchy and Accumulation on a World Scale: Women in the International Division of Labour*. London: Zed Books Ltd.

Mikdashi, Maya and Jasbir K. Puar. 2016. 'Queer Theory and Permanent War'. *GLQ: A Journal of Lesbian and Gay Studies* 22 (2): 215–22. https://doi.org/10.1215/10642684-3428747.

Mir-Hosseini, Ziba. 1996. 'Women and Politics in Post-Khomeini Iran. Divorce, Veiling, and Emerging Feminist Voices'. In *Women and Politics in the Third*

World, edited by Haleh Afshar, 142–70. Women and Politics. London: Routledge.

2009. 'Towards Gender Equality: Muslim Family Laws and the Shari'ah'. In *Wanted: Equality and Justice in the Muslim Family*, edited by Zainah Anwar, 23–63. Selangor: Musawah.

Mittermaier Amira. 2012. 'Dreams from Elsewhere: Muslim Subjectivities beyond the Trope of Self-cultivation'. *Journal of the Royal Anthropological Institute* 18 (2): 247–65. https://doi.org/10.1111/j.1467-9655.2012.01742.x.

Moallem, Minoo. 2005. *Between Warrior Brother and Veiled Sister*. Berkeley: University of California Press. https://www.ucpress.edu/book/9780520243 453/between-warrior-brother-and-veiled-sister.

Moghadam, Valentine M., ed. 1994. *Gender and National Identity: Women and Politics in Muslim Societies*. London: Zed Books.

Moghnieh, Lamia. 2017. '"The Violence We Live in": Reading and Experiencing Violence in the Field'. *Contemporary Levant* 2 (1): 24–36. https://doi.org/10 .1080/20581831.2017.1318804.

Mohanty, Chandra Talpade. 1988. 'Under Western Eyes: Feminist Scholarship and Colonial Discourse'. *Feminist Review* 30: 60–81.

2013. 'Transnational Feminist Crossings: On Neoliberalism and Radical Critique'. *Signs: Journal of Women in Culture and Society* 38 (4): 967–91. htt ps://doi.org/10.1086/669576.

Mohanty, Chandra Talpade, Ann Russo, and Lourdes Torres, eds. 1991. *Third World Women and the Politics of Feminism*. Bloomington: Indiana University Press.

Mojab, Shahrzad. 2000. 'Vengeance and Violence: Kurdish Women Recount the War'. *Canadian Woman Studies* 19 (4): 89–94.

ed. 2001. *Women of a Non-State Nation: The Kurds*. Costa Mesa: Mazda Publishers.

2004. 'No "Safe Haven": Violence Against Women in Iraqi Kurdistan'. In *Sites of Violence: Gender and Conflict Zones*, edited by Wenona Giles and Jennifer Hyndman, 108–33. Berkeley: University of California Press.

Moser, Caroline and Fiona Clark, eds. 2001. 'The Gendered Dynamics of Armed Conflict and Political Violence'. In *Victims, Perpetrators Or Actors? Gender, Armed Conflict and Political Violence*, 13–29. London: Zed Books.

Mulholland, Jon, Nicola Montagna and Erin Sanders-McDonagh, eds. 2018. *Gendering Nationalism: Intersections of Nation, Gender and Sexuality*. Cham: Palgrave Macmillan.

Najmabadi, Afsaneh. 2013. *Professing Selves: Transsexuality and Same-Sex Desire in Contemporary Iran*. Durham: Duke University Press.

2017. 'State-Building, Science and Religion: Sexuality in Iran'. *Economic & Political Weekly* 52 (42/43).

1997. '"The Erotic Vatan [Homeland] as Beloved and Mother: To Love, to Possess, and To Protect." *Comparative Studies in Society and History* 39 (3): 442–67.

2005. *Women with Mustaches and Men without Beards*. Berkeley: University of California Press.

Nakhal, Jana. 2015. 'Women as Space/Women in Space: Relocating Our Bodies and Rewriting Gender in Space'. *Kohl* 1 (1): 15–22.

Naples, Nancy A. 2003. *Feminism and Method: Ethnography, Discourse Analysis, and Activist Research*. New York: Routledge.

Nash, Jennifer C. 2014. 'Institutionalizing the Margins'. *Social Text* 32 (1 118): 45–65. https://doi.org/10.1215/01642472-2391333.

2019. *Black Feminism Reimagined: After Intersectionality*. Next Wave. Durham: Duke University Press.

Neven, Brecht and Marlene Schäfers. 2017. 'Jineology: From Women's Struggles to Social Liberation'. ROAR Magazine. 2017. https://roarmag.org/essays/ji neology-kurdish-women-movement/.

Newaya Jin, ed. 2016. *Jineolojiye Giriş*. Mezopotamien Verlag.

Öcalan, Abdullah. 2009. *Özgürlük Sosyolojisi: Demokratik Uygarlık Manifestosu, no. 3*. Neuss: Mezopotamien Verlag.

2010. *Jenseits von Staat, Macht und Gewalt*. Neuss: Mezopotamien Verlag.

2011. *Democratic Confederalism*. Cologne: Transmedia Publishing Ltd.

2013a. *Liberating Life: Woman's Revolution*. Cologne: International Initiative.

2013b. *Demokratik Uygarlık Manifestosu. Uygarlık: Maskeli Tanrılar ve Örtük Krallar Çağı*. Vol. 1. Kitab. Azadi Matbassı.

2015. *Demokratik Kurtuluş Ve Özgür Yaşamı İnşa (İmralı Notları)*. Neuss: Mezopotamien Verlag.

2016. *Democratic Nation*. Cologne: International Initiative.

2017. *The Political Thought of Abdullah Öcalan: Kurdistan, Women's Revolution and Democratic Confederalism*. London: Pluto Press.

n.d. *Apocu Militan Kişilik 2.CİLT*. Bilim Aydinlanma Yayinlari. Accessed 4 September 2018. https://www.scribd.com/document/34893644/Apocu-Militan-Ki%C5%9Filik-2-C%C4%B0LT-Abdullah-Ocalan.

O'Keefe, Theresa. 2013. *Feminist Identity Development and Activism in Revolutionary Movements*. New York: Palgrave Macmillan.

Olson, Robert W. 1996. *The Kurdish National Movement in the 1990s: Its Impact on Turkey and the Middle East*. Lexington: The University Press of Kentucky.

Orhan, Mehmet. 2016. *Political Violence and Kurds in Turkey: Fragmentations, Mobilizations, Participations and Repertoires*. Routledge Studies in Middle Eastern Politics 77. New York: Routledge.

Ortner, Sherry B. 1978. 'The Virgin and the State'. *Feminist Studies* 4 (3): 19. https://doi.org/10.2307/3177536.

Özarslan, Asli. 2017. 'Türkei – Der Vergessene Krieg Im Osten'. ZDF info. https://www.youtube.com/watch?v=MIeqmaHnP5A&has_verified=1.

Özgür Kadın Akademisi ed. 2016. *Jineoloji Tartışmaları*. First Edition. Diyarbakir: Mezopotamien Verlag.

Özsoy, Hisyar. 2010. *Between Gift and Taboo: Death and the Negotiation of National Identity and Sovereignty in the Kurdish Conflict in Turkey*. PhD thesis: University of Texas.

Pankhurst, E. Sylvia. 2015. *The Suffragette: The History of the Women's Militant Suffrage Movement, 1905-1910*. London: Forgotten Books.

Parashar, Swati. 2009. 'Feminist International Relations and Women Militants: Case Studies from Sri Lanka and Kashmir'. *Cambridge Review of International Affairs* 22 (2): 235–56. https://doi.org/10.1080/09557570902877968.

2014. *Women and Militant Wars: The Politics of Injury*. London: Routledge.

Parashar, Swati and Janet Andrew Shah. 2016. '(En)Gendering the Maoist Insurgency in India: Between Rhetoric and Reality'. *Postcolonial Studies* 19 (4): 445–62. https://doi.org/10.1080/13688790.2016.1317397.

Pateman, Carole. 1988. *The Sexual Contract*. Cambridge: Polity Press.

Peteet, Julie. 1991. *Gender in Crisis: Women and the Palestinian Resistance Movement*. New York: Columbia University Press.

1997. 'Icons and Militants: Mothering in the Danger Zone'. *Signs* 23 (1): 103–29.

Peterson, Abby. 1985. 'The Revolutionary Potential of the "Private": A Critique of the Family as a Revolutionary Force Position'. *Acta Sociologica* 28 (4): 337–48.

Peterson, V. Spike. 2010. 'International/Global Political Economy'. In *Gender Matters in Global Politics: A Feminist Introduction to International Relations*, edited by Laura J. Shepherd, 204–17. New York: Routledge.

Philips, John W. P. 2014. 'Becoming Female with Derrida and Nietzsche: Algebra of Deconstruction'. *Parallax* 20 (1): 54–66.

PKK. 1995. 'PKK Örgütü Programi ve Parti Tüzüğü. PKK 5. Kongresi'. 1995. https://yadi.sk/i/fOTXtxnob7GiGw.

Pottier, Johan, Laura Hammond, and Christopher Cramer. 2011. 'Navigating the Terrain of Methods and Ethics in Conflict Research'. In *Researching Violence in Africa: Ethical and Methodological Challenges*, edited by Christopher Cramer, Laura Hammond, and Johan Pottier, 1–12. Boston: Brill.

Puar, Jasbir. 2007. *Terrorist Assemblages: Homonationalism in Queer Times*. Durham: Duke University Press Books.

2017. *The Right to Maim: Debility, Capacity, Disability*. Durham: Duke University Press Books.

Pugliese, Joseph. 2016. 'Drone Casino Mimesis: Telewarfare and Civil Militarization'. *Journal of Sociology* 52 (3): 500–521. https://doi.org/10.1177/1440783316655630.

Puwar, Nirmal. 2004. *Space Invaders: Race, Gender and Bodies out of Place*. Oxford: Berg.

Rajasingham-Senanayake, Darini. 2001. "Ambivalent Empowerment: The Tragedy of Women in Conflict." In *Women War and Peace in South Asia: Beyond Victimhood to Agency*, edited by Rita Manchanda, 102–30. New Delhi: Sage Publications.

Rêwîtiya Berbi Mexmûre Ve (Travelling to Maxmûr). 2014. Maxmûr.

Richter-Devroe, Sophie. 2011. 'Palestinian Women's Everyday Resistance: Between Normality and Normalisation'. *Journal of International Women's Studies* 12 (2).

Riley, Robin Lee, Chandra Talpade Mohanty, and Minnie Bruce Pratt. 2008. *Feminism and War: Confronting US Imperialism*. London: Zed Books.

Rubin, Gayle. 1992. 'Thinking Sex: Notes for a Radical Theory of the Politics of Sexuality'. In *Pleasure and Danger: Exploring Female Sexuality*, edited by Carole S. Vance, 267–93. London: Pandora.

Rudaw. 2020. 'Turkey Carries out Multiple Strikes in Northern Iraq: Officials'. Rudaw.Net. Accessed 15 May 2020. https://www.rudaw.net/english/kurdi stan/150420203.

Rudi, Axel. 2018. 'The PKK's Newroz: Death and Moving towards Freedom for Kurdistan'. *Zanj: The Journal of Critical Global South Studies* 2 (1): 92. https://doi.org/10.13169/zanjglobsoutstud.2.1.0092.

Sahin-Mencutek, Zeynep. 2016. 'Strong in the Movement, Strong in the Party: Women's Representation in the Kurdish Party of Turkey'. *Political Studies* 64 (2): 470–87. https://doi.org/10.1111/1467-9248.12188.

Salhi, Zahia Smail. 2010. "The Algerian Feminist Movement between Nationalism, Patriarchy and Islamism." *Women's Studies International Forum* 33 (2): 113–24. doi:10.1016/j.wsif.2009.11.001.

Said, Edward W. 1978. *Orientalism*. London: Vintage Books.

Saigol, Rubina. 2000. 'Militarisation, Nation and Gender: Women's Bodies as Areas of Violent Conflict'. In *Women and Sexuality in Muslim Societies*, edited by Pınar İlkkaracan, 107–21. Istanbul: Women for Women's Human Rights (WWHR).

Salih, Ruba. 2017. 'Bodies That Walk, Bodies That Talk, Bodies That Love: Palestinian Women Refugees, Affectivity, and the Politics of the Ordinary': *Antipode* 49 (3): 742–60. https://doi.org/10.1111/anti.12299.

Sayegh, Ghiwa. 2017. 'Talking Sex as a Necessity'. *Kohl: A Journal for Body and Gender Research* 3 (2): 134–37.

Schäfers, Marlene. 2018. '"It Used to Be Forbidden": Kurdish Women and the Limits of Gaining Voice'. *Journal of Middle East Women's Studies* 14 (1): 3–24. https://doi.org/10.1215/15525864-4296988.

    2019. "Troubled Terrain: Lines of Alliance and Political Belonging in Northern Kurdistan." In *Methodological Approaches in Kurdish Studies: Theoretical and Practical Insights from the Field*, edited by Bahar Baser, Mari Toivanen, Begum Zorlu, and Yasin Duman, 69–83. Kurdish Societies, Politics, and International Relations. Lanham: Lexington Books.

    2020. "Walking a Fine Line: Loyalty, Betrayal, and the Moral and Gendered Bargains of Resistance." *Comparative Studies of South Asia, Africa and the Middle East* 40 (1): 119–32. doi:10.1215/1089201X-8186126.

Schippers, Mimi. 2007. 'Recovering the Feminine Other: Masculinity, Femininity, and Gender Hegemony'. *Theory and Society* 36 (1): 85–102. https://doi.org/10.1007/s11186-007-9022-4.

Schmidinger, Thomas. 2014. *Krieg und Revolution in Syrisch-Kurdistan: Analysen und Stimmen aus Rojava*. Wien: Mandelbaum.

    2018. *Rojava: Revolution, War and the Future of Syria's Kurds*. London: Pluto Press.

Schneider, Jane. 1971. 'Of Vigilance and Virgins: Honour, Shame and Access to Resources in Mediterranean Societies'. *Ethnology* 10 (1): 1–24.

Segal, Lynne. 2007. *Slow Motion: Changing Masculinities, Changing Men*. Third Edition. Basingstoke: Palgrave Macmillan. https://doi.org/10.1057/978023058 2521.

    2008. 'Gender, War and Militarism: Making and Questioning the Links'. *Feminist Review*, no. 88: 21–35.

Sehlikoglu, Sertaç. 2016. 'Exercising in Comfort: Islamicate Culture of *Mahremiyet* in Everyday Istanbul'. *Journal of Middle East Women's Studies* 12 (2): 143–65. https://doi.org/10.1215/15525864-3507606.

——— 2018. 'Revisited: Muslim Women's Agency and Feminist Anthropology of the Middle East'. *Contemporary Islam* 12 (1): 73–92. https://doi.org/10.1007/s1 1562-017-0404-8.

Serxwebûn. 1995. 'PKK (Partiya Karkerên Kurdistan) Program ve Tüzgüğû'. *Serxwebûn*, no. Weşanên 71.

Shah, Alpa. 2018. *Nightmarch: Among India's Revolutionary Guerrillas*. London: Hurst & Company.

Shahvisi, Arianne. 2018. 'Beyond Orientalism: Exploring the Distinctive Feminism of Democratic Confederalism in Rojava'. *Geopolitics*, 1–25. https://doi.org/10 .1080/14650045.2018.1554564.

Sharoni, Simona. 2001. 'Rethinking Women's Struggles in Israel-Palestine and in the North of Ireland'. In *Victims, Perpetrators or Actors? Gender, Armed Conflict and Political Violence*, edited by Caroline O. N. Moser and Fiona C. Clark, 85–98. London: Zed Books.

Shaw, Martin. 2004. 'New Wars of the City: Relationships of "Urbicide" and "Genocide"'. In *Cities, War, and Terrorism: Towards an Urban Geopolitics*, edited by Stephen Graham, 141–45. Studies in Urban and Social Change. Malden: Blackwell Publishing.

Sirman, Nüket. 2016. 'When Antigone Is a Man: Feminist "Trouble" in the Late Colony'. In *Vulnerability in Resistance*, edited by Judith Butler, Zeynep Gambetti, and Leticia Sabsay, 191–210. Durham: Duke University Press.

Sjoberg, Laura and Caron E. Gentry. 2015. 'Introduction: Gender and Everyday/ Intimate Terrorism'. *Critical Studies on Terrorism* 8 (3): 358–61. https://doi .org/10.1080/17539153.2015.1084204.

Sjoberg, Laura and Sandra Via. 2010. *Gender, War, and Militarism: Feminist Perspectives*. Santa Barbara: ABC-CLIO, LLC.

Smith, Helena. 2007. 'When Wrong Boyfriends or Clothes Lead Daughters to Kill Themselves'. *The Guardian*, 23 August 2007. World news. https://www .theguardian.com/world/2007/aug/23/turkey.gender.

Smith, Linda Tuhiwai. 1999. *Decolonializing Methodologies: Research and Indigenous Peoples*. London: Zed Books.

Snitow, Ann Barr, Christine Stansell, and Sharon Thompson, eds. 1983. *Powers of Desire: The Politics of Sexuality*. New Feminist Library. New York: Monthly Review Press.

Solina, Carla. 1997. *Der Weg in die Berge: Eine Frau bei der kurdischen Befreiungsbewegung*. Hamburg: Edition Nautilus.

Sorkin, Michael. 2004. 'Urban Warfare: A Tour of the Battlefield'. In *Cities, War, and Terrorism: Towards an Urban Geopolitics*, edited by Stephen Graham, 251–62. Studies in Urban and Social Change. Malden: Blackwell Publishing.

Spivak, Gayatri C. 1988. 'Can the Subaltern Speak?' In *Marxism and the Interpretation of Culture*, edited by Carl Nelson and Lawrence Grossberg, 271–316. Urbana: University of Illinois Press.

——— 1996. 'Subaltern Studies: Deconstructing Historiography'. In *The Spivak Reader*, edited by Donna Landry and Gerald MacLean, 203–36.

1990. 'The Post-Colonial Critique: Interviews, Strategies, Dialogues'. In *The Post-Colonial Critique: Interviews, Strategies, Dialogues*, edited by Sarah Harasym. New York: Routledge.

2009. *Outside in the Teaching Machine*. New York: Routledge.

Steflja, Izabela and Jessica Trisko Darden. 2020. *Women as War Criminals: Gender, Agency, and Justice*. Stanford: Stanford University Press.

Strangers in a Tangled Wilderness, ed. 2015. *A Small Key Can Open a Large Door: The Rojava Revolution*.

Sylvester, Christine. 2001. *Feminist International Relations: An Unfinished Journey*. Cambridge Studies in International Relations. Cambridge: Cambridge University Press.

ed. 2011. *Experiencing War*. War, Politics and Experience. London: Routledge.

2013. *War as Experience: Contributions from International Relations and Feminist Analysis*. First Edition. New York: Routledge.

Tax, Meredith. 2016. *A Road Unforeseen: Women Fight the Islamic State*. New York: Bellevue Literary Press.

Tejel, Jordi. 2009. *Syria's Kurds: History, Politics and Society*. Routledge Advances in Middle East and Islamic Studies. London: Routledge.

2017. 'Le Rojava: heurs et malheurs du Kurdistan syrien (2004-2015)'. *Anatoli. De l'Adriatique à la Caspienne. Territoires, Politique, Sociétés*, no. 8 (October): 133–49. https://doi.org/10.4000/anatoli.610.

Tank, Pinar. 2017. "Kurdish Women in Rojava: From Resistance to Reconstruction." *Die Welt Des Islams* 57 (3–4): 404–28. doi:10.1163/15700607-05734p07.

Tickner, Ann J. 2011. 'Retelling IR's Foundational Stories: Some Feminist and Postcolonial Perspectives'. *Global Change, Peace and Security* 23 (1): 5–13.

1992. *Gender in International Relations: Feminist Perspectives on Achieving Global Security*. New York: Columbia University Press.

Tong, Rosemarie Putnam. 1998. *Feminist Thought: A More Comprehensive Introduction*. Second Edition. Boulder: Westview Press.

True, Jacqui. 2010. 'Feminism and Gender Studies in International Relations Theory'. Oxford Research Encyclopaedia of International Studies. 1 March 2010. https://doi.org/10.1093/acrefore/9780190846626.013.46.

Vali, Abbas, ed. 2003. *Essays on the Origins of Kurdish Nationalism*. Costa Mesa, CA: Mazda Publishers.

2011. *Kurds and the State in Iran: The Making of Kurdish Identity*. London: I.B. Tauris.

Vinthagen, Stellan and Anna Johansson. 2013. '"Everyday Resistance": Exploration of a Concept and Its Theories'. *Resistance Studies Magazine* 1 (1): 1–46.

Viterna, Jocelyn. 2006. 'Pulled, Pushed, and Persuaded: Explaining Women's Mobilization into the Salvadoran Guerrilla Army'. *American Journal of Sociology* 112 (1): 1–45.

2009. "Negotiating the Muddiness of Grassroots Field Research: Managing Identity and Data in Rural El Salvador." In *Women Fielding Danger: Negotiating Ethnographic Identities in Field Research*, edited by Martha Knisely Huggins and Marie-Louise Glebbeek. Lanham, MD: Rowman & Littlefield.

2013. *Women in War: The Micro-Processes of Mobilization in El Salvador*. Oxford: Oxford University Press.

Walton, Olivia Rose. 2016. 'How the Toxic Patriarchy of War Plays Out on Kurdish Women's Bodies'. *Kurdish Institute Brussel* (blog). 15 February 2016. http://www.kurdishinstitute.be/how-the-toxic-patriarchy-of-war-plays-out-on-k urdish-womens-bodies/.

Watts, Nicole F. 2010. *Activists in Office: Kurdish Politics and Protest in Turkey*. Studies in Modernity and National Identity. Seattle: University of Washington Press.

Weber, Cynthia. 2016. *Queer International Relations: Sovereignty, Sexuality and the Will to Knowledge*. Oxford Studies in Gender and International Relations. New York: Oxford University Press.

Wedeen, Lisa. 1999. *Ambiguities of Domination: Politics, Rhetoric, and Symbols in Contemporary Syria*. Chicago: Chicago University Press.

Weiss, Nerina. 2010. 'Falling from Grace: Gender Norms and Gender Strategies in Eastern Turkey'. *New Perspectives on Turkey* 42: 55–76. https://doi.org/10 .1017/S0896634600005574.

2014. 'The Power of Dead Bodies'. In *Histories of Victimhood*, edited by Steffen Jensen and Henrik Rønsbo, 161–78. Philadelphia: University of Pennsylvania Press.

Welchman, Lynn and Sara Hossain, eds. 2005. *'Honour': Crimes, Paradigms, and Violence Against Women*. London: Zed Books.

White, Aaronette M. 2007. 'All the Men Are Fighting for Freedom, All the Women Are Mourning Their Men, but Some of Us Carried Guns: A Raced-Gendered Analysis of Fanon's Psychological Perspectives on War'. *Signs* 32 (4): 857–84.

White, Paul. 2000. *Primitive Rebels or Revolutionary Modernisers? The Kurdish Nationalist Movement in Turkey*. London: Zed Books.

2015. *The PKK: Coming down from the Mountains*. Rebels. London: Zed Books.

Wibben, Annick T. R. 2010. *Feminist Security Studies: A Narrative Approach*. London: Routledge.

2016. *Researching War: Feminist Methods, Ethics and Politics*. Interventions. London: Routledge.

Wikan, Unni. 2008. *In Honor of Fadime*. Chicago: Chicago University Press.

Wilcox, Lauren B. 2015. *Bodies of Violence: Theorizing Embodied Subjects in International Relations*. Oxford: Oxford University Press.

Wolf, Judith. 2004. 'Aspekte Des Geschlechterverhältnisses in Der Guerrilla Der PKK/KADEK Unter Besonderer Berücksichtigung Des Ehrbegriffs'. In *Gender in Kurdistan Und Der Diaspora*, edited by Hajo, Siamend et al., Bd. 6:183–216.

Wood, Elisabeth Jean. 2006. 'The Ethical Challenges of Field Research in Conflict Zones'. *Qualitative Sociology* 29 (3): 373–86. https://doi.org/10 .1007/s11133-006-9027-8.

Wudud, Amina. 2009. 'Islam beyond Patriarchy through Gender Inclusive Qur'anic Analysis'. In *Wanted: Equality and Justice in The Muslim Family*, edited by Zainah Anwar, 95–110. Selangor: Musawah.

Wylie, Alison. 2003. 'Why Standpoint Matters'. In *Science and Other Cultures: Issues in Philosophies of Science and Technology*, edited by Robert Figueroa and Sandra G. Harding, 26–48. New York: Routledge.

Yılmaz, Arzu. 2016. *Atruş'tan Maxmûr'a*. Istanbul: Iletişim.

Yüksel, Metin. 2006. 'The Encounter of Kurdish Women with Nationalism in Turkey'. *Middle Eastern Studies* 42 (5): 777–802. https://doi.org/10.1080/00263200600828022.

Yuval-Davis, Nira. 1997. *Gender and Nation*. London: Sage.

Yuval-Davis, Nira, Floya Anthias, and Jo Campling, eds. 1989. *Woman, Nation, State*. Basingstoke: Macmillan.

Zengin, Asli and Sertaç Sehlikoglu. 2016. 'Everyday Intimacies of the Middle East'. *Journal of Middle East Women's Studies* 12 (2): 139–42. https://doi.org/10.1215/15525864-3507595.

Zengin, Aslı. 2015. 'Cemile Cagirga: A Girl Is Freezing under State Fire'. Jadaliyya. 2015. http://www.jadaliyya.com/Details/32470/Cemile-Cagirga-A-Girl-is-Freezing-Under-State-Fire.

Zeydanlıoğlu, Welat. 2012. 'Turkey's Kurdish Language Policy'. *International Journal of the Sociology of Language* 2012 (217). https://doi.org/10.1515/ijsl-2012-0051.

Zeynep Kinaci (Zilan). 1996. PKK Online. 1996. http://pkk-online.com/en/index.php/sehitlerimiz/103-zeynep-kinaci-zilan.

Multimedia

Aynur Doğan. n.d. *Dayê Dayê*. Accessed 5 September 2018. https://www.youtube.com/watch?v=F-x2rmOAL00.

Ayşe Şan. n.d. *Lêlê Dayê*. Accessed 5 September 2018. https://www.youtube.com/watch?v=faJZeD4TMFs.

Binevş Agal. 2011. *Bêrîvan* XE "Bêrîvan". Accessed 11 September 2018. https://www.youtube.com/watch?v=d7eaD9JJSdM

Gençlerden Kobra Skeci 'Kobra Ket, Saet Xweş'. 2016. https://www.youtube.com/watch?v=yDNKFHP4nbE.

Grup Munzur. n.d. *İsyan Ateşi*. Accessed 5 September 2018. https://www.youtube.com/watch?v=8MB6RLCCUxI.

Hozan Serhat. n.d. *Dayê Dayê*. Accessed 11 September 2018. https://www.youtube.com/watch?v=aF4FXtf1JR0.

Koma Azad. n.d. *Êdî Bese Lê Dayê*. Accessed 5 September 2018. https://www.youtube.com/watch?v=EbU3lahXsEA.

M4zlum. 2016 'Graffiting by Turkish State Forces as a Form of Psychological Warfare in Kurdistan'. Tumblr. Accessed 12 September 2018. http://teachmeviolence.tumblr.com/post/148120973545/graffiting-by-turkish-state-forces-as-a-form-of.

Özarslan, Asli. 2017. 'Türkei – Der Vergessene Krieg Im Osten'. ZDF info. https://www.youtube.com/watch?v=MIeqmaHnP5A&has_verified=1.

Wa Şehîd. n.d. Accessed 5 September 2018. https://www.youtube.com/watch?v=Sv9CXSeS9sk.

Xemgîn, Xelîl. n.d. *Ey Şehîd*. Accessed 5 September 2018. https://www
    .youtube.com/watch?v=MK0fl7Qr5Pc.

Xezal û Gerîla. n.d. Accessed 12 September 2018. https://www.youtube.com/wa
    tch?v=QcpgMHeeGVU.

Index

abstinence contract, 22, 23, 163, 164, 170,
176, 194, 203
activist, xi, 3, 4, 7, 8, 10, 13, 14, 17, 22, 29,
30, 31, 33, 34, 35, 37, 41, 48, 49, 60,
66, 67, 70, 71, 72, 73, 74, 89, 91, 94,
95, 101, 133, 134, 139, 148, 163, 165,
166, 172, 183, 185, 189, 191, 193,
197, 199, 203
agency, 15, 20, 21, 25, 26, 40, 71, 92, 98,
100, 127, 129, 134, 142, 143, 160,
168, 200
Agirî, Leyla, 16, 102, 116, 162, 163,
187, 194
AKP, xiv, 29, 48, 93, 172
Al-Ali, Nadje, xi, 6, 11, 13, 19, 24, 25, 27,
29, 43, 44, 46, 60, 61, 63, 80, 99, 135,
147, 165, 170, 193, 199
asexuality, 63

bargain, 24, 41, 167, 184, 194, 204
party bargain, 23, 41, 163, 164, 165, 167,
173, 194, 201, 204, 205
patriarchal bargain, 23, 156
barricades, 66, 69, 72, 81, 84, 85, 90, 94, 95
Bayık, Cemîl, 3, 46, 56, 57, 64, 151, 191
Bêrîtan, 52, 64, 97, 102, 107, 108, 127
Bêrîvan, 52, 64
body politics, 6, 11, 18, 26, 27, 33, 40, 69,
163, 164, 167, 168, 190, 195
Bookchin, 122
border, 4, 29, 30, 31, 32, 85, 87, 88, 97,
145, 158, 165
Botan, 90, 131
bourgeoisie, 76, 86, 193
petit-bourgeois, 54, 61, 128
Bozarslan, Hamit, xi, 44, 45, 46, 51, 68, 90,
100, 126, 127, 132, 144, 201

Çağlayan, Handan, 6, 43, 44, 50, 51, 55,
61, 76, 114, 127, 155, 182
Cansız, Sakine, 45, 46, 47, 175, 176,
184

capitalism, 2, 27, 49, 58, 61, 63, 70, 124,
184, 186, 188, 192, 197, 198
civil life, 18, 31, 33, 180
Cizre, viii, 47, 52, 66, 69, 78, 80, 82, 85, 87,
90, 91, 158
Cizre, Newroz, 102, 190
class, 17, 20, 27, 28, 33, 46, 50, 73, 76, 86,
92, 108, 155, 169, 180, 200
class struggle, 169
co-chair system, 59, 60
Cockburn, Cynthia, xi, 6, 18, 19, 24,
69, 198
communal life, 10, 22, 98, 100, 109, 118,
128, 129, 169, 180, 205
communist movements, 168
Communist Party, 14, 46, 169
Congress of Free Women. See KJA
conservative, 23, 31, 134, 165, 176, 186,
187, 191, 201, 202
continuum of violence, 4, 7, 18, 68, 70, 95,
97, 107, 189

daesh, 3, 22, 29, 44, 62, 112, 129, 135, 138,
146, 149, 153, 159, 163, 165, 201, 203
daily life, 31, 40, 43, 53, 101, 134, 136, 160,
180, 183
De Volo, Bayard, 6, 9, 11, 19, 132,
133
decolonising, 35, 61
democracy, 44, 61, 64, 93, 151, 197
Radical democracy, 3, 73, 203
Democratic Confederalism, 3, 4, 24, 25, 29,
31, 58, 59, 61, 64, 102, 115, 126, 128,
130, 154, 163, 171, 198, 202
Democratic Free Women's Movement. See
DÖKH
Democratic Society's Congress. See DTK
desexualisation, 11, 22, 23, 40, 163, 167,
178, 194
development, 31, 43, 50, 64, 87, 163,
193, 202
displacement, 138, 155

For EU product safety concerns, contact us at Calle de José Abascal, 56–1°,
28003 Madrid, Spain or eugpsr@cambridge.org.

www.ingramcontent.com/pod-product-compliance
Ingram Content Group UK Ltd.
Pitfield, Milton Keynes, MK11 3LW, UK
UKHW020354140625
459647UK00020B/2470